A CALENDAR
OF DELAWARE WILLS

NEW CASTLE COUNTY

A CALENDAR
of DELAWARE WILLS
NEW CASTLE COUNTY

1682-1800

ABSTRACTED AND COMPILED

By THE HISTORICAL RESEARCH COMMITTEE
OF THE COLONIAL DAMES OF DELAWARE

CLEARFIELD

Originally Published
New York, 1911

Reprinted
Genealogical Publishing Company
Baltimore, 1969

Reprinted for
Clearfield Company, Inc., by
Genealogical Publishing Co., Inc.
Baltimore, Maryland
1989, 1996, 2000, 2006

Library of Congress Catalogue Card Number 71-76816
International Standard Book Number: 0-8063-0079-5

Made in the United States of America

PREFACE

The Historical Research Committee of the Delaware Society of the Colonial Dames of America, in preparing this calendar of wills, has worked upon the original wills as far as they exist in the Register's office, and upon the original Record of Probate, where the wills are missing.

Abstracts have been made of many wills, which, because of technical irregularities, were not probated, and consequently are not matters of record. The genealogical data thus presented gives the volume a unique advantage. For a period of years, in the early life of this Colony the law did not require that the probated wills filed in the Register's office should be recorded. Because of this, genealogists, and others interested in research work, were permitted to use the original wills, with the natural result that many were carried away, and many others suffered destruction or defacement from constant and careless handling.

When the Committee realized that immediate action was necessary, if the contents of these unrecorded papers were to be preserved, it undertook the work of safeguarding them, by making abstracts of all the wills of New Castle County from the earliest times to 1800. In compiling these abstracts, the simplest plan of chronological arrangement, with full index of names, has been adopted.

The dates, in order, show when the will was made, and when probated. The lines (thus ———) indicate that the date is missing. The annexed letters and numbers refer to the Will Record and pages, where the full will is recorded in the Register's office. Other abbreviations are noted elsewhere.

It is the hope of the Committee that a labor that has been long, but of continuous interest in its accomplishment, may be of value to the interested public in establishing lines of descent, and in linking the present to the far past of our early Delaware settlers.

WILMINGTON, DELAWARE.
May, 1910.

ABBREVIATIONS
OF THE NAMES OF HUNDREDS OF
NEW CASTLE COUNTY

Appoquinimink..........................Appo. Hd.
Brandywine............................B'wine Hd.
Christiana............................Chris. Hd.
Mill Creek............................Mill Crk. Hd.
New Castle............................N. C. Hd.
Pencader..............................Pen. Hd.
Red Lion..............................Red Lion
St. Georges...........................St. Geo. Hd.
White Clay Creek...............W. Clay Crk. Hd.

OTHER ABBREVIATIONS

Administered ....Adm.
Borough ....Bor.
Codicil ....Dec'd.
Daughter ....Dau.
Estate ....Est.
Executor (trix) ....Exc.
Miscellaneous ....Misc.
Nuncupative ....Nunc.
Wilmington ....Wil.

Errata

Page 82, line 35: For "Ingebor and Elenor Stedham" read
                  "Ingebor and Elenor Derrickson."
Page 86, line 33: For "Higgins" read "Huggins."
Page 89, line 40: For "Mary Wilson" read "Mary Nelson."
Page 92, line 24: For "Aug. 23, 1779," read "Aug. 23, 1777."
Page 98, line 44: For "Raukin" read "Rankin."
Page 110, line 39: For "Nehemiad" read "Nehemiah."
Page 126, line 20: For "1791" read "1792."
Page 131, line 30: For "Elcles" read "Eccles."
Page 133, line 35: For "1791" read "1794."

CALENDAR OF DELAWARE WILLS
NEW CASTLE COUNTY

Dirick Lawrence. Filed —— 1682. Dirick Williams, Brother Hybert, Sister Gretia.

Ralph Hutchinson. Feb. 16, 1679. Dec. 31, 1683. A. 61. Peter Alrichs, Thomas Wolleston, Daniel Tilewant (of Fairfield), John Ogle's two sons, Joanes Arskin, John Smith, John Anderson, Ann Wolleston, uncle John Bedford, my brother Robert. Exc. Peter Alrichs, James Waliams, James Matthews.

Gysbert Direckson. Town of New Castle. Dec. 3, 1682. 2nd day of 11th mo. called January, 1682-3. A. 64. Three children, named Susanna, Anna, and Adetie; wife, Cattalanty Gertrude; Emelius de King, married eldest dau. of Gysbert Dereckson.

John Barnes. On Delaware River. Nov. 12, 1683. 11th of 11th mo. vulgarly called January, 1683-4. A. 60. Wife, Engeltie; two children, Engeltie and Barite. Guardian, Peter Maeslander.

Pelle Mathysen. Sept. 24, 1683. ——. A. 62. Wife, Metze.

Cornelius Johnson. Oct. 20, 1683. — 29, 1683. A. 61. Sons, Johannes and Poule Johnson; wife, Elizabeth. Exc. wife, Elizabeth Pieterson.

Hon. Peter Maeslander. Swanwicke. Oct. 25, 1683. Jan. 1683-4. A. 62. Wife, Barbary; children, not named. Exc. John Paul Jacquet, Hubert Lawrence.

Peter Themis De Witt. (Nunc.) Swanwick. Sept. 26, 1683. Letters granted Mar. 14, 1684. A. 63. Wife, Annita; son, Themis De Witt. "One of the daughters married to John Jacquet, administrator." Attested by John Barnes, Ambrose Baker, Peter Ffalcher, Edmund Cantwell.

Christopher Elliott. (Nunc.) Mar. 17, 1684-5. A. 67. Wife, Ann; Exc. wife, Ann Ellitt.

Pella Parker. (Nunc.) A. 65. Letters granted Oct., 1684, to Conrad Constantine, in behalf of his wife Christian, late widow of Pella Parker, wife, eight children.

John Smith. (Nunc.) Dec. 9, 1684. A. 66. Wife, Sarah; child, Mary. Will attested by Joseph Powell and Margaret Smith. Eye and ear witness, Joseph Cookson, Joseph Bowles, Jonas Arskin.

Edmund Cantwell. N. C. Oct. 28, 1679. Jan. 17, 1685. A. 78. Wife, Mary Cantwell; children, Richard Cantwell, Johanna Cantwell and Elizabeth Cantwell; Mr. Johanos De Haas, Mr. Peter Allrick, Mr. Epharim Henman, Mr. John Williams; brother-in-law Johannes De Haas. Exc. wife, Mary Cantwell and three children.

John Taylor. Drawyers Crk. Hd. Mar. 20, 1684-5. A. 67. Son, John Taylor, his mother-in-law. Exc. wife, Jane.

Lassee Oalson (Lawrence Olleson) (Nunc.). He died Aug. 3, 1684. Feb. 16, 1684. Wife, Annitee Clement's dau., his children; his two biggest sonns; his other & youngest son. Attested by Benedict Stidem. Letters granted to Peter Andrus Hallman in behalf of his wife, Annity Clements, late widow of Lassa Oalson.

Dr. Thomas Spry. Apr. 6, 1685. Dec. 7, 1685. A. 69. Four children, Annesky Egbert and Abiah Egbert and Abraham, and Dau. Sarah Spry of Plymouth; my adopted son, Joseph Bisse—alias Spry; John Mandy, Mr. James William, Dr. Latwoop. Exc. James Williams, John Mandy.

Hans Corderus. Cooper. Swanwick. Dec. 24, 1686. Mar. 18, 1686-7. A. 81. Brother's youngest child named Jacquininta Magdelina Baonsona, Mrs. Mary Block, Isaac Lind, Hybert Laurance, Martin Seider, John Abram's son-in-law John Harmonson, Brother —— Corderus. Exc. John Harmonson.

John Walker. Sas. Crk. Hd. Mar. —, 1686. Mar. 19, 1686-7. A. 87. Wife, Dorothy Walker, "Walter Smith having marryed Dorothy Walker, ye widdow and relict of John Walker, Sr. Exc. Dorothy Walker.

William Welsh. (Nunc.). Mar. 7, 1686-7. A. 83. Sarah Welsh, the widow and relict of William Welsh, late of New Castle co., Gent. Dau., Susannah Welsh.

Timon Stedham (Stiddom). Chris. Hd. Feb. 1, 1686. Apr. 24, 1686. A. 73. Wife, Christina; dau., Ingabor Stiddom; little dau., Magdolena Stiddom; sons, Lucas Stiddom, Erasmus Stiddom.

John Anderson—alias Stalcup. Aug. 29, 1679. July 20, 1686. A. 79. Wife, Christina Carlos; son-in-law, Lucas Stiddom; eldest son named Auchin; children, viz: Charlos, John, Peter, Mary, Jonas.

Dirk Williams. Feb. 27, 1686. Aug. 10, 1686. A. 75. Wife, Funcha; children, not named. Exc. Adam Peterson.

Herman Janson. Farmer. Port Hook. Apr. 1, 1684. Nov. 10, 1686. A. 74. Wife, Begchy; daus., Anneky and Catharina. Exc. wife, Begchy (or Bilchy).

John Wattkings. W. Clay Crk. Hd. Dec. 13, 1685. Dec. 28, 1685-6 A. 70. John Nomerson's daughter, Mary Nomerson. Exc. John Nomerson.

William Hatten. Dk. Crk. Hd. Feb. 9, 1687. Misc. 1. 174. Wife Elizabeth, two daughters, youngest Martha, James Harrison, kinswoman, Mary Hall. Exc. wife, Elizabeth Whuldon, Rebecca Hatton, Joseph Houlding, Isaac Whuldon.

Thomas Laws. Feb. 24, 1687. Misc. 1. 282. Wife, Ann Laws; my children.

Isack Decow. Chelsey. 23rd day of 11th mo., 1686-7. 15th day of 4th mo., 1687. A. 89. Dau., Elizabeth Decow; wife, Rebecca; five children; sons, Jacob Decow, John and Isack Decow; dau.,

Susannah. Trustees, Thomas Langhorn, Robert Ashton, bro. Jacob.

Francis Hutchinson. Dk. Crk. Hd. Mar. 6, 1686. Apr. 21, 1687. A. 85. Wife, Ann. Hutchinson.

Hannah Prime. May 14, 1687. Ralph Prime. Guardians for said children are Thomas Snelling and Benjamin Gumly.

Henry Lemmons. Nov. 14, 1687. A. 94. Wife, Ann; children not named. Wife's first children.

Urin Urinson, Senior. Aug. 13, 1688. Feb. 5, 1690. Misc. 1. 467. Wife, Brita; youngest son, Henry Uronson, my undutiful son, Uron. Exc. wife, Brita.

John Hendrickson. Jan. 18, 1689. Jan. — 1689. Misc. 1. 175. Wife, Mary; sons, Hendrick and William, unborn child. Exc. bro. John Hannson, John White.

Thomas Harriss. Dk. Crk. Hd. July 10, 1690. ———. Misc. 1. 177. Wife, Elizabeth; son, Thomas; two daus., Elizabeth and Hannah; unborn child. Exc. wife, Elizabeth Harriss.

Magnus White, Mariner. Late of Boston—now of N. C. May 6, 1690. June 10, 1690. Only dau. Hannah White. Exc. John McKenzie, Richard Reynolds, James Halliday.

John Mattson Skrika. Apr. 14, 1689. Mar. 15, 1691. Misc. 1. 425. Wife, four sons, dau. Annika, dau. Mary.

John MacKony (McAnthony). N. C. Hd. Dec. 6, 1690. Nov. 30, 1691. Misc. 1. 348. Wife, Mabel MacKony. Exc. friends, John Donaldson, Robert French.

Da Ringh. N. C. Mar. 17, 1692. Misc. 2. 30. Wife, Susannah de Ringh; oldest son, Nicholaes de Ringh; three children, Lucretia, Nicolaes and Gysbert de Ringh. Exc. brother, Mattheis de Ringh.

Thomas Gasper. July 22, 1692. Oct. 5, 1692. Misc. 1. 76. Wife, Mary. Exc. wife, Mary Gasper.

Peter Alrichs. Town of N. C. Jan. 25, 1694. Eldest son, Sigfridus Aldrichs; sons, Hermanns Alrichs, Jacobus and Wessell. Exc. four sons.

John Garretson. Nov. 28, 1694. Mar. 5, 1694. B. 13. Three sons, Garott, Casper and Cornelius. "Thayor mother," Ann; daughters; wife, Ann.

Hiburd Lawrence. Dec. 24, 1694. Mar. 5, 1694. Misc. 1.283. Sister's sonns, Hans Lawrence and Markus Sheear, my three kinsmen; my three kinswomen, namely: Gertrit Crane, Roseman and Elizabeth Sheear. Exc. Edward Gibb, Robert Ashton, Wm. Padison.

Wallraven Otto. Nov. 7, 1694. Nov. 30, 1694. B. 25. Two children, Garret and Mary. Exc. bro.-in-law., John Willson.

John McCarty (MacKarta). Blk. Bd. Crk. Hd. Dec. 1, 1694. Misc.

1.348. Wife, Mary MacKarta; Percival Westingdale. Exc. Mary McCarty.

Edward Blake. N. C. Nov. 15, 1695. Feb. 14, 1695. B. 42. Wife, Hannah; two children, Sarah and Edward; Abraham and Hannah Decon. Exc. wife, Hannah, Richard Halliwell.

Benjamin Gill, late of N. C. Co., now of Monmouth River, Salem Co., N. J. Ship carpenter. July 15, 1695. Feb. 6, 1695. Misc. 1.178. Wife, Ann. Estate in England and America. Exc. wife, Ann.

Henry Williams. N. C. Nov. 10, 1694. Feb. 20, 1695. B. 16. Eldest son, John Williams; eldest dau., Sarah Williams, my six children; dau. Mary. Exc. brother, John Williams Neering, Richard Halliwell, Richard Cantwell.

John Taylor. Dk. Crk. Hd. B. 49. Wife, Grace; son, John; dau., Elizabeth. Exc. Grace Taylor.

Reynier Vanderculine. Apr. 24, 1695. Misc. 1. 470. To eldest dawter; to dawter Caterine; to two youngest dawters; to wife, Margaret; Widow Walberry, Cornelyus Dericson. Estate in Holland; Bridget Henrickson. Exc. Peter Stallcups, Henry Bronson.

Zacharias Vanderculine. Nov. 2, 1694. June 14, 1695. B. 2. Brother, Reynier Vanderculine; brother-in-law, Cornelius Cectel and wife, Emmetje; brother-in-law, Silvester Garland and wife, Soetje; wife, ———.

Ellen (Ellinor) Grantham. Widow and relict of John Grantham. N. C. Mar. 13, 1694-5. July 1, 1695. B. 9. Loving friend Dorcas Hogg; widow, Mary Williams; Hannah Black; son, John Grantham. Exc. son, John Grantham.

John Grantham. N. C. Oct. 30, 1694. July 1, 1695. Misc. 1.77. Wife, Eleanor Grantham; son, John Grantham. Exc. Eleanor Grantham.

Richard Huddon. Jan. 2, 1694. July 1, 1695. B. 8. Son, Andrew Huddon. Exc. mother-in-law.

Johannes de Haes. N. C. Nov. 4, 1694. July 1, 1695. B. 14. Eldest son, Rowlif De Haes; son, Johannes De Haes; wife, Elizabeth. Guardians, Peter Alrichs, Richard Hallywell. Exc. wife, Elizabeth.

Lawrence Eustason. Nov. 11, 1694. July 1, 1695. B. 11. Wife, Ann; dau., Wallabor. Exc. wife, Ann Eustason.

James Halliday. Nov. 19, 1694. Aug. 7, 1695. B. 27. Dau., Elizabeth; wife, Katharine.

Morgan Druett. Yeoman. Newport. 27th day of 7th m. 1695. Mar. 16, 1695. B. 46. Wife, Cassandra; six children, Elizabeth Judson, Hannah Albertson, William Druett, Benjamin Druett, Mary Druett and Sarah Druett; son-in-law, William Albertson. Exc. Cassandra Druett. Overseers, Jacob Chandler and William Albertson, Sr.

John Ball. Nov. 19, 1694. Sept. 7, 1695. B. 30. Ralph; son, James Ball; Mary Snelling, dau. of Thomas Snelling. Exc. wife, Ann. Trustees, Richard Halliwell, Richard Hambly.

Mary Williams. N. C. Oct. 22, 1695. Oct. 28, 1695. B. 33. Thomas and John Land, sons of Samuel Land; Henry Land; Darem Hog, wife of George Hog and mother of said children; Mary Hutchinson, dau. of Robert Hutchinson; Peter Alrichs, John Donaldson, John Williams, Richard Hallywell, Robert French, Edw. Blake, James Claypool, and his wife, Mary. Exc. James Miller.

George Baker. Oct. 31, 1695. Nov. 18, 1695. B. 36. Sons, Joseph and George Baker; daughters, not named. Exc. friend, Ellihu Anderson.

Mary Smith. N. C. Nov. 19, 1694. Dec. 4, 1695. B. 38. Brother-in-law, John Read—son of my father-in-law, James Read of New Castle. Exc. James Read, Mr. John Donaldson.

Elizabeth Fforat. Before 1696. B. 57. Johannes Dehaes and Elizabeth, his wife; granddau., Elizabeth Dehaes. Exc. Mr. Edw. Blake, Mr. Richard Hallywell, John Dehaes.

Ambrose Baker. N. C. Apr. 19, 1695. Mar. 29, 1696. B. 57. Wife, Alihee Baker; dau., Marthy. Exc. wife, Alihee Baker.

Jacob Young. Sisill Co., Md. Feb. 22, 1696. Mch. 20, 1696. B. 66. Three children; son, Joseph; dau., Mary; Bonomy Clark intermarried to dau. of said Jacob Young. Exc. dau., Mary.

John Forat. Ship carpenter. N. C. Jan. 12, 1691. Apr. 27, 1696. B. 55. Wife, Elizabeth Fforat; children of former wife. Wife, Elizabeth named as executor, but she was not living. Exc. Richard Halliwell.

Thomas Child. 10th of 3rd m. 1694. July 20, 1696. B. 61. Michael Harland and George, his son. Mary Malings, the daughter by Thomas Pomeroy, Dinah Harland, Hannah Harland, Samuel Underwood, Elizabeth Dirckson, Michael Harland's dau. Abey. Exc. George Harland.

Hans Hanson. Aug. 11, 1696. Nov. 17, 1696. son, Peter; son, Hanson; son, Joseph Hanson; young son, Henry Hanson; dau., Ann Hanson.

Wibrough Walker. Executrix of John Walker. N. C. May 6, 1697. Nov. 9, 1697. B. 68. Son, John Walker; grandson, Andrew Hudde; son, Powall Barnes; dau., Christian Calvert. Exc. son, John Walker.

Jacob Clemenson. Feb. 7, 1698. June 17, 1698. B. 74. Wiffe, Bridget Gurning; daughters and sons, not named. Exc. wife, Bridget.

William Pooll. 2nd m. 11th, 1698. May 21, 1698. B. 73. Brother, Nathaniel Cartmill. Exc. Nathaniel Cartmill.

Christian Stidham (widow of Timothy Stidham) (Nunc.). Jan. 24, 1698-9. Mar. 13, 1698. B. 75. Sons, Gilbert and Jonas; Peter

Anderson's dau. Bridget; son, Jonas' dau. Christian; three daughters, Mary and Ann and Christena. Exc. Jonas Walraven.

William Crosse. N. C. Nov. 20, 1697. Jan. 31, 1697-8. B. 70. Elizabeth Bisk, youngest dau. of John Bisk; Elizabeth McDonnold, dau. of Donnald McDonnold; Thomas Janvier. Exc. Thomas Janvier.

Jacob Vandeveer. Apr. 15, 1698. Mar. 30, 1699. B. 79. Wife, Katharine; my sons, John, Cornelius and William; my fourth son, Jacob.

John Holt. N. C. Dec. 14, 1699. Apr. 29, 1700. B. 86. Margaret Liston, wife of Edward Liston. Exc. Margaret Liston.

John Williams Nerring. Merchant. N. C. June 4, 1698. Aug. 27, 1700. Misc. 1, 366. Son, Jacobus Williams Nerring; four daughters, Sarah, Lydia, Elizabeth and Joanna Williams Nerring. Wife deceased. Adm. daughters, Sarah and Lydia; Mr. Richard Halliwell; Dr. Samuel Staats, Capt. Johannes Kip.

Robert Hartup. Blk.bd. Crk. Hd. Oct. 12, 1700. B. 188. Wife, Anna Hartup. Exc. wife, Anna.

John Donaldson. Merchant. N. C. Feb. 12, 1701-2. Apr. 8, 1702. G. 416. Youngest dau. Mary Donaldson; eldest dau. Katherine; bro. William Donaldson; Dorcus Hogg, wife of George Hogg. Exc. Richard Hallywell, Robert French, Dennis Dakey.

Richard Clark. N. C. Oct. 14, 1702. C. 34. Son, Richard Cark; dau. Anne. Exc. George Hogg, Benjamin Swett.

Thomas Sawyer. Feb. 19, 1705-6. Feb. 19, 1706. B. 120. Wife, Jeny; sons, ·Robert and Thomas; daus. Anne Sawer and Mary Sawer. Exc. wife.

Robert Ashton. Chelsey. Nov. 11, 1706. Feb. 27, 1706. B. 123. Son, John Ashton; son, Joseph Ashton; dau. Ann Richardson; dau. Sarah Wyatt, her mother. Exc. sons, John and Joseph Ashton.

John Johnson. Merchant. Late of London. Town of Salem, within the western division of the province of Nova Cesaria. Oct. 5, 1705. Apr. 1, 1706. B. 102. Three children, John, Thomas and Martha Johnson, who are living with my mother and are to be heard of at Dr. Rothers in Bewford Buildings in Strand in London. Exc. William Hall, Nathaniel Breading, John Valentine.

Bryan Pearl. Artificer. Of the thoroughfare to Dk. Crk. Hd. Jan. 1, 1705-6. Apr. 18, 1706. B. 104. Dau., Ann Slather; dau., Margrett; wife, Jane; children, viz: William Pearl, Benjamin Pearl, Ralph Pearl and Rachel Pearl. Exc. wife, Jane Pearl; son, William Pearl.

John Hussy. May 8, 1707. Feb. 18, 1707. B. 137. Son, Christopher; son, Jededeah; dau. Rebecca, wife of Samuel Collins; dau. Mary, wife of Moses Swett; dau. Ann, wife of James Stanyon;

dau. Susannah, widow of Richard Otis; dau. Bathshabo, wife of Thomas Babb; dau. Charity, wife of Garit Garitson; dau. Content, wife of Henry Land; son, John Hussy. Exc. son, John Hussy.

Powel Thomason. R. Clay Crk. Hd. Feb. 24, 1707. B. 172. Wife, Fileshe; child, ——; daughter; bro. Chitzoney.

Bryan McDonnel. Feb. 23, 1707. March 19, 1707. B. 153. Wife, Mary McDonnel; sons, William and Bryan McDonnel; eldest son, John MacDonnel; son, James McDonnel; dau. Mary Dangor; son, Richard McDonnel; dau. Anable McDonnel. Exc. wife, Mary McDonnel; son, William McDonnel; son, Bryan McDonnel.

Aaron Johnson. Jan. 3, 1694. Aug. 5, 1707. B. 131. Wife, Barbara James; Rev. minister of Swedes' church, Mr. Errious Bioerk. Exc. wife, Barbara.

Peter Godin. Yeoman. N. C. Dec. 23, 1704. Aug. 8, 1707. B. 129. Dau. Esther, the wife of Anthony Funson; two children, Philip and Elizabeth; wife, Ann; son, Peter. Exc. George Fogg, Joseph Griffin.

Joseph Perkins. Husbandman. 4th day of 11th m. 1706-7. Aug. 19, 1707. Eldest son, Joseph Perkins; son, John; son, Caleb; son, Humphrey; son, Joshua; eldest dau. Marey; dau. Marthay; wife. Exc. Mar. Perkins, wife; George Robinson.

Bartholomew Bassett. Dk. Crk. Hd. Dec. 11, 1707. ——. Misc. 1. 3. Wife, Elizabeth; Hannah Lambert; children of my bro. Thomas Bassett; bro.-in-law, John Mitchell. Exc. wife, Elizabeth.

Morris Liston. Sept. 9, 1708. Feb. 15, 1708. Misc. 1. 284. Wife, Jane Liston; two children, John and Edmund Liston; two grandchildren, Rachel and Ruth Russell. Exc. wife, Jane Liston.

John Grubb. Tanner. Chester Co., Penna. Feb. 12, 1707-8. Mar. 26, 1708. Misc. 1. 82. Dau. Charity, wife of Richard Beeson; dau., Phoebe Grubb; wife, Francis Grubb; sons, Emanuel, John Joseph, Henry, Samuel, Nathaniel, Peter. Exc. son, John; wife, Frances.

Hugh Marsh. Dk. Crk. Hd. Mar., 1708. Apr. 10, 1708. Misc. 1.349. Former wife and daughter: wife, Penelopy Marsh; three sons, John, Joseph and Robert Marsh; brother Robert. Exc. wife, Penelopy Marsh, bro. Robert Marsh and Benjamin Richardson.

Henry Williams. Shipright. N. C. Mar. 8, 1707. Apr. 26, 1708. B. 139. Son, Henry; wife, Ann. Exc. friend and brother, James Sinnex; wife, Ann.

Richard Reynolds. Yeoman. Mar. 21, 1707. May 19, 1708. B. 162. Wife, Ann; children, Mary Reynolds, John Reynolds, Sarah and Richard Reynolds. Exc. wife, Ann Reynolds, John French; son, John Reynolds.

John Guest. Feb. 1, 1706. May 22, 1708. Misc. 1. 79. Brothers,

Thomas Guest and Samuel; wife, Susannah. Exc. Susannah Guest.

Hance Defoss. Jan. 21, 1707. May 27, 1708. B. 145. Brother, Johannes Defoss; wife and children, apprentice, Richard Hanly. Exc. Johannes Defoss.

Mathias Defoss. May 7, 1705. May 27, 1708. B. 142. Wife, Sarah Defoss; sons, Hans and Johannes Defoss; daus., Margaret and Helena and Ingebor and Anne and Elizabeth; dau. Helena's children and husband. Exc. Sarah Defoss.

Christopher Stanley. N. C. May 11, 1708. June 2, 1708. B. 151. Wife, Mary; two sons, Christopher and Robert. Exc. wife, Mary Stanley.

Gisbort Walraven. Apr. 19, 1708. June 4, 1708. B. 147. Wife. Christana; sons, Gisbort, Jonas; daus., Sarah, Catran; brother, Jonas Walraven; son, Richard. Exc. bro. Jonas Walraven; Mathias Peterson: Edward Robinson.

Michael Trombalt (Trumell). N. C. Oct. 20, 1706. June 28, 1708. B. 149. Ann Godin, wife of Peter Godin; Elizabeth Bell; Thomas Allett. Exc. Samuel Sillsbee.

Thomas Medcalfe. Yeoman. N. C. Aug. 26, 1708. ———. B. 206. Wife, Martha; four sons, Thomas, Henry, Joseph and William; dau., Mary. Exc. wife, Martha.

Richard Mankin. Weaver. N. C. Aug. 9, 1708. Sept. 8, 1708. B. 166. Son. George Mankin; son, Richard Mankin; daus., Ann Mankin and Mary Mankin. Exc. son, George, James Robinson.

William Dickson. Weaver. R. Clay Crk. Hd. 31st day of 1st m. 1708. Sept. 20, 1708. B. 164. Wife, Ann; children. Advisors and guardians, Brothers Mirthwell Jearlan and John Grigg. Exc. wife, Anna Dickson.

James Hayes. Aug. 1, 1708. Sept. 22, 1708. B. 157. Son-in-law, William Burrowes; son-in-law, Johr Burrowes; son-in-law, Richard Burrowes; dau.-in-law, Rebecca Burrowes. Exc. Naomi Hayes.

William Grant. Sept. 26, 1708. ———. Misc. 1.80. Eldest son, William Grant; son, John Grant. Appo. Hd.; youngest dau., Mary Grant; dau. Elizabeth Munrow; William Cook. Exc. Richard Cantwell, Absalom Cuff.

Elline Gouldsmith. Dk. Crk. Hd. 26th of 6th m., 1708. Oct. 2, 1708. B. 169. Ann Ashton, dau. of John Ashton; Rebecca Freeland, dau. of William Freeland, dec'd.; Absalom Cuff's three children, viz: Jacob, Esther and Patience; Thomas Shaw, Jane Emran; two nieces. Rebecca England and Martha Cuff; Absalom Cuff and Martha, his wife. Exc. Friend and nephew, Absalom Cuff. Property in Old England.

Philip England. 7th day of 7th mo., 1708. Nov. 3, 1708. B. 174. Wife, Elizabeth, deceased; sons, Joseph and James England;

sons-in-law, William Wells and Abraham Cuffe; dau., Elizabeth Wells; dau.-in-law, Martha Cuffe; twenty grandchildren; Joseph England's 8 children; William Wells' 7 children; Absalom Cuffe's 3 children and Hannah Berwick and her child. Exc. son, Joseph and sons-in-law.

John Smith, Senior. Husbandman. Chris. Crk. 9th day of 10th m., called Dec., 1708. B. 158. Wife, Sarah Smith; dau., Mary Smith. Attested by Joseph Cookson, Joseph Bonnelle, Jonas Arskain.

Brewer Sinnexen. Nov. 25, 1708. Dec. 15, 1708. B. 205. Wife, Sophia; sonn, James Sinnexson; eldest sunn, Brude; Dorcas, the wife of my sunn James. Exc. wife; sunn, James. Original will in Phila. Wills Office.

Katharine Flaherty. (Nunc.) Dec. 22, 1708. Dec. 27, 1708. Attested by John Healy. Filed. "Testator departed this life on the 24th inst., 1708." Martha Williams of Appo. Hd.; two children, John Flaherty and Margaret Flaherty; "boy John Flaherty she left unto John Healy of Appo. Hd., girl, Margaret Flaherty she left unto Martha Williams."

Lewes Owen. Dk. Crk. Hd. Jan 22, 1708. ——— Misc. 1. 371. Eldest dau., Ann; dau. Ellen; youngest dau., Jane; wife, Lowry Owen; two sons, Lewis Owen and John Owen. Exc. wife, Lowry.

Nicholas Smith. Yeoman. Forest near Blk. bd. Crk. 28th of 12th m., called Feb., 1708. ———. B. 202. Wife, Hannah Smith; two children, Jacob Smith and Hannah Smith; dau., Ann Russell. Exc. wife, Hannah Smith.

Morris Vander Winghouse (Mourits Vanwidwenhuysen). Nov. 1, 1709. Misc. 1. 471. Unkle, Jacob Mourits and his wife, of New York; sisters, Elizabeth Vanwidwenhuysen and Catrina Lamberts; cousin, Janntye De Hart; consins, Paul Maurits, Jacob Maurits, Jr.

William Ball. Blacksmith. N. C. Jan. 30, 1709. Feb. 13, 1709. B. 195. Eldest son, John Ball; eldest dau., Sarah Anderson; youngest son, Thomas Ball; sons, John and Jeremy Ball; wife, Esther Ball; dau., Mary McDonnell; Elizabeth and Anne Ball. Exc. wife, Esther Ball, James Robinson.

Peter Andree. Appo. Crk. Hd. Feb. 15, 17—. Mar. 18, 1709. B. 200. Sister, Susannah Andree; Jacob and Abraham Martin, the sons of Jeffry Martin. Exc. sister, Susannah Andree.

James Withe. Shoemaker. Dk. Cr. Hd. Jan. 1, 1708. Nov. 17, 1709. B. 191. Son, John Withe. Exc. William Wells, yeoman.

Clement Clementson. Three-tree Hook. Feb. 4, 1709. Apr. 7, 1710. B. 203. Mother, Bridget Giljohnson; coson, John Clementson, my mother's youngest son; sister-in-law, Sarah Clementson; coson, John; John John Jeans, his two girls. Exc. mother, Bridget Giljohnson.

Henry Halso. Merchant. Apr. 20, 1710. Apr. 27, 1710. B. 198. Joseph Hill; Joshua Story; Wessel Alrichs, goldsmith; Andrews Peterson, yeoman; wife, Anna Halso. Exc. Wessell Alrichs.

Ann Hartup. Widow. Apr. 19, 1710. May 18, 1710. B. 190. Eldest son, John; sons, Hendry, Robert. Exc. Peter Walraven, Samuel Vane.

Adam Hyke. Husbandman. Swanwicke. Apr. 8, 1709. June 28, 1710. B. 215. Wife, Gartrude; sons, Henry Hyke, Adam Hyke, Solomon Hyke; Widow Stork, grandmother of Solomon Hyke; son, Peter Brank; daus., Margaret, Barbara, Alkey. Exc. wife, Gartrude.

Peter Stallcop. Sept. 3, 1709. May 16, 1710. B. 193. Wife, Katherine; son-in-law, Rev. Ericus Biork; son, John Stalcop; son, Andrew; dau., Margaret Stallcop; son-in-law, John Justasson. Exc. wife, Katherine; son-in-law, Rev. Ericus Biork; son, John. ·Leaving small children.

Jacob De fraux (Dutrux). Planter. N. C. Dec. 27, 1709. June 21, 1710. B. 209. Son, William Dutrux; wife, Elizabeth Dutrux; three youngest sons, Isaac, Benjamin and Cornelius. Exc. Elizabeth Dutrux.

John Tilton. Planter. N. C. Jan. 1, 1709-10. June 21, 1710. B. 208. Wife, Elizabeth; son, John Tilton. Exc. Elizabeth Tilton.

John Richardson. N. C. Nov. 10, 1710. Dec. 2, 1710. B. 223. Wife, Elizabeth; two sons, John and Richard; grandson, John Anderson; the son of James Anderson; granddau., Mary Anderson; nephew, John Richardson, son of brother, Joseph of Glamford Bridge, Great Britain. Exc. wife, Elizabeth Richardson; son, John Richardson.

Cornelius Empson. Gentleman. Goal Grange, N. C. Dec. 12, 1710. B. 224. Son, Richard Empson; Ebenezar; daus., Sarah and Elizabeth and Susannah; son, Charles; son, James; wife, Mary; daus., Ann. and Susannah and Mary. Exc. wife, Mary; George Robbeson, Isaac Taylor, Thomas Babb, Ebenezer Empson.

James Middleton. Late of Kingdom of Ireland. Late dweller in Chester in province of Pennsylvania. 10th month 1st, 1710. Dec. 23, 1710. B. 227. Shipmates, William and John Hill, Richard Dobson, James Downe, James Hambleton, Margaret Ray, Sarah Hill, John Salkild, John Bell, Hannah Verina, six children of Geo. Robinson, viz: Ann, Mary, Catrin, George, Valentine and Rebackah. To Jos. Gilpin near Concord and Geo. Robinson of Rockland, cousins William and John Davis, sons to James Davis of Ireland. Exc. Joseph Gilpin, George Robinson.

Jane Liston. Blk. bd. Crk. Hd. Jan. 6, 1711. Jan. 10, 1711. Misc. 1. 286. Two granddaughters, Rachel and Ruth Russell; son, Edmund Liston. Exc. Joseph England. Memo. dated Jan. 18, 1711, mentions Daniel Blowitt and Joan Liston.

George Cummins. Late of Staten Island, N. Y. Nov. 25, 1709. Oct. 27, 1711. B. 218. Brother, Wm. Comans; sister, Jone George Garrison; my father-in-law, John Brown of Staten Island. Exc. brother, Wm. Comans.

William ' Houston. Sometime merchant. Burgess of, Whithorn. Burgess and gild brother of City of Glascow, both in Scotland. Otherwise called Wm. Houston of New Castle, etc. May 25, 1707. Dec 11, 1711. Misc. 1. 178. Sisters, Jannott, Katharn, Agnes and Mary Houston; only brother, Anthony Houstown of London; Mr. John Wilson, Jasper Yeats, Dr. Sproys; son of Sarah Howes, London; Sir Wm. Naxfield. Exc. Benj. Sweet.

Matthew Walton. Dk. Crk. Hd. Mar. 28, 1712. Apr. 25, 1712. B. 229-230. Father-in-law, Abraham Lackerman; wife, Rebekah; two sons, Abraham and Matthew; daughter, Mary. Exc. wife, Rebekah Walton.

John Thomas. Oct. 28, 1711. May 3, 1712. B. 234. Oldest son, David; two sons, Thomas and Joseph Thomas; eldest dau., Mary Thomas, and her two children; dau., Sarah Thomas. Exc. Sarah Thomas, David Thomas.

Jean Reall, wife of Jacob Reall. Appo. Hd. Jan. 11, 1702. May 6, 1712. B. 232. Dau., Jean Andree; dau., Elizabeth Andree; son, Peter Andree; dau., Ann Andree; dau., Susannah Andree; dau., Mary Martin, the wife of Jeffrey Martin. Exc. daus., Jean and Elizabeth Andree.

Thomas Lloyd. Yeoman. W. Clay Crk. Hd. Apr. 7, 1712. June 3, 1712. B. 230-233. Wife, Sarah Lloyd; grandson, Thomas Rice; son-in-law, Evan Rice and Katherine, his wife; brother-in-law, Evan Howell. Exc. Sarah Lloyd.

Asmund Stedham. Husbandman. N. C. Aug. 26, 1711. Aug. 22, 1712. B. 237. Sons, Samuel, Asmund, Adam; wife, Margarett; daus., Sarah, Mary, Christeen; dau., Bridget (married); Overseers, Edward Robinson and Mathias Peterson. Exc. wife. Margaret; eldest son, Samuel; brother, Lucas Stedham.

Cornelius Vandever. Dec. 18, 1712. Feb. 18, 1712. B. 253-254. Wife, Margaretha; son, John; two youngest sons, William and Henry; children, Jacob, Phillip, John, Elizabeth, Margaretha, Catherine, William. Exc. son, Phillip; friend, Peter Peterson.

Robert French. Merchant. N. C. Jan. 23, 1712. C. 1. Wife, Mary French; son, David French; eldest dau., Katherine French; dau., Ann French; dau., Elizabeth French; dau., Mary French; brother, Thomas French of Kent Co.; Col. John French, Isabella Trent; Elenor Trent, Andrew Hamilton of Chester, Maryland. Exc. Mary French (wife), David French (son). Trustees, Andrew Hamilton, Thomas French (brother).

Peter Walraven. Sept. 24, 1712. Oct. 13, 1712. B. 19. Sons, Jacob Walraven, John Walraven and Isaac Walraven. Exc. Henry Walraven, Thomas Boyor.

Edward Jeoffreys. Cordwainer. N. C. Dec. 5, 1712. Dec' 12, 1712. B. 249. Wife, Jean. Exc. wife, Jean.

Humphrey Best. N. C. 1st day of 4th m., called June, 1710. Dec. 22, 1712. B. 179. Wife, Ellnor Best; sons, William and Humphrey Best. Exc. wife.

John Houie. Yeoman. Drayer Crk. 11m. 16th, 1711-12. Dec. 27, 1712. B. 180. Coozin, John NaCoole; wife, Mary Houie. Exc. wife, Mary.

Robert Hayes. Blk. bd. Crk. Hd. Oct. 9, 1713. C. 13. Wife, Hannah Hayes; dau., Isabella Hayes. Exc. Richard Cantwell.

Mathias Lossan. N. C. Nov. 27, 1712. Jan. 10, 1712-13. A. 251. Son, Wholle; children, Ingebor, Wholle, Annikie, Sarah and Mary; father-in-law, Lucas Stedham; brother, Wholle Lossan. Exc. Wholle Lossan, Lucas Stedham.

Thomas Shaw. Duck Creek. Nov. 19, 1713. Feb. 12, 1713. C. 15. Wife, Hannah Shaw; children. Exc. Hannah Shaw.

Robert Smith. Yeoman. Geo. Crk. Jan. 11, 1713. Mar. 15, 1713. C. 17. Son, Thomas Smith; wife, Anne Smith; son, Richard Smith; son, Robert Smith; son, William Smith. Exc. Anne Smith (wife), Richard Empson, John Ashton.

Reynier Harmens Van Burkloe. Bombay Hook. Nov. 19, 1713. Mar. 19, ——. C. 16. Wife, Mary Van Burkloe; eldest son, Peter; other children, Mary, Margarette, Daniel, Susanna, William, Herman, Jacob, Samuel and Rebecca. Exc. wife, Mary; friend, Daniel Pastories.

John Lewis. Sept. 17, 1708. April 10, 1713. B. 185. Wife and children. Exc. Sarah Lewis, Thomas Reece (brother-in-law).

George Read. Yeoman. St. Geo. Hd. Mar. 22, 1712. May 4, 1713. B. 182. Eldest son, George Read; son, Robert; dau., Elizabeth; dau., Lidiah Read. Exc. son, Robert Read. Guardians, James Robinson, Richard Empson.

Abraham Cartwright. May 16, 1713. Aug. 15, 1713. C. 10. Father, Thomas Cartwright, deceased, of Christian Creek. Age of Absolam, 19 yrs., 11 mo. Brother-in-law, Cornelius Williams. Exc. brother-in-law, Cornelius Williams.

Patrick Fitzgerald. Husbandman. July 10, 1714. ——. C. 111. Rowland Fitzgerald. Exc. Rowland Fitzgerald.

Isaac Sheffer. Yeoman. N. C. May 11, 1714. May 27, 1714. C. 19. Wife, Cartwright Sheffer. Exc. wife, Cartwright Sheffer, Thomas Boyer.

Rachel Colvert. Widow. N. C. July 15, 1714. July 27, 1714. C. 20. Daus., Mary Inlow and Elizabeth Colvert; brother-in-law, Tobias Tussey. Exc. Tobias Tussey, John Land.

John Cox. Dec. 3, 1713. Aug. 10, 1714. Misc. 1. 38. "Children;" two daughters, Anna; "the youngest brother, Elias Cox;" son,

Peter Cox; son, Charles Cox; John Cox, Jr., Magnus Cox, Augustine Cox. Adm. by wife, Bridget.

Bartle Bartleson. Nov. 29, 1711. Nov. 4, 1714. C. 24-25. George Wakford. Exc. George Wakford.

John Bolton. Farmer. St. Geo. Hd. Nov. 15, 1713. Dec. 2, 1714. C. 22. Wife, Ann Bolton, Mary Sawier, dau. of Thomas Sawïer (dec'd.) and grandchild to Ann, my wife. Exc. Isaac Gooding of Reedin Island, Ffloren Sorency.

John Garland. Merchant. N. C. Dec. 2, 1714. Dec. 11, 1714. C. 26. Wife, Mary Garland; dau., Susannah Garland; brother, Anthony Green; brother, Abraham Garland; sister, Sodt Anderson. Exc. wife, Mary; father, Silvester Garland.

John Vardamon. Appo. Crk. Mar. 17, 1714. Apr. 5, 1715. Misc. 1.472. Wife, Margaret; son, Johannes; other children, Christopher and William and Jane Margrtia. Exc. Margaret Vardamon.

Isaac Gooding. Province of Penna. April 20, 1715. May 3, 1715. Misc. 1.83. Son, John; sons, Isaac and Jacob Gooding; son, Abraham; dau., Mary; wife, Judith; daus., Elizabeth Garbarock and Susan Gooding. Exc. Judith Gooding, Jacob Gooding.

Job Brewster. N. C. Apr. 14, 1715. May 31, 1715. C. 30. Wife, Elizabeth; three daus., Elizabeth, Sarah and Ann. Exc. father, John Brewster, Cornelius Cooch, John Wood.

Richard Mankin. Weaver. Mar. 16, 1715. June 1, 1715. C. 27. Uncle, James Robinson; brother, George Mankin; sister, Ann James' eldest son, (viz.), Joseph James, Mary Chandler. Exc. George Mankin, Thomas Chandler.

John Frogg. Merchant. Philadelphia. Aug. 17, 1706. Feb. 11, 1716. C. 69. Wife, Mary Frogg. Exc. wife, Mary Frogg.

Roeloff Dehaes. Merchant. Widower. N. C. Jan. 4, 1716. Feb. 23, 1716. C. 74. Dau., Elizabeth De Haes, Catherine De Haes, Mary De Haes, Joanna De Haes, Sarah dehaes. Exc. Richard Halliwell, Col. John French, Rowland Fitzgerald.

Richard Cantwell. Gentleman. Appo. Hd. Oct. 17, 1715. Mar. 18, 1716. C. 77. Wife, Mary Cantwell; son, Richard; dau., Mary; sister, Elizabeth Garretson's three children, Edmund Garretson, Cantwell Garretson and Mary Garretson. Exc. wife, Mary Garretson.

Thomas Turner (Tournier). Harlem, New York. July 25, 1709. Mar. 28, 1716. C. 85. Son, Daniel Turneur; wife, Mary Turneur; other children, Jacob Turneur, Peter; Frederick Devow. Exc. Mary Turneur (wife).

David Griffith. Farmer. (Nunc.) Apr. 24, 1716. Apr. 27, 1716. C. 46. Eldest son, Griffith Griffith, "upon arrival in this counttry;" eldest dau., Jane Lewis, wife of William Lewis; dau., Mary Watkin, wife of Peter Watkin; second son, John Griffith. Exc. John Griffith.

William Grant. Yeoman. Appo. Hd. May 17, 1716. July 21, 1716. N. 350. Wife, Mary Grant; son, William Grant. Exc. Samuel Vance, John Peterson, wife, Mary Grant.

Hadadiah Offley. Dk. Crk. Hd. Sept. 19, 1716. Oct. 1, 1716. C. 54. Wife, Laurana Offley; nephew, William Shaw. Exc. wife, Laurrana Offley, father-in-law, Charles Hilliard.

Gertrude Tussey. Stoney Penn. Sept. 23, 1716. Oct. 12, 1716. C. 57. Eldest sons, Peter and John Mounce; son, Stephen Tusey. Exc. Lasey Peterson, brother; Peter Mounce, son.

Christian Urinson. Yeoman. Late of Chris. Crk., now of Fifth Point, N. C. C. Oct. 16, 1716. Nov. 6, 1716. C. 60. Wife, Elizabeth; son, Christian; dau., Sophia; unborn child; brother, Peter Anderson. Exc. wife, Elizabeth, Peter Hance, Mathias Peterson.

Thomas Grimes, Graham or Grahm. Dec. 29, 1705. Oct. 29, 1716. C. 65. Sons, James and John; son, Thomas. Exc. son, James Grimes.

Charles Ford. Labourer. St. Geo. Hd. Jan. 24, 1716-7. Feb. 20, 1716-7. C. 72. Aliley Eyky, the dau. of Adam Eyky; Hannah King, dau. of Frances King; Marinus King, Grace Whittaker (servant). Exc. Frances King.

Sigfreedus Alrichs. Jan. 5, 1715. March 28, 1716. C. 40. Wife, Mary. In default of issue, children of my brothers, Hermanus and Jacobus (deceased) and children of my bro. Wessell. Peter Alrichs, son of bro. Jacobus. Exc. wife, Mary. Silvester Garland.

Phillip Gooding. Feb. 24, 1717. ——. C. 112. Sister, Elizabeth, wife of William Wright; father, Peter Gooding, Anne Johnson. Exc. brother, William Wright.

Stephen Wilcox. (Nunc.) Blk. bd. Crk. Hd. 18th day of 1st m. 1717-8. Mar. 19, 1717. C. 123. Wife, Magdalen Willcox. Exc. Magdalen Willcox (wife). Witnesses, High Conyer, James Askew, Martha Askew.

John Laws. Yeoman. N. C. Mar. 15, 1716-7. Mar. 29, 1717. C. 82. Sister, Jane Ireland; friend, John McCoole; brother, John Ashton, and Anna, his wife; mother, Ann Bolton; sister, Mary Houie. Exc. John McCoole.

James Anderson. Mar. 20, 1716-7. Apr. 20, 1717. C. 86. Dau., Hannah Anderson; son, John Anderson; dau., Mary Anderson; son, James Anderson; son, Peter Anderson; son, Samuel Anderson. Exc. son, James Anderson. Bro. David Miller.

Robert Hutchinson. Yeoman. Apr. 11, 1717. May 3, 1717. C. 88. Cousine and friend, Gunning Bedford, and his son, William Bedford; uncle, Josiah Tailer; Rev. James Anderson, minister at New Castle; Martha Turnnor. Mrs. Poulson, formerly widow Sumaker; my mother, Margaret Hutcheson; sisters, Mary Hutcheson and Hannah Richeson; my niece, or sister's daughter, Mary, Mercy or Morey. Exc. mother, Margaret Hutcheson, brother-in-law, John Richeson, Gunning Beford.

Mary Marrarty. Widow. Blk. bd. Crk. Hd. Mar. 28, 1717. May 22, 1717. C. 91. Dau., Elizabeth Harding; John and William Russell, the sons of John and Mary Russell. Exc. Elizabeth Harding, (dau.).

James Alexander. Carpenter. New Minister, Cecil Co., Md. July 12, 1717. C. 103. Wife, Mary; youngest son, Ffrancis; sons, Joseph and John; another child, not named; father-in-law, John Steel, Yeoman, of New Castle Co.; brother, Ffrancis Alexander of Cecil Co., Md. Exc. wife, Mary; father-in-law, John Steel; brother Ffrancis Alexander.

John Evans. Sept. 3, 1717. C. 100. Four sons. Exc. Thomas Evans, brother; Morgan Morgans.

Howell James, Senior. Yeoman, of Welsh tract. Aug. 17, 1717. Oct. 1, 1717. C. 96. Granddau., Margaret James; granddau., Jane James; grandson, William James, son of William James; wife, Phoebe; son, Howell James; sons, James and Phillip James; dau., Mary; dau., Ann; dau., Sarah; grandson, James James, the son of William James. Exc. James James, Phillip James, Howell James.

Jeremiah Cloud. Cordwainer. Rexland Manor. Feb. 20, 1715-6. Dec. 21, 1717. C. 118. Wife, Elizabeth; son, William Cloud; sons, Jeremiah and Mordecai, Daniel, John; daus., Hannah, Sarah, Elizabeth. Exc. Elizabeth Cloud, William Cloud.

Cornelius Vangosoll. Nov. 8, 1717. May 22, 1718. C. 126. Mother, Gertrude; brother, Johannes; sister, Catherine. Exc. Gertrude Vangosoll.

Benjamin Richardson. Yeoman. Blk. bd. Crk. June 10, 1718. July 26, 1718. G. 131. Son, John; wife, Ann; son, Edward; six children, Benjamin Richardson, Sarah Liston, Ann, Joseph, Thomas and Catherine Richardson; son-in-law, Thomas Ward. Exc. son, Edward; wife, Ann.

Lewis Thomas. N. C. June 22, 1718. July 24, 1718. C. 128. Brother, John; brother, Richard; my father; brother, David; brother, Joseph; sister, Mary; sister, Anna; brother, Richard's son, David. Exc. brothers, Richard and John.

Urian Anderson. July 22, 1718. Aug. 12, 1718. Wife, Mary Anderson; sons, James, John and Urian; brothers, James Anderson, and Peter Anderson; son, Elias; son, Jonah; daus., Mary and Annie Anderson; sons, Peter and Mounse Anderson. Exc. wife, Mary Anderson.

William Vandervare of B'wine Ferry. Jan. 29, 1717. Oct. 13, 1718. C. 236. Wife, Alice. Exc. Alice Vandevare.

Robert Witherspoon, Minister. St. Geo. Hd. June 4, 1718. Aug. 22, 1718. C. 142. Rebecca Premson; wife, Mary Witherspoon;

Elias and Sedyer Naudain, son and dau. of Sedyer Naudain. Exc. Mary Witherspoon, Elias Naudain, Isaac Vigoreaux.

Phillip Peirce. N. C. Nov. 26, 1718. Dec. 3. 1718. Misc. 1. 389. Jonas Jonas, Rebekah Nicholl. Exc. Joseph England.

Thomas Ward. Dk. Crk. Hd. Aug. 20, 1719. ———. Misc. 2.20. Wife, ———; son, Thomas. Exc. Joseph England, Henry Shadden.

Richard Hallowell. Merchant. Dec. 4, 1716. Dec. 17, 1719. C. 162. Richard and Mary Cantwell, the son and dau. of Richard Cantwell; three eldest sons of Henry Garretson, (namely) Richard, Edmund and Cantwell; Hallowell and Bridget Garretson, the son and dau. of said Henry Garretson; Mary Garretson. dau. of said Henry Garretson, four god-children, viz: Jasper Yeats, Jr., William Bedford, John Ross, and Priscilla Robinson; brother, Thomas Halliwell; nephew, Thomas Halliwell; nieces, Bridget and Mary Halliwell, (daus. of Thomas); Elizabeth Garretson, widow. Exc. John Moore; Rev. George Ross.

Benjamin Swett. Farmer. N. C. Dec. 21, 1719. Jan. 7, 1719. C. 169. Dau., Sarah De haes; grandson, Joseph Hamerton; granddau., Rebecca Hamerton; grandson, Benjamin Swett; Rowland Fitzgerald; grandson, John Swett; James Merriweather; dau.-in-law, Ann Fitzgerald. Exc. James Cooper, Gerald Garrison, Brother Jedediah Hussey.

Edward Cole. Cooper. Feb. 6, 1719. Feb. 16, 1719. C. 176. Wife, Hester Cole; dau., Ann Cole. Exc. Hester Cole.

Richard Elson. Appo. Hd. Dec. 13, 1719. Feb. 17, 1719. C. 173. William Williams. Exc. William Williams.

Mathew Corbet. Yeoman. Dk. Crk. Hd. 10th day of 12th m., called February. Feb. 25, 1719. C. 180. Two daughters, Jane Corbett, Mary Corbett; son, James Corbett. "These three all my children." Exc. son, James.

Ellinor Fowke. Widow. Dk. Crk. Hd. Feb. 14, 1719. Mar. 5, 1719. C. 188. Son, Henry Fowke; dau., Ann; grandchild, Ann, the widow of Thomas Gillett; grandchild, Ellinor; Mary Owens, John Sanders, Steven Sanders, Lydia Sanders, James Sanders, Peter Sanders, John Owens, Ellinor Fowke, Owen Fowke, Stephen Fowke, Sarah Fowke, Rebecca Banto, Jane Gano. Exc. James Gano.

Silvester Garland. Merchant. N. C. Oct. 7, 1710. June 19, 1719. C. 232. Wife, Anne Garland; son, Abraham Garland; son, Silvester Garland; dau., Sodt Anderson; granddau., Susannah Garland, the dau. of my son John Garland; son-in-law, James Cebron. Exc. wife, Anne Garland; son-in-law, James Anderson.

Jeremiah Lautman. Farmer. Dk. Crk. Hd. Aug. 9, 1718. 9. 15, 1719. C. 151. Wife, Hana; sons, John Lantman, Matthew Lantman, Jacob. Exc. wife.

John Brewster. Innholder. N. C. Nov. 22, 1718. Dec. 11, 1719. C. 158. Three grandchildren, Sarah, Mary and Elizabeth, daughters of Job Brewster. Wife, Elizabeth. Exc. wife, Elizabeth.

Adam Sharpley. Shilpots Crk. Nov. 16, 1686. Apr. 20, 1720. C. 207. Wife, Mary. Exc. wife, Mary.

Jasper Yeates. Merchant. N. C. Feb. 6, 1718. May 2, 1720. C. 211. Son, George Yeates; son, John Yeates; son, Jasper Yeates; dau., Mary Yeates; dau., Ann McCall; wife, Katherine Yeates. Exc. wife, Katherine Yeates; son, George Yeates, George McCall.

John Houghton. Mar. 10, 1720. May 27, 1720. C. 221. Wife, Ann Houghton; dau., Martha Houghton; dau., Mary; dau., Rebecca; dau., Dina Dixon; dau., Ann Dixon; son, George Dixon; four sons, viz: Henry, William, John, and Thomas Dixon. Exc. wife, Ann Houghton, John Gregg.

George Peterson. Yeoman. Swanwick. June 8, 1720. Aug. 4, 1720. C. 238. Wife, Catharine; sons, Peter, William; daus., Elinor, Alice; sons, Jacobus, Corneluss and George.

William Hackett. Apr. 16, 1720. Aug. 19, 1720. C. 248. Eldest son, John Hackett; eldest dau., Prudence; two sons, Joseph Hackett and William Hackett. Exc. wife, Sarah Hackett.

Charles Wallace. (Nunc.) Pigeon run. Aug. 20, 1720. Attested by Margaret Hutchinson, aged 20 years. Mr. Cross, executor.

James Deming (Dunnen). July 31, 1720. Sept. 23, 1720. C. 252. Wife; children, John, Robert, Jane, James and Ezekial. Adm. by wife, Mary Deming.

Thomas John. W. Clay Crk. Hd. May 17, 1720. Oct., 1720. C. 253. Wife, Rebecca John; son, John; son, Enoch; son, Thomas; son, Benjamin; dau., Sarah; dau., Mary; dau., Ruth.

Paul Poulson. Blk. bd. Crk. Hd. Apr. 13, 1720. Nov. 29, 1720. C. 260. Wife, Elizabeth Poulson. Exc. wife, Elizabeth Poulson.

George Hogg, Senior. Cordwainer. N. C. Jan. 11, 1721. Jan. 22, 1721. Misc. 1 179. Son, George Hogg; wife, Anne; son, John; John White; son, James; dau., Sarah Gregg, wife of George Gregg. Exc. Anne Hogg, (wife); John Hogg, (son).

John Greenwater. Yeoman. Apr. 7, 1721. Feb. 19, 1721. Misc. 1.85. Son, John Greenwater; wife, Elizabeth; dau., Isabel Greenwater; brother, William Patterson; John and Jacob Godding, Charles Robison, cordwainer. Exc. wife, Elizabeth; friend, John Stewart.

Henry Garretson. Yeoman. Chris. Hd. Dec. 28, 1721. Feb. 19, 1721-2. Misc. 1.86. Eldest son, Henry Garretson; other three children, Conrad Garretson, John Garretson and Mary Garretson. Exc. wife, Christian Garretson.

Baldwin Johnson. Appo. Hd. Feb. 28, 1720. Mar. 6, 1721. C. 283.

Mother-in-law, Ann Eyre; dau., Mary Johnson; son, Edward Johnson. Exc. Alexander Hamilton, of Philadelphia; James Heath, of Maryland; Mary Heath, his wife; John Rees, of New Castle; brother, Edward Johnson; Richard Oliver, of Antigua.

Thomas Griffith. Cooper. Mar. 17, 1720-1. Mar. 25, 1721. Thomas and Mary Brown, children of my sister, Margaret Brown. Exc. John Daniel Tomay.

Isaac Bellarby. Yeoman. St. Geo. Hd. ———. Mar. 27, 1721. C. 288. Sons, Isaac Bellarby and John Bellarby; daus., Mary and Susannah Bellarby; wife, Temperance Bellarby. Land in Dunster Parish, Summersetshire, Old England. Trustees, Brother Henry, John Ashton, Joseph Ashton, John McColle. Exc. Isaac Bellarby, Junior.

Sarah West. May 5, 1721. May 18, 1721. C. 298. Son, John West; dau., Mary Read; son, William West. Exc. son, John West. Guardians for sons, Joseph England, John Ashton, Andra Peterson.

Peter Jubart. St. Geo. Hd. May 2, 1721. May 18, 1721. C. 295. Children, viz. Peter Jubart, Andra Jubart, John Jubart, Abraham Jubart; dau., Magdalene Jubart; son, David Jubart; son, Jacob Jubart. Exc. son, Peter Jubart.

John Wallace. Yeoman. Nov. 15, 1720. Sept. 2, 1721. C. 309. Son-in-law, John Dixon, in Ireland; Robert Langham, of Bellmanagonaugh, in County of Doron, Ireland. Exc. John Brian, farmer; Thomas Reed.

Rees Meredith. W. Clay Crk. Hd. Sept. 5, 1721. 8., 2, 1721. C. 341. Wife, Mary Meredith; dau., Margaret Meredith. Hannah Fallow. Exc. James Robinson, Evan Rice.

Paul Saunders. Namens Crk. Mar. 24, 1716. Sept. 20, 1721. C. 346. Sister, Hannah Saunders; cousin, Joseph Tomlinson, the son of Samuel Tomlinson. Exc. Samuel Tomlinson, Thomas Whitehurst.

Thomas Allett. Innholder. N. C. Sept. 20, 1721. Oct., 1721. C. 324. Cousins, Margaret Allett and Navran Allett, the two daughters of my brother, William Allett, of Country of Antrim in Ireland. Exc. John Silsbee, carpenter; Joshua Storrie, innholder; wife, Ann Allett.

Joseph Wheeldon. Husbandman. N. C. Feb. 28, 1721. Oct. 2, 1721. C. 334. Wife, Bridget; son, Isaac; son, Joseph. Exc. wife, Bridget Wheeldon.

Mordecai Moore. Practitioner in Physick. Ann Arundel Co., Maryland. 2d d. of 9th m., 1713. Oct. 29, 1721. N. 57. Three daus., viz: Deborah, Mary and Elizabeth; son, Richard Moore; kinswomen, Mary Coleman, Mordica Burgess; Joseph Coleman; children of my son-in-law, Charles Burgess, viz: Francis Hanslop; William Burgess, Ursula Burgess, Mordica Burgess, Charles Burgess, Benjamin Burgess; dau.-in-law, Susannah Mitchell; her children, Burges Mitchell, Mordica Mitchell, John Mitchell, and Hennerietta Mitchell. Exc. Deborah Moore, (wife); Richard Moore, (son).

Samuel Stidham. (Nunc.) Yeoman. Chris. Hd. Oct. 31, 1721. Nov. 6, 1721. C. 327. Wife; younger brother, Adam; son, Jacob. Attested by Timothy Stidham and Jonas Stidham.

Henry Garreson. Yeoman. Chris. Hd. Oct. 24, 1721. 9. 18. 1721. (O. S.) C. 315. Sons, John Garrason, Garrett Garrason, Henry Garrason, Peter Garrason; wife, Ann; three daughters, Catherine, Ann, Elizabeth; brother, Powell Garrason. Exc. wife, Ann; son, John.

Ambrose London. (Nunc.) Dec. 4, 1721. C. 350. House of George Mankin. Attested by Lucas Stidham, Jr., Robert Robinson, son of Edward Robinson, Brewer Senexson. Exc. Edward Robinson.

Joseph Wood, Esquire. N. C. Dec. 12, 1721. Dec. 21, 1721. C. 361. Granddau., Ann Clerk; wife; son, Joseph Wood; dau., Jean Clerk; dau., Susannah Empson; son-in-law, Ebenezer Empson; dau., Letitia; dau., Rebecca Wood. Exc. son, Joseph Wood; son-in-law, Ebenezer Empson.

John Taylor. Blk. bd. Crk. Hd. Dec. 7, 1721. Feb. 15, 1722. Misc. 1.451. Son, William Taylor; sons, John, Ephraim and Abraham; wife, Eamie; John Berrows, William Holiday. Exc. wife, Amy.

Samuel Underwood, Senior. June 11, 1722. Feb. 18, 1722. Misc. 1.468. Wife; son, Samuel; son, Joseph; son, Benjamin; sons, Alexander and Thomas; dau., Elizabeth Harris. Exc. sons, Benjamin and Joseph.

John Harvey. Mar. 26, 1722. May 17, 1722. Misc. 1.182. William Garden, John Burges, Richard Hambly. Exc. William Garden, John Burgess, Richard Hambly.

James Williams. Mar. 30, 1722. May 17, 1722. Misc. 2.22. Friend and Exc. James James.

Edward Gray. Red Lyon Hd. May 3, 1722. Aug. 7, 1722; Misc. 1.88. Wife; daus., Mary, Ann; sons, Joseph, Benjamin and John. Exc. Wm. Courson, John McCook, James Armitage.

John Davis. Yeoman. Pen. Hd. Sept. 6, 1722. Sept. 28, 1722. C. 331. Parents; landlord, William Lewis; Jenkin John. Exc. William Lewis, David Evans, Gent.; Jenkin Evan, Yeoman.

John Hunter. Mar. 16, 1722. Mar. 22, 1723. Misc. 1.182. William Carden, Gasberry Carden.

Peter Mounce. Yeoman. B'wine Hd. Apr. 19, 1723. ———. Misc. 1.353. Wife, Annaka Mounce; eldest son, William Mounce; son, John Mounce; son, Benjamin Mounce; unborn child.

Neal O'Neal. Planter. Appo. Hd. June 6, 1720. Oct. 1, 1723. Misc. 1.372. My children; mother, Mary O'Neal; Mary Cantwell,

widow of Richard Cantwell; her two children, viz: Richard
Cantwell and Mary Low. Exc. Mary Cantwell.

Obadiah Holt. Jan. 20, 1725. Feb. 16, 1725. Misc. 1.183. Wife,
Sarah; oldest son, Martin Holt; 2nd son, Obadiah; 3rd son,
George. Exc. Sarah Holt.

Richard Lewis. Yeoman. Mill Crk. Hd. Apr. 24, 1725. ———.
Misc. 1.287. Wife, Helen; son, John Lewis; son, David Lewis;
my dau., Jane Cann, wife of William Cann; grandchild, Elizabeth Cann, dau. of William Cann; grandchild, Hellina Cann, dau.
of William Cann; grandson, William Cann, son of William Cann;
grandchild, Mary Cann. Exc. wife, Helen Lewis; son, John
Lewis.

Christopher Huston. Mill Crk. Hd. Dec. 6, 1726. Jan. 6, 1726. Misc.
1.184. Son, Samuel; daus., Joan, Martha and Ann; son-in-law,
Hugh Linn, John Porter; Samuel's brother, Robert; grandchildren, Christopher and James Huston; Charles Simons. Exc.
wife, —— Huston; son, Samuel Huston.

Casparus Garritson. Yeoman. Chris. Crk. Hd. 12th m. 3, 1726.
Feb. 6, 1726. Misc. 1.90. Wife, Ann; eldest son, John; sons,
William and Joseph; daughters. Exc. wife, Ann.

Richard Green. Mar. 15, 1725. July 12, 1726. Misc. 1.89. Brother,
Jacob Weldin; couzen, Mary William. Exc. mother, Mary
Green.

Ellis Humphries. Yeoman. Nov. 26, 1726. ———. Misc. 1.185.
Brother Lennard; Abraham Humphries, son of brother Richard
Humphries, deceased; Stephen Humphries, son of brother Richard Humphries, deceased; father-in-law, John Ashton. Exc.
brother, Lennard.

Thomas Bird. Carpenter. Chris. Hd. Nov. 20, 1726. Dec. 10, 1726.
Misc. 1.6. Eldest son, Robert; son, John; son, Joseph; daus.,
Franciss and Rebecca; sons, Richard and James; wife, Sarah;
son, Empson; daus., Mary, Elizabeth and Susannah; unborn
child. Exc. Ebenezer Empson; wife, Sarah.

James Robinson. Yeoman. Dec. 4, 1726. Dec. 30, 1726. Misc. 1.408.
Son, George; dau., Cathren Mack Donald; dau., Ann Hollings-
worth; wife, Cathren; children, James, Thomas, William, Joseph,
John, Priscilla, Daniel or David, and boy, Robinson; brothers,
George and Joseph Robinson. Exc. wife, Cathren, and son,
James.

John Grant. Yeoman. St. Geo. Hd. Dec. 26, 1726. Misc. 1.89.
Children, John Grant and Rachel Grant. Exc. William Goddart,
merchant; James Merryweather, tanner.

Caleb Offley. Yeoman. 12th day of 8th m., 1727. Mar. 9, 1727.
Misc. 1.373. Wife, Elizabeth Offley; eldest son, Michael Offley;
son, Caleb Offley; son, Daniel Offley; son, David; my sister's
son, Hazadiah Shaw. Exc. wife, Elizabeth.

John Little John. B'wine Hd. Mar. 4, 1726. Apr. 1, 1727. Misc. 1.291. Wife ———; children. Exc. wife, ———.

Richard Lewis. Mar. 21, 1722. Apr. 5, 1727. Misc. 1.287. Daus., Esther and Ann; unborn child; Elishah Thomas, Enoch Morgan, Owen Thomas; wife, Elizabeth. Exc. wife, Elizabeth Lewis.

Thomas Hollingsworth. Chris. Hd. Oct. 30, 1725. Apr. 13, 1727. Misc. 1.186. Wife, Grace; sons, Abraham, Thomas, Jacob and Joseph; dau., Elizabeth Strode; dau., Hannah Dixson; dau., Sarah Dixson, Grace Hollingsworth, William and Litisher Obery. Exc. wife, Grace Hollingsworth; son, Thomas Hollingsworth.

Isaac Vandike. Aged 47. Middlesex Co., New Jersey. Recorded in Perth Amboy. B. 45. Mar. 31, 1727. May 15, 1727. Misc. 1.479. Wife, Barber; son, Thomas; son, Isaac; dau., Mary. Exc. Andross Vandike, John Vandike.

George Plum. Yeoman. St. Geo. Hd. 6th mo. 3, 1727. ———. Misc. 1.399. Wife, Hannah Plum; sons, James, Joseph and George; dau., Phoebe. Trustees, John Ashton, John McCool. Exc. wife, Hannah.

John Vancoolin (Vanquilon). N. C. Hd. Apr. 15, 1727. Aug. 9, 1727. Misc. 1.475. Son, John Vanqulion; son, Andrew Vanqulion; son, Jacob Vanqulion; dau., Marey; dau., Christiana; son, Peetter. Exc. Peetter Clowson; George Vanqulion, Inkoss Slotham.

John Vance. Mill Crk. Hd. Oct. 23, 1727. Nov. 27, 1727. Misc. 1.476. Wife; children; father. Adm. Mary Vance.

William Monro. Yeoman. Dec. 5, 1728. Mar. 14, 1728. Misc. 1.352. Son, John Monroe; dau., Hana Monroe. Exc. John MaColl, Peter Holsteen.

Col. John French. N. C. Nov. 22, 1728. Dec. 12, 1728. Misc. 1.72. Wife; Eves French; Capt. William Battell; dau., Mary; son-in-law, Robert Robertson; dau., Sybilla; grandson; granddau., Mary Battell; granddau., Eves; granddau., Mary Robertson; dau., Mary French, Mr. George Ross, John Reynolds. Exc. wife, Eves; son-in-law, William Battell.

Trustram Sholand. Farmer. Drawyer's Crk. Feb. 8, 1729-30. Feb. 14, 1729. Misc. 1.428. Godson, Richard Lewis, son of David Lewis; relations in England; Solomon Hall, John Bishop. Exc. friend, Bishop.

John Boulton. Feb. 14, 1720-21. May 29, 1729. Misc. 1.5. Wife, Mary Boulton; brother, Francis Boulton; sister, Elonor Boulton; sister, Jain Boulton. Exc. wife, Mary Boulton.

Henry Goodwin. St. Geo. Hd. July 25, 1729. Aug. 24, 1729. Misc. 1.91. Wife, Elizabeth Goodwin; dau., Sarah Goodwin; dau., Mary Goodwin; my son, Frances Goodwin; my son, Mathew Goodwin; dau., Jean Blackburn and her husband, Richard Blackburn. Exc.

wife, Elizabeth and all my daughters except Jean, and Hermanus Allrich.

Nicholas VanDyke. Yeoman. St. Geo. Hd. Mar. 19, 1728. Nov. 19, 1729. Misc. 1.481. Sons, John and Nicholas; wife, (Juan saney?); eldest son, Thomas; dau., Catharine, wife of Hendrick Vanboorin (?); former wife; youngest son, Daniel; dau., Grace VanDike, wife of Owen Carty; dau., Mary Van, wife of William ———— (?); dau., Margaret, wife of Standly Van Dike; dau., Ann Van Dike, wife of James Anderson; son, Abraham; son, Hendrick; son, Daniel. Exc. sons, John and Nicholas.

Mary Miller. Widow. Sept. 9, 1729. Dec. 15, 1729. Misc. 1.353. Three children; eldest son, John; second son, James. Exc. son, John Miller.

William Williams. Yeoman. N. C. Oct. 13, 1729. Dec. 6, 1729. O. 493. Wife, Catharine; only son, William; daughters. Exc. wife, Catharine; son, William.

Samuel Griffing. Dec. 17, 1729. Dec. 19, 1729. Misc. 1.92. Son, William Griffing; son, James Griffing; daus., Elizabeth, Naomi; wife.

Griffith Lewis. Weaver. Mill Crk. Hd. Dec. 31, 1730. Jan. 15, 1730. Misc. 1.292. Wife, Cathrin; cuson kinsman, Phillip Thom. Exc. wife, Catharine Lewis.

James Lafarty. Mill Crk. Hd. Jan. 16, 1730. Jan. 25, 1730. Misc. 1.291. Wife, Isabel; son, John; daus., Margrat and Sara. Exc. James McCall, William Cochran.

James Haley (Healey). Blk. bd. Crk. Hd. Feb. 14, 1729. May 21, 1730. Misc. 1.187. Child; son-in-law, Will Harraway. Exc. Anne Haley and Thomas Noxan.

James Sykes. Feltmaker. N. C. Aug. 6, 1726. Feb. 18, 1729-30. Misc. 1.427. Wife, Mary Sykes; two sons, Stephen Sykes and James Sykes. Exc. wife, Mary. Trustees, Richard Grafton, William Read.

John Land. Bricklayer. N. C. Feb. 26, 1730. ————. Misc. 1.293. Wife, Rebekah Land; sons, Samuel Land and John Land; brother, Henry Land; son, Joseph Land; son-in-law, Henry Gonne; dau. Elizabeth Gonne. Exc. wife, Elizabeth Land.

William Graham. (Gent.) N. C. June 24, 1730. July 6, 1730. Misc. 1.93. Jeremiah Ball and Morgan Morgan, church wardens; wife, Jane. Exc. Jane Graham (wife).

Jacob King. Yeoman. St. Geo. Hd. May 5, 1730. June 15, 1730. Misc. 1.248. Wife, Catherine; children. Exc. brother, Francis King; brother, Cornelius King; wife, Catherine.

Andreas Vandike. Yeoman. May 20, 1730. June 15, 1730. Misc. 1.484. Wife, Jemima; sons, Abram, Andreas and Jacob; unborn child; son, John; two daus., Mary and Elizabeth. Exc. son, John Vandike.

Cornelius Truax. Yeoman. Rd. Lion Hd. Aug. 22, 1730. Sept. 5, 1730. N. 62. Wife, Magdalene Truax; mother, Elizabeth Truax; son, Jacob Truax; son, Peter Truax; son, Phillip Truax. Exc. Magdalene Truax, wife; Elizabeth Truax, mother; Christopher Eaton.

John Harris. Pen. Hd. Dec. 1, 1730. Dec. 11, 1730. Misc. 1.188. Wife, Esther; Mr. Ross; dau., Ann Lewis.

John Gosard. Yeoman. Mar. 25, 1729. Dec. 22, 1730. Misc. 1.94. Wife, Joan; sons, William and James. Exc. Joan Gosard.

Peter Hanson. Yeoman. Feb. 26, 1731. Mar. 4, 1731. Misc. 1.189. Brother, John Hance; Katharine Truax, Philip Truax; brother, Hans Hanson, Joseph Hanson. Exc. brothers, Hans Hanson and Joseph Hanson.

Evan Lewis. Feb. 11, 1731. Feb. 20, 1731. Misc. 1.296. My stepson, David Davies; stepdau., Rachel David; wife, Ann Lewis.

Alice Thomson. Nov. 3, 1729. Sept. 29, 1731. Misc. 1.453. Children, Matthew and John Thompson. Exc. Robert Black.

Moses Kenny. Yeoman. Mill Crk. Hd. Dec. 18, 1732. Feb. 20, 1732. Misc. 1.251. Wife, Eleanor; my sister's dau., Jane; Moses Kenny, son of my brother, Matthew Kenny; brother, John; brother, Robert. Exc. wife, Eleanor.

Alice Kirk. (Spinster). Chris. Hd. Mar. 12, 1731-2. Apr. 19, 1732. Misc. 1.294. Husband, Samuel; Jacob Vand (owen-?-, Jr.); brother-in-law, Henry (Pedrew?); my cousin, Richard (?), and his children. Exc. husband, Samuel Kirk.

Thomas Gozell. Yeoman. N. C. Oct. 14, 1732. Misc. 1.95. Friend, Robert Robertson; Israel Blake, son of Edward Blake of New Castle; John Robertson, son of above Robert. Exc. James Merriwether and Benj. Swett of New Castle. Administrator, Galbetha Gozell, wife of Thomas, testator.

John Starling. Planter. Oct. 16, 1732. ———. Misc. 1.431. My son, William, and dau., Sarai; rest of my children. Trustees and exc. above-mentioned son and dau., and in case of their death and their Uncle Francis Caran and his wife, Elizabeth.

Samuel Shennan. Taylor. April 2, 1732. Dec. 9, 1732. Misc. 1.429. Mother, Agnes Shennan (widow); brother, Hugh Shennan and his sons, Jeremiah Shennan, Samuel and John Shennon; brother, John Shennan; brother, Roger Shennan; sister, Kathrine Shennan; cusen, Mary Shennan; brother, Edward Shennan. Exc. mother, Agnes Shennan; brother, Hugh Shennan.

Rebecca Land. Widow. Dec. 4, 1732. Dec. 27, 1732. Misc. 1.296. Oldest son, Samuel Land; dau., Elizabeth Gonne; her husband, Henry Gonne; dau., Dorcas McGhee; son, John Land; son, Joseph Land. Exc. son, Samuel; son-in-law, Henry Gonne.

John Curtis. St. Geo. Hd. Feb. 27, 1733. Mar. 10, 1733. Sons, John and Richard; daus., Catherine and Rebecca Curtis; brother,

Isaac; wife, Rebekkah. Trustee, Thomas Noxon. Exc. Rebeccah Curtis.

Mary Van Bebber. Widow and exc. of Jacob Van Bebber. St. Geo. Hd. Jan. 16, 1733. Mar. 14, 1733. Misc. 1.486. Son, Jacob; dau., Mary Ashton; grandson, Joseph Hart, only son of my dau., Grace Hart, deceased; Peter Vⁿ Bebber, brother of my dec. husband, Jacob; sister of dec. husband, to wit—Hester Gooding and Veronica Birmingham; children of my brother, Nathaniel Fitz-Randolph of Woodbridge, New Jersey; my sister, Experience Moor, wife of Samuel Moor.

John Hussey. Yeoman. Chris. Hd. 6th m. (called Aug.) 28, 1729. April 12, 1733. Misc. 1.192. Wife, Anne Hussey; sons, John Hussey, Stephen Hussey, Nathan Hussey and Christopher Hussey; Christopher Hussey, dec'd.; dau., Mary, wife of Henderson Housstown; dau., Anne Hussey, Theodate Hussey, Content Hussey. Exc. wife, Ann Hussey; son, John Hussey. Trustees, brother, Garret Garretson, and friend, John Richardson.

Jacob Van Bebber. Merchant. St. Geo. Hd. Aug. 14, 1733. Sept. 16, 1733. Misc. 1.485. Wife, Mary; son, Jacob. Exc. Mary Van Bebber.

Jacob Vandiver. Yeoman. B'wine Hd. Oct. 19, 1732. Dec. 8, 1733. Misc. 1.488. Wife, Mary; son, John Vandiver; son, Cornealous Vandiver; dau., Catherine; dau., Elizabeth; son, Tobias Vandiver; son, Peter; Jonathan Stilley and Maudlin, his wife. Exc. wife, Mary; Samuel Scot, Elias Tassey.

Garret Veight. Staten Island, Co. of Richmond, province of New York. Nov. 26, 1732. Jan. 2, 1734. K. 224. Son, John Veighte; two grandsons, Garret Veighte and Garret Lockerman; dau., Lumetic Lockerman; grandson, Nicholas Veighte. Exc. John Veighte (son), Nicholas Lasillier.

Isaac Gravenraet. N. C. Jan. 24, 1734. ———. Misc. 1.96. Oldest son, Andrew Gravenraet; oldest dau., Ann; daus., Elizabeth and Mary; sons, John and Henry; daus., Lucretia and Cornelia; brother-in-law, John Hoops; wife, (dec'd.). Exc. son, Andrew; dau., Anne.

George Garretson. Appo. Hd. Jan. 19, 1733. Apr. 23, 1734. Misc. 1.98. Wife, Sarah Garretson. Exc. wife, Sarah.

Mary Rees, widow of William. Apr. 30, 1734. May 10, 1734. Misc. 1.412. Dau., Rebecca Thomas; dau., Jane James; children of Evan James by my dau. Rachel, dec'd.; grandchildren, John and Dinah Williams, children of son Jacob, dec'd., and to his dau., Hannah Williams; Benj. and Chesia David, children of Thomas David, by my dau., Gweullian; dau., Anna. Exc. two sons, Elias and Nathaniel Williams.

Thomas Huff. Yeoman. Appo. Hd. May 1, 1734. May 22, 1734. Misc. 1.192. Wife, Elizabeth. Exc. wife, Elizabeth.

Benjamin Stout, Senior. Apr. 25, 1734. June 10, 1734. Misc. 1.43r. My son, Jacob Stout; my wife. Exc. wife and son.

James Ogle. Mill Crk. Hd. Aug. 18, 1734. Sept. 6, 1734. Misc. 1.378. Two daus., Elizabeth and Anne; wife, Grissel Ogle; son, Thomas. Exc. Grissel Ogle. Trustees, brother, Thomas Ogle; Jonathon Hays.

Richard Moore. Ann Arundel Co., Maryland. Apr. 6, 1734. Sept. 3, 1734. N. 63. Wife, Margaret Moore; son, Samuel Moore; son, Mordecai Moore; three younger children, viz: Richard, Thomas and Charles. Exc. Margaret Moore, wife; Samuel Moore, son; Mordecai Moore, son.

Elizabeth Ogle. Widdow and relick of Thomas Ogle. Wh. Clay Crk. Hd. Sept. 18, 1734. Misc. 1.376. Eldest son, Edward Ogle; five of my children, viz: David, Alexander, Elizabeth, Susannah, and Jane Ogle; eldest son, Francis Graham (by my first husband); son, William Graham; two daus., Grissel and Anne Graham; daus., Anne Land, Elizabeth Ogle. Exc. Francis Graham and William Armstrong.

Jedediah Hussey. N. C. Dec. 9, 1734. Dec. 29, 1734. Misc. 1.193. Wife, Esther; dau., Rebeccah, wife of Stephen Lewis; son, Sylvanus Hussey; James Cooper; dau., Esther, (children, viz: Rebeccah, Sylvanus, Jedediah and Esther). Exc. son-in-law, Stephen Lewis; friend, Cornelius Garretson; son, Sylvanus Hussey.

Jean Moor. Rd. Lion Hd. Feb. 2, 1735. Feb. 19, 1735. Misc. 1.355. Son-in-law, Samuel Moor; son, Robert; son, John Moor; my brother, John Shields. Exc. cousin, Patrick Porter and friend, Peter Anderson.

Moses White. Schoolmaster. N. C. March 12, 1735. March 16, 1735. Misc. 2.22. Children, David White of Octarrara; dau., Jane Edwards; son, Joseph; son, James; dau., Mary Jones; son, John. Exc. David White (son), James Byron.

Thomas Pearson. Yeoman. Sept. 20, 1735. Oct. 17, 1735. Misc. 1.390. Wife, Christian Perison; son, Edward. Exc. wife, Christian; Edward Hawkins.

Edward Green. Mill Crk. Hd. Jan. 11, 1745-6. Dau., Martha Bracken; son, Thomas Bracken; dau., Margaret Reed. Exc. Thomas Bracken.

John Griffith. Oct. 28, 1735. Jan. 20, 1735-6. Misc. 1.99. Sons, Daniel, Benjamin, Samuel and John; granddau., Jane, dau. of Benjamin; " dau. Sarah's children." Exc. son, John.

John Harriss. (Nunc.) St. Geo. Hd. May 20, 1736. May 25, 1736. Misc. 1.199. Died at house of John Simpson.

Cornelius Kettle. Farmer. Apr. 3, 1733. Apr. 15, 1736. Misc. 1.252. Son, John; son, Zachariah; grandson, Samuel Silsby; granddau., Mary Janvier. Exc. sons, John and Zachariah.

Francis Land. July 23, 1735. Dec. 8, 1736. Misc. 1.299. Eldest dau.; eldest son, Samuel; son, John; dau., Dorcas; dau., Mary; son, Thomas; dau., Sarah; wife, Christian. Exc. wife, Christian Land and three sons, John, Samuel and Thomas Land.

Elias Thomas. Jan. 2, 1737. Misc. 1.453. Dau., Sarah; wife, Mary; Enoch Morgan, Sr.; son, Zachariah.

Thomas Smith. Merchant. N. C. Son of William Smith, chemist and citizen of York in Great Britain. May 4, 1737. June 13, 1737. Misc. 1.432. Wife, Mary; son, William; sister, Anne Smith of the city of York. Exc. Richard Grafton, Margaret Williamson (widow).

Daniel Von Burkelow. Farmer. Nov. 13, 1735. May 19, 1737. Misc. 1.490. Brother, Jacob Von Burkelow; son-in-law, Isaac Truax; wife, Mary. Exc. Mary Von Burkelow.

Samuel Wilson, lately from Ireland. Aug. 18, 1737. Nov. 1, 1737. Misc. 2.21. Brother, William Wilson (malter) in Lisburn, Co. of Antrim, Ireland, his wife and children; brother, David Wilson; my brother and sister Caldwell. Exc. William Nevin, John Legate, John Armoz.

John Gregg. Yeoman. Chris. Hd. Apr. 27, 1738. March 6, 1738. Misc. 1.99. Wife, Elizabeth; "Wm., my eldest son"; son, Thomas; son, Joseph; son, Samuel; dau., Hannah; dau., Rebeccah; dau., "Emey." Exc. son, William; son, Samuel.

John Griffith. B'wine Hd. Dec. 25, 1739. Jan. 24, 1739. Misc. 1.103. Wife, Cateren Griffith. Exc. friend, Adam Buckley.

Patrick Cannon. Taylor. Mill Crk. Hd. March 15, 1738-9. Apr. 23, 1739. Misc. 1.41. Eldest brother, Daniel Cannon in parish of Temple Moor, in Barrony of Gusowen (?) in ye county Donegal, for my four brethren and sister. Exc. Wm. McGaughy.

Holliwell Gerritson. Yeoman. Appo. Hd. Sept. 6, 1739. Oct. 19, 1739. Misc. 1.102. Mother, Elizabeth; widow. Exc. mother, Elizabeth Gerritson.

Mary Lewis. Tayloress. Willingtown. 4th m. 10th, 1739. Sept. 20, 1739. Misc. 1.301. Brothers and sisters. Exc. Trusty friends, Wm. Shipley and Joshua Way.

Edward McFarlan. Weaver. Willingtown. July 24, 1739. Aug. 11, 1739. Misc. 1.357. Wife, Mary. Exc. William Patton.

Hugh Creagan. Dealer. Mill Crk. Hd. Oct. 17, 1739. Oct. 17, 1739. Misc. 1.43. Sister, Catharine Creagan (allias Divine), wife of Patrick Divine in Ireland. Exc. friend and cozon, Samuel Littler in Wilmington.

Benj. Griffis. Yeoman. B'wine Hd. Jan. 1, 1740. Jan. 4, 1740. Misc. 1.104. Wife, Mary. Exc. wife, Mary.

Matthew Walton. Farmer. Appo. Hd. March 19, 1738. March 19, 1740. Misc. 2.17. Son, Matthew; wife, Mary; John Taylor, Jr., Isaac Truax. Exc. wife, Mary; Abraham Lockerman.

Minshall Littler. Cordwainer. Wilmington. May 22, 1740. June 2, 1740. Misc. 1.303. Wife, Lydia Littler; brother, Joshua Littler. Exc. brother, Joshua Littler and friend, Alexander Seaton.

Owen O'Shaveling. Sept. 24, 1741. Jan. 9, 1741. Misc. 1.379. Brother in Ireland. Exc. brother, Forlagh (Ireland), and Alexander Moor.

Rebecca Baird. N. C. Jan. 28, 1740. March 3, 1741. Misc. 2.8. Son, Robert Baird; dau., Mary, wife of Archibald Baird; dau., Margaret, wife of Robert Walker; dau., Jane, wife of Thomas Barry; dau., Elizabeth, wife of Ezekial Boggs; grandson, James Boggs, son of Elizabeth and Ezekial; granddau., Rebecca Boggs (same). Exc. Ezekial Boggs.

John Bonbonous. Christin Bridge. Feb. 23, 1740-1. Mar. 26, 1741. Misc. 2.4. Wife, Susannah; William Jones. Exc. Dr. Rees Jones and William Jones.

Jacob King. Appo. Hd. June 20, 1741. July 2, 1741. Misc. 1.254. Brother, Thomas King; sister, Rachel King; other brothers and sisters. Exc. uncle, Jacob Hyatt.

Rodger (Roger) Williams. Yeoman. Pen. Hd. July 12, A. D. 1741. Oct. 5, 1741. Misc. 2.15. Wife, Margaret; sons, William, Maurice, Roger, Thomas; daus., Martha, Mary Rees and Margaret; grandson, Jehu Rees. Exc. wife, Margaret; son, Thomas.

Samuel Greave. Yeoman. Chris. Hd. 21st day of 7th m., 1741. Nov. 3, 1741. Misc. 1.107. Wife, Sarah Greave; son, John Greave; son, Samuel Greave; son, Jonathon; dau., Martha and her husband, Jacob Chandler. Exc. three sons, John, Samuel and Jonathon.

David Nevin. Mill Crk. Hd. Feb. 21, 1742-3. March 9, 1742. Misc. 1.369. Wife, Isabel Nevin; son, John; son, William; dau., Mary. Exc. wife, Isabel; brother, William Nevin.

Elizabeth Garretson. Appo. Hd. May 22, 1742. June 9, 1742. Misc. 1.107. Dau. Bridget, wife of Richard Colegate; granddau., Eliz. Garretson, eldest dau. of my son, Richard, dec.; granddau., Eliz. Cadogan, only child of my dau., Mary, deceased; Andrew Garretson, eldest son of my son, Edmund Garretson; Edmund Garretson, son of my son, Cantwell Garritson; John Colegate, eldest son of Richard Colegate; other sons of Richard, Richard and Henry Colegate; Richard Holliwell, dec.; son, Hallowell Garretson, deceased. Exc. son, Edmund Gerritson; son-in-law, Richard Colegate and Adam Peterson, son of Andrew.

Catherin Leolin. Widow. Pen. Hd. Oct. 26, 1742. Misc. 1.305. Son, Thomas Leolin; son, William Leolin. Exc. son, William Leolin.

Evan Reece (Rice). Farmer. Mill Crk. Hd. Oct. 21, 1742. Dec. 21, 1742. Misc. 1.409. Wife, Katrina; son, Thomas; son, Thomas's 2nd son, William; his eldest son, Evan; dau., Sarah Wallace; her dau., Rachel; son, Evan. Exc. son, Evan.

Richard Grafton. Merchant. N. C. June 27, 1737. Jan. 12, 1743. Misc. 1.109. Four godchildren, viz: Jane Read, George Ross, —— Ogle, son of Thomas Ogle, dec'd., George Gonne, —— ——; brothers and sisters in England; George Grafton, Joseph Grafton, Benjamin Grafton, Elizabeth Denham; friend, John Willis. Exc. dau., Mary Grafton; wife, Mary Grafton. Dau. Mary will be 18 years old on the 4th day of September, 1749. Guardian, Clement Plumstead.

John Kettle. Yeoman. Rd. Lion Hd. March 11, 1742. March 29, 1743. Misc. 1.256. Wife, Elizabeth; two sons, Cornelius and John Kettle; two brothers, Zacharias Kettle and Henry Colesberry; four daus., Susanna, Mary, Catherine and Elizabeth Kettle. Exc. two brothers, Zacharias Kettle and Henry Colesberry.

Andrew Stalcop. Farmer. Chris. Hd. April 5, 1743. Misc. 1.434. Son, Philip Stalcop; wife, Anna Barbery, who is Philip's mother; my apprentice, Elizabeth Tussey; dau., Catherine; dau., Margaret. Exc. wife, Anna Barberry Stalcop and son, Philip.

Joseph Rodes, Sr. Yeoman. N. C. Jan. 10, 1743-4. N. 142. Dau., Abigail Rodes; dau., Ann Rodes; son, William Rodes; son, John Rodes; dau., Hannah; dau., Elizabeth Rodes; dau., Mary Rodes; son, Joseph Rodes; son, Richard Rodes; son, Benjamin Rodes; brother, Benjamin Rodes, at Jamaica. Exc. John Rodes, son; and Joseph Rodes, son.

Shusan Claghorn. Pen. Hd. Jan. 31, 1744. ——. G. 137. Son, Charles; son, Mathew Claghorn. Exc. dau., Jane Claghorn.

George Gregg. Yeoman. Chris. Hd. 3rd mo. 23rd, 1744. Sept. 14, 1744. Misc. 1.112. Wife, Sarah; sons, John, Richard and George. Exc. son, Richard.

Thomas Hyatt. Yeoman. St. Geo. Hd. April 19, 1742. Sept. 17, 1744. Misc. 1.195. Wife, Rachel; sons, Thomas, David, Jacob, Peter, Caleb and Joseph; grandson, Thomas Peterson, son of John Peterson; dau., Cathren Johnson; dau., Mary Holland, wife of John. Exc. wife, Rachel and son, Caleb.

Matthew Kenney. Yeoman. Mill Crk. Hd. Aug. 20, 1744. Oct. 1, 1744. Misc. 1.257. Wife, Rebeccah; son, Matthew; son, Moses; daus., Elizabeth, Helen and Mary; son, Robert. Exc. wife.

John Baldwin. Yeoman. Chris. Hd. Nov. 18, 1744-5. March 21, 1744-5. Misc. 2.12. Eldest son, Francis; two young children; dau., Hannah; son, William; 'dau., Elizabeth, wife of James Huklin; dau., Mary, wife of Nicholas Pyle; dau., Sarah, wife of John Pyle; son, John. Exc. son, Francis.

George Morriss. Appo. Hd. April 26, 1745 (?). June 2, 1745. Misc. 1.358. Wife, Mary; brother, Joseph Morriss. Exc. wife, Mary Morriss and Alexander Armstrong.

Philip Vanluveneigh. N. C. Jan. 12, 1744. June 5, 1745. Misc. 1.492.

Sons, Philip, Richard and Isaac; daus., Catharine, Mary and Susanna; wife, Eleanor. Exc. wife, Eleanor.

Thomas McCrea. June 10, 1745. June 13, 1745. Misc. 1.359. Wife, Esther McCrea; son, Thomas McCrea, Rodger Anderson. Exc. friend, Daniel Hamilton.

John Lewden, Senior. Yeoman. May 20, 1744. June 25, 1745. Misc. 1.305. Son, Joseph; son, John Lewden; son, Josiah; John Richardson; granddaus., Elizabeth Houston and Margaret Harris; Ann Ravy. Exc. sons, John and Joseph.

John White. Mill Crk. Hd. May 5, 1742. Aug. 2, 1745. Misc. 2.14. Friend, James Jordan; son, James; son, Robert; son, Samuel; wife, Francis; two youngest sons, William and Broak. Exc. James Jordan.

John Hendrickson. Farmer. Chris. Hd. Oct. 8, 1731. Nov. 7, 1745. Misc. 1.199. Wife, Bridgett; son, John Hendrickson; son, Peter Hendrickson; daus., Mary, Catherine, Elizabeth, Bridgett, Sarah and Susannah; father-in-law, John Anderson. Exc. wife, Bridgett.

Joseph Cloud. B'wine Hd. Nov. 30, 1745. Misc. 1.44. Wife, Sisley; son, Robert Cloud; son, Joseph; son, Nathaniel; dau., Susannah Edwards; dau., Elizabeth Cloud; dau., Phebey Cloud. Exc. son, Robert.

Nicholas Bishop. Mill Crk. Hd. July, 1745. Dec. 6, 1745. Misc. 2.11. Wife, Elizabeth; sons, Henry, John and Nicholas; daus., Elizabeth, Mary and Susanna. Exc. son, John Bishop.

William Rinkin, Sr. Mill Crk. Hd. Oct. 12, 1745. Dec. 26, 1745. Misc. 1.411. Wife, Margaret; son, William; son, John; dau., Susannah; dau., Jannet Alexander. Exc. wife, Margaret; son, William.

Robert Marsh. Appo. Hd. Jan. 8, 1746. Feb. 4, 1746. G. 149. Dau., Mary Donew; son, William Marsh; son, John Marsh; dau., Margaret Marsh; son, Robert Marsh. Exc. Robert Marsh, son.

Isaac Weldon. Carpenter. Feb. 1, 1746. March 9, 1746. Misc. 2.13. Wife, Anne; son, Joseph; son, William; youngest son, Abraham. Exc. wife, Anne.

Elias King. Miller. B'wine Hd. Feb. 14. 1746. Mar. 10, 1746. Misc. 1.259. Wife, Mary; son, Frederick King; dáu., Christianer Gussey; son, John. Exc. wife, Mary and Luke Mounce.

John Pugh. Missionary of St. Ann's Parish. Aug. 27, 1745. May 21, 1746. Misc. 1.391. Wife, Christiana; son, Jacob; wife's sister(?), Naudain; her sister, Rebecca Van bebber; her brother, Jacob Van bebber's daughter, Ester Van bebber. Exc. wife, Christiana.

Jonathan Strange. Sept. 2, 1746. G. 285. Wife; children, viz: Catherine, Mary, Elizabeth, Susannah, Elenor, Francis and Sarah. Exc. wife, John Thomas and Lewis Thomas, wife's brothers.

Samuel Greave. Yeoman. Chris. Hd. 3rd day of 7th m. 1746. Sept. 13, 1746. Misc. 1.114. Children: dau., Hannah Greave; dau.,

Rachel Greave; son, Isaac Greave; brother, Jonathon. Exc. brothers, Jonathon and John Greave.

Samuel Guthrey. St. Geo. Hd. Sept. 1, 1746. Sept. 13, 1746 Sons, Addam, Robert, Samuel; daus., Jane, Mary, Elizabeth and Rachel; wife, Mary. Exc. wife, Mary and son, Robert.

Robert Lucas. Cecil Co., Maryland. April 10, 1744. Nov. 3, 1746. Misc. 1.308. Wife, Mary. Exc. wife, Mary.

Jared Harron. W. Clay Crk. Hd. Sept. 15, 1746. Nov. 20, 1746. Misc. 1.202. Brother, Ollipher; J. Seans, William Peary.

Charles Tussey (Elias). Farmer. B'wine Hd. Oct. 18, 1746. Dec. 2, 1746. Misc. 1.454. Wife, Christian Tussey; son, Alexander Tussey; dau., Ann Tussey; son, John Tussey; son, Elias Tussey. Exc. Elias King; Christian Tussey (wife), and Luke Mounce.

John Baldwin. Chris. Hd. Sept., 1740. Dec. 8, 1746. Misc. 2.14. Wife, Elizabeth; mother, Mary Lewis; sons, William and Thomas; daus., Mary, Lydia and Hannah. Exc. wife, Elizabeth and Jacob Hollingsworth.

John Webster. Weaver. Province of Pennsylvania, County of New Castle. Dec. 20, 1747. Jan. 7, 1747. G. 71. Wife, Ruth; sons, Thomas, John and Henry; daus., Mary and Ann; eldest son. Exc. wife, Ruth, and John Marshall.

Margaret Crawford. Widow. Mill Crk. Hd. Feb. 20, 1744-5. Jan. 26, 1747. G. 103. Son, Andrew Craford; son, Robert Craford; dau., Margaret Alexander; dau.-in-law, Elinor Craford. Exc. Robert Craford, son.

Thomas Bullock. Weaver. Wil. Jan. 19, 1747-8. Feb. 2, 1747-8. G. 90. Wife, Margaret; son, Samuel Bullock; daus., Sarah Bullock, Ann Bullock, and Alice Bullock. Exc. wife, Margaret; Matthew McKinnie, (cooper).

William McClearn. Merchant. B'wine Hd. Jan. 30, 1747. Feb. 17, 1747. G. 93. Brother, James McClearn; sister, Margaret McClearn; sister, Mary McClearn; father, Matthew McClearn; eldest brother, John; William Reah. Exc. James Huston, cordwainer; William Reah, farmer.

Francis Beavis. Jan. 13, 1747. Feb. 18, 1747. G. 89. Sister, Hannah Ryley. Exc. Thomas Quonb and Edward Ryley.

Agnus Hunter. Wil. Feb. 9, 1747. Feb. 18, 1747. G. 92. Daughter, Agnus. Exc. Robert Wright, John Burnet and Matthew W. Kinney.

Catherine Lewis. "Widdow." Mill Crk. Hd. Nov. 8, 1746. April 1, 1747. Misc. 1.309. Rev. Owen Thomas. Exc. trusty friend, Sarah Thomas

Abraham Vandike. Feb. 1, 1746-7. April 11, 1747. Misc. 1.493. Wife, Elizabeth. Exc. wife, Elizabeth.

Edward Lowder. N. C. Hd. Feb. 25, 1745-6. April 11, 1747. Misc. 1.312. Wife, Mary; mentions children. Exc. wife, Mary.

William Gregg. Miller. Chris. Hd. Jan. 10, 1746. April 13, 1747. G. 477. Wife, Ann; son, Harmon; son, William; three younger sons, viz: Joshua, Jacob and Abraham; daus., Elizabeth, Hannah and Margory; "Bros. Samuel Gregg and George Robinson my trustees." Exc. wife, Anne; son, Harmon.

David Griffeth. Yeoman. Pen. Hd. April 5, 1747. April 14, 1747. Wife; dau., Mary John; seven grandchildren, David John, Joseph John, Catherin John, Mary John, Thomas John, Dinah John; Sarah John, my maid; Elinor William. Exc. dau., Mary John and grandson, David John.

Peter Petersonsmith. Husbandman. B'wine Hd. Mar. 14, 1746-7. May 11, 1747. Misc. 393. Sons, Samuel and Mathias; wife, Bridget; other two sons, Tobias and Andrew; step-son, John Morton. Exc. wife, Bridget Petersonsmith.

Ebenezer Grubb. Farmer. B'wine Hd. May 7, 1747. June 27, 1747. Misc. 1.120. Brother, Henry Grubb; brother, William Grubb; brother, Jesse Grubb. Exc. brother, Henry.

John William Lurkingsiler. St. Geo. Hd. Sept. 5, 1745. June 29, 1747. Misc. 1.311. Son-in-law, John Michell Sigmund; Swedesminister, Peter Thronburg, Timothy Steadham. Exc. John Michell Sigmund.

John Penn. Esquire. Hitcham in Co. of Buckingham. Oct. 24, 1746. Nov. 12, 1746 in England. July 20, 1747 in New Castle Co., America. G. 1. My dear sister, Mary Freame; my servant, John Travers; my old and worthy servant, Thomas Penn; servant, Hannah Roberts; Jane Aldrige, wife of Henry Aldrige of White Waltham Co. of Berks; nephew, John Penn, eldest son of brother Richard; my late grandfather, Thomas Callowhill; my dear brother, Richard Penn; my dear brother, Thomas Penn; Thomas Hyam and David Barclay, friends of London; nephew Richard Penn 2nd, son of brother Richard Penn; niece, Hannah Penn; my sister, Margaret Freame; my niece, Philadelphia Hannah Freame; my great niece, Mary Margaretta Fell; my nephew of the half blood (William Penn of Cork, Eng.); Springett Penn, the eldest son of said William Penn; Christian Gulielma Penn, dau. of sd. Wm. Penn; my grandnephew (of the half blood) Robert Edward Fell, who is only son of late Gulielma Maria Fell. English Exc. Wm. Nigor of London, merchant; Joseph Freame, citizen and banker of London; Lascelles Metcalf of Westminster, Esquire. American Exc. Thomas Penn, brother.

Henry Priest. Tallow chandler. Wil. Sept. 5, 1747. Oct. 13, 1747. G. 36. Dau., Elizabeth Priest of Portsmouth, in Hampshire, England; Susannah Dinsdale (dau. of John Dinsdale of Boston, butcher). Exc. Susannah Dinsdale.

Christian Land. Widow. N. C. July 25, 1743. Sept. 30, 1747. G. 37. Son, Thomas Land; two daus., not named; three sons,

Thomas, Samuel and John. Exc. sons, Samuel, John and Thomas Land.

Elizabeth Vandike. Aug. 10, 1747. Oct. 1, 1747. G. 39. Brother, Benjamin; Joseph and William Roads; sister, Abigail Roads; John Roads; father, Joseph Roads, deceased; John Vandike, Abraham Cannon; cousin John Vandike, sone of above said John; cousin, Grace Vandike, dau. of said John. Exc. John Vandike, first named.

William Ball. Mill Crk. Hd. Aug. 17, 1747. Oct. 1, 1747. G. 41. Wife; son, John; son, Joseph; son, Jasper; daus., Mary and Sarah. Exc. wife; Hugh Clerke.

Robert Aiken (Eiken). Blacksmith. Red Lyon Hd. Sept. 18, 1747. Oct. 1, 1747. G. 43. Wife, Isabel Aiken; children, not named; brother Alexander Aiken. Exc. Thomas Reynolds, Alexander Aken and wife, Isabel Aken.

James Ball. Yeoman. Mill Crk. Hd. Feb. 16, 1739-40. Oct. 17, 1747. G. 56. Wife, Mary; brother, John Ball; children, John, James, William McFarlin. Exc. wife, Mary Ball; brother, John Ball.

Daniel Makkary. Appo. Hd. June 2, 1747. Nov. 17, 1747. G. 58. Wife, Elizabeth Makkary; son, Richard Makkary.

Thomas Norman. N. C. Nov. 12, 1747. Nov. 26, 1747. G. 60. Rev. Charles Tennant; wife, Isabel; the dau. of Patrick Flynn. Exc. wife, Patrick Flynn, James King.

William Nevin. Farmer. Mill Crk. Hd. Nov. 28, 1747. Dec. 7, 1747. Wife, Margaret Nevin; son, William; daus., Mary Montgomery, Martha Nevin, Margaret Nevin, Agnes Nevin and Isabell Nevin. Exc. wife, Margaret Nevin; Thomas Montgomery.

John Stalcop. Wil. Nov. 6, 1747. Dec. 26, 1747. G. 140. Wife, Elizabeth; son, Peter Stalcop; mother, Susannah Turner.

John Heath. Chris. Hd. Dec. 8, 1747. Jan. 11, 1748. G. 69. Wife, Hannah Heath; dau., now Elizabeth John; cuson, Allice Cantrol. Exc. wife, Hannah.

John Gray. Jan. 4, 1748. Jan. 17, 1748. G. 227. Wife, Elas; children (not named). Exc. wife, Elas; Alexander Porter.

Jonas Robinson. Blacksmith. Chris. Hd. Jan. 4, 1748-9. Jan. 17, 1748. G. 221. Wife, Rebeckah Robinson; son, Charles Robinson; son, William Robinson; sons, Edward and Joseph Robinson; daus., Mary and Ann Robinson. Exc. wife, Rebeckah Robinson; Robert Armstrong.

George Moore. Pen. Hd. Feb. 23, 1747. Jan. 17, 1748. G. 222. Wife, Elizabeth Moore; son, Alexander Moore; dau., Mary; dau., Isable; dau., Isable's children. Exc. wife, Elizabeth Moore; Patrick Flynn.

John Bourgardin. St. Geo. Hd. Jan. 27, 1748-9. Misc. 1.17. Wife, Iszabell. Exc. wife, Iszabell; Andrew Bryan.

John Macky. Town of New Castle. Mar. 19, 1746. Jan. 31, 1748. G. 237. Wife, Araminta Macky. Exc. wife, Araminta.

Samuel Ruth. Yeoman. Jan. 28, 1748. Feb. 7, 1748. G. 233. Wife, Mary; sons, James, Joseph, Alexander, George, Samuel, John and William; dau., Mary.

Zachariah Derrickson. Yeoman. B'wine Hd. Jan. 21, 1748. Feb. 22, 1748. G. 277. Wife, Elizabeth Derrickson; son, Cornelius Derrickson; sons, Zeckrias and Peter; son, William. Exc. wife, Elizabeth Derrickson; Nels Justison.

Thomas Bullock. Weaver. Borough of Wilmington. Jan. 19, 1747-8. Feb. 2, 1747-8. G. 90. Wife, Margaret; son, Samuel Bullock; dau., Sarah Bullock; dau., Ann Bullock; dau., Alice Bullock. Exc. wife, Margaret; Matthew McKinnie (cooper).

Christopher Rie. Farmer. Feb. 9, 1748. Feb. 24, 1748. G. 278. Dau., Rebecca 'Rie; son, John Rie; two grandchildren, Abraham and Catherine Booth; my children, Joseph, Stephen, Christopher, James and George. Exc. John Rie, son; Solomon Simmons.

Joseph England. West Nottingham Township, Chester Co., Penna. 16th day of 10th m:, 1748. Mar. 4, 1748. G. 281. Dau., Joanna Townsend; son, Samuel England; son, Joseph England; son John's three children, namely: David England, Mary England, John England. Exc. sons, Samuel England, Joseph England.

Francis Robinson. 4th of 12th mo., 1748. March 7, 1748. G. 288. Son, Francis Robinson; dau., Rebecca Robinson; son, Nicholas; son, James; wife. Exc. wife; son, James Robinson.

Abraham Hyatt. St. Geo. Hd. Mar. 2, 1748. Mar. 8, 1748. G. 283. Wife, Ann Hyatt; children, Stephen Hyatt, Abraham Hyatt and Alvin Hyatt. Exc. wife, Ann Hyatt; John Vance.

William Andrews. Yeoman. Chris. Hd. 23rd d. of 11th mo., 1747. Mar. 25, 1748. G. 109. Wife, Miriam Andrews; daus., Ruth and Hannah Andrews; son, Ezekial Andrews; son, John Andrews; James Hash. Exc. wife, Miriam; friend, Mr. Jos. Hewes.

John Daniel Thony. Miller. St. Geo. Hd. Mar. 12, 1748. Apr. 6, 1748. G. 115. Wife, Elizabeth Thony; William Goforth; dau., Mary Thony; dau., Elizabeth Dushane, Valentine Dushane; John Rees, Lewis Rees and Thomas Rees, sons of my wife's brother, John Rees of Mill Creek Hd. Exc. dau., Elizabeth Dushane and Mary Thony.

Thomas Nelson. Labourer. Pen. Hd. March 1, 1748. April 6, 1748. G. 107. Son, Girard Nelson; daus., Francis and Rebecca; son, James' child, if she live until she comes of age. Exc. Benjamin Elder, James Siner.

Ann Dushane. Spinster. Swan Hook. Feb. 15, 1747-8. April 6, 1748. G. 106. Youngest son, Joseph Jaquot; dau., Judith; grand-dau., Ann Jaquot, daughter to son, Nicholas Jaquot; dau., Catherine; son, Peter Jaquot; dau., Susannah. Exc. son, Peter Jaquot.

Thomas Evans. Yeoman. Pen. Hd. Mar. 30, 1748. Apr. 9, 1748. G. 111. Wife, Mary; son, Samuel Evans; three daus., Rachel, Catherine and Hannah. Exc. wife, Mary Evans.

Lewis Goton or Geton. Yeoman. St. Geo. Hd. Feb. 18, 1732. April 12, 1748. G. 113. Sons, Lewis and Peter Geton; dau., Jean Bellow; dau., Mary Vandegrift; dau., Sary Jeton. Exc. sons, Lewis and Peter.

William Jack. Mariner of Londonderry, Ireland; now of New Castle. Mar. 13, 1747-8. Apr. 18, 1748. G. 119. Brother, Thomas Jack; father, James Jack; "my mother." Exc. Geo. Munro.

Gerard Nillson. Labourer. Pen. Hd. Apr. 7, 1748. Apr. 18, 1748. G. 117. Wife, Elizabeth; daus., Rebeckah and Mary. Exc. wife, Elizabeth; James Reed.

Peter Poulson. Yeoman. N. C. March 20, 1748. Apr. 20, 1748. G. 139. Sister, Susannah Stalcop; brother, Willam Poleson. Exc. William Poleson.

Daniel McAlister. Apr. 27, 1748. Apr. 29, 1748. G. 152. Son, Daniel McAlester; brother's son, Daniel McAlester. Exc. Daniel Clark, Thomas Moor.

Jemima Sonney. Widow to Jacob. April 18, 1747. May 3, 1748. Misc. 1.436. Eldest son, John Sonney; son, Silas Sonney; two youngest sons, Samuel and Jacob. Exc. William Hammond, Isaac England. (This name is either Sonney or Soreney.)

George Cummins. (Nunc.) N. C. May 6, 1748. May 14, 1748. G. 153. His children. Taken by Jacob Corbit, Rebecca Brown.

Francis Johnson. Cooper. N. C. May 11, 1748. May 17, 1748. G. 148. Wife, Sarah; nephew, Francis Johnson, the son of brother, Nathaniel; sister, Jane; nephew, Thomas Holland; nephew, John Grimes. Exc. wife, Sarah Johnson; nephew, Thomas Holland; nephew, John Grimes.

Robert Maccay. Farmer. St. Geo. Hd. March 7, 1747. May 18, 1748. G. 142. Wife, Elizabeth; sons, Charles and John; grandson, Leonard Maccay; daus., Mary, Elizabeth; dau., Rebeckah. Exc. wife, Elizabeth Maccay.

Howell James. (Nunc.) May 23, 1748. May 26, 1748. G. 154. Mother, Ann James; brother, Mankin James; sister, Mary Robinson; Ann and Rebecca, daughters of Mary Robinson; brother, Phillip James. Attested by Alexander Montgomery and Ann Baldwin.

Thomas Hays. Dec. 2, 1747. May 26, 1748. G. 164. Sister, Jane Love. Exc. Peter Noxon, James Crawford. Adm. Benjamin Love.

Henry Dyer. ——, 1748-9. ——. G. 430. Wife, Mary. Exc. Mary Dyer, wife.

James Leanord. Farmer. May 20, 1748. June 14, 1748. G. 145.

Two sons, James and Clement; James Dunnahoue, son of John Dunnahoue, Sr., of Kent Co., Maryland. Exc. John Dunnahoue.

George Hogg. Jan. 11, 1740-41. June 16, 1748. G. 134. Son, George Hogg; dau., Elizabeth Hogg; brother, John Hogg. Exc. dau., Elizabeth.

John Hogg. Jan. 10, 1742. June 16, 1748. G. 134. Nephew, John Gregg, son of George Gregg; nieces, Elizabeth and Susanna Hogg, the daus. of brother, James, deceased; niece, Elizabeth, dau. of brother, George Hogg. Exc. Benjamin Swett, Jacob Chandler.

John Garretson. Yeoman. N. C. Hd. Aug. 24, 1748. June 31, 1748. G. 231. Dau., Abiah Garretson; wife, Hester; son, John Garretson. Exc. wife, Hester Garretson and her brother, Daniel Turner.

William Goforth. Yeoman. Red Lyon Hd. June 18, 1748. July 17, 1748. G. 147. Wife, Ann; "my children"; son, William. Exc. wife, Ann.

William Cloud. Yeoman. B'wine Hd. May 12, 1747. July 18, 1748. G. 150. Dau., Mabel Askew; dau., Elizabeth; son, Mordica; dau., Margaret Cloud; son, Henry Cloud; son, Jeremiah Cloud; son, Daniel Cloud; son, William; son, Joseph; wife, Elizabeth. Exc. wife, Elizabeth Cloud.

Evan David, Senior. Pen. Hd. Aug. 21, 1748. ——, 1748. G. 207. Eldest son, John David; son, Joshua David; dau., Margret; wife, Jane David; son, Thomas. Exc. wife, Jane David; son, Thomas David.

Zachiras Thomas. Farmer. Pen. Hd. June 24, 1748. Aug. 1, 1748. G. 166. Cousin, Mary Evan; sister, Sarah. Exc. James James, brother-in-law.

John Webb. Shipwright. Wil. 3rd mo. 20, 1748. Aug. 2, 1748. G. 169. Sons, Joseph and John; dau., Margaret; dau., Hannah. Exc. William Warner, Margaret Tucker, dau.

David Howell. Yeoman. Pen. Hd. Mar. 10, 1746. Aug. 3, 1748. G. 167. Son, Daniel Howell; daus., Rachel Rees, wife of Rees Rees and Sarah Williams, wife of John Williams. Exc. sons, Daniel and David.

Thomas Babb. Aug. 17, 1748. ——. G. 484. Granddau., Lydia Gregory; granddau., Rebecca Gregory; grandson, John Gregory; son, Peter Babb; son, Thomas Babb; son, Phillip Babb; dau., Mary; dau., Rebecca; dau., Lydia. Exc. Peter Babb, son.

David Jones. Pen. Hd. Aug. 18, 1748. Aug. 27, 1748. G. 179. Dau., Rachel Williams; grandson, David Jones; dau., Mary Deal; dau., Jane Jones; wife, Esther; son, Morgan Jones; son, James Jones; Esther Jones, dau. of John Jones; son, John Jones; son, Daniel Jones; son, David Jones. George Brown's children, viz: Thomas, John, William and George Brown; grandson, Benjamin Jones, son of John Jones. Exc. wife, Esther Jones; sons, Morgan Jones, James Jones and Daniel Jones.

Catharine Woodland. Widdow. Kent Co., Maryland. Dec. 20, 1747. Sept. 10, 1748. G. 176. Mother; two brothers, Richard and Joshua; William Woodland's two younger children, Jonathan Woodland and Martha Woodland; brother, John Curtis. Exc. Dr. Lewis Williams.

Samuel McInteer. Yeoman. White Clay Crk. Hd. Sept. 7, 1748. Sept. 18, 1748. G. 191. Wife, Mary; Sam'l McAnteer; son, Robert McAnteer, William McAnteer; dau., Elinor; John McAnteer, son of Mary; Elizabeth McAnteer, dau. of Mary. Exc. sons, Alexander McAnteer, Andrew McAnteer.

Richard Moore. Wil. Nov. 28, 1742. Sept. 19, 1748. G. 178. Wife, Dorothy. Exc. Dorothy Moore (wife).

Richard Sturges. Yeoman. Appo. Hd. Aug. 15, 1748. Sept. 22, 1748. G. 199. Richard Edinfield; brother, William Sturgis; Dorcas Edinfield, Stotely Sturgis, Aaron Pearceson. Exc. brother, William; Dorcas Edinfield.

Augustine Constantine. Yeoman. Newport. Aug. 29, 1748. Sept. 27, 1748. G. 189. Conrad Garretson; wife, Jannet; daughters. Exc. Jonas Walraven, Joseph Abraham.

Thomas Nugin. Labourer. Mill Crk. Hd. Sept. 5, 1748. Sept. 29, 1748. G. 198. Wife, Jane Nugin. Exc. wife, Jane.

Thomas Shane. Weaver. Appo. Hd. Feb. 20, 1747-8. Oct. 6, 1748. G. 104. Wife, Mary Shane; son, Thomas; dau., Phabey Shane. Exc. wife, Mary Shane.

John Turner. Chris. Hd. Oct. 1, 1748. Oct. 8, 1748. G. 205. Nephew, Hugh Neal; nephew, David Neal; nephew, Matthew Neal; nephew, Mary Neal; sister, Lettice Neal. Exc. sister, Lettice Neal.

Valentine Robinson. Cecil Co., Maryland. May 16, 1748. Oct. 10, 1748. G. 185. Eldest son, Charles Robinson; youngest son, Thomas Robinson; wife, Elizabeth Robinson. Exc. Elizabeth Robinson, wife; George Robinson, brother.

David Thomas. Bricklayer. Pen. Hd. Sept. 29, 1748. Oct. 10, 1748. G. 204. Mother, Catharine; sisters, Rachel Griffiths and Sarah Thomas; sister, Ann Bush; brothers, Lewis and Richard. Exc. brother, Lewis Thomas; brother, Richard Thomas.

John Hill. Farmer. N. C. Hd. Aug. 29, 1748. Oct. 13, 1748. G. 187. Son, Thomas Hill; dau., Susannah Whitesides; her brother, John Hill; dau., Lydia Lewis; son, Joseph Hill. Exc. son, John.

James Crawford. Sept. 27, 1748. Oct. 22, 1748. G. 202. Son, Robert Huston and Jane Huston; wife, Mary; child, Mary Crawford; child, Catharine Crawford. Exc. Robert Bannell; wife, Mary Crawford.

Geoorge Alford. Mill Crk. Hd. Sept. 13, 1748. Nov. 3, 1748. G. 201. Wife, Alse Alford; son, Charles. Exc. son, Charles Alford.

Adam Short, Senior. Yeoman. N. C. Hd. Mar. 29, 1748. Nov. 6,

1748. G. 181. Wife, Martha; son, Adam Short; son, Henry Short; son, Abram Short; dau., Miriam Daley; two grandsons, namely, Abraham and Isaac Bush; John Daley. Exc. Martha Short (wife).

Robert Creighton. Nov. 16, 1748. ———. G. 208. Wife; sons, James Creighton and Robert Creighton and William Creighton. Exc. friend, William Brotherton and William Creighton. Guardian, friend, James McMechen.

Alvan Hyatt. Sept. 16, 1743. Nov. 19, 1748. G. 195. Brother, Abraham Hyatt. Exc. brother, Abraham Hyatt.

Philip Smith. Taylor. Chris. Hd. Nov. 20, 1748. Nov. 23, 1748. G. 208. Son, Charles Smith; son, James Smith; father, Barnard Smith; James Hall or John Hall, son of James Hall of Monahon, Ireland. Exc. William Armstrong.

Richard Enos. Farmer. N. C. April 30, 1748. Dec. 3, 1748. G. 183. Elizabeth Rebecca Hill; wife, Susannah; son, Abraham; dau., Mary; son, Stephen; son, Joseph; son, Samuel. Exc. Robert Mitchell, son-in-law; Samuel Enos, son.

John Stanley. Appo. Hd. Sept. 1, 1747. Dec. 8, 1748. G. 210. Wife, Winnifred; son, Christopher; son, William; son, Joseph; son, Robert; dau., Elenor. Exc. sons, Joseph Stanley, Robert Stanley.

Edmond Garritson. Appo. Hd. Sept. 22, 1748. Dec. 10, 1748. G. 225. Children, Andrew, Henry, Elizabeth, Lydia, Edmund, Mary, Sarah, Halliwell and Adam Garreson; John Anderson's two daughters. Exc. wife, Elizabeth.

John Van Coolen. Sallopman. Apr. 25, 1741. Dec. 19, 1748. G. 226. Brother, Jacobus Van Coolen. Exc. brother, Jacobus Van Coolen, Daniel Turner.

Samuel Eves. Woodberry, New Castle Co. March 6, 1742-3. Dec. 25, 1748. G. 193. Two daus., Susannah and Elizabeth Peterson; wife, Elenor Eves; grandson, John Peterson; sons, John and James Eves; eldest son, Samuel, deceased. Exc. sons, John and James Eves.

Peter Tranberg. Will. Jan. 23, 1744-5. Dec. 27, 1748. G. 196. Sister in Sweden, Annika Tranberg; wife, Ann Catharine; eldest son, Andrew Tranberg; daus., Rebecca and Elizabeth Tranberg; son, Peter Tranberg. Exc. Ann Catharine Tranberg, (wife); Andrew Tranberg, (son).

James Miller. March 7, 1742. Codicil'd, Dec. 28, 1749, (O. S.). Jan. 4, 1749. G. 357. Wife, Sarah; son, John; son, David; dau., Mary Gilmer; daus., Elizabeth and Susannah. Exc. Sarah Miller, wife; John Miller, son. Codicil, Exc. David Miller, John Miller, sons.

William McDowell. Mill Crk. Hd. July 26, 1749. Feb. 13, 1749. (O. S.) G. 367. Wife, Margaret; son, Joseph; grandson, William McDowell (son of Joseph); son, Robert Kirkwood; dau., Mary

Kirkwood; son, Hugh Owen and his wife, Elizabeth, and son, William Owen. Exc. wife, Margaret; son, Robert Kirkwood.

Eliz. Cloud. Widow. B'wine Hd. Feb. 3, 1749-50. Feb. 22, 1749-50. G. 375. Dau., Margaret Cloud; son, Daniel Cloud; son, William Cloud; three daus., Elizabeth Boothe, Mable Askew and Margaret Cloud. Exc. Joseph Grub (cooper).

William Bannet. St. Geo. Hd. Jan. 20, 1749-50. Feb. 22, 1749-50. G. 368. Dau., Mary; dau, Francis; son, Nicholas; wife, Mary; son, William; three grandsons, sons of eldest dau., Ansanty, wife of John Vansant. Exc. Nicholas Bannet, (son); Nicholas Vandike, (brother).

James King. Pigeon Run. N. C. Hd. Feb. 13, 1749. Feb. 22, 1749. G. 370. Rev. Mr. Charles Tennent; wife, Margaret; Rev. Mr. Gilbert Tennent. Exc. wife, Margaret; John Parkinson, Thomas Reynolds.

Michael Butcher. St. Geo. Hd. Feb. 9, 1749-50. Mar. 5, 1749-50. G. 380. Brother, Thomas Butcher; uncle, Michael Butcher; cousin, John Butcher. Exc. Thomas Butcher, (brother); John Butcher, (cousin).

John Meldrom. St. Geo. Hd. Feb., 1749. March 6, 1749. G. 373. Son, Robert Meldrom; Elizabeth Dollos, dau. of Robert Dolloss; brother-in-law, Thomas Walker; brother-in-law, George Walker; William Dolloss, John Dolloss. Exc. Andrew Bryan.

Hugh McWhirtor. Pen. Hd. Feb. 17, 1749. Mar. 6, 1749. G. 372. Wife, Jean McWhirtor; son, John McWhirtor; daus., Agnes and Jean; son, Alexander. Exc. Jean McWhirtor, (wife).

William Wollaston. Yeoman. Mill Crk. Hd. Mar. 1, 1749-50. Mar. 9, 1749-50. G. 377. Dau., Lebiah Ogden, wife of David Ogden; dau., Mary Clerk; wife, Charety; son, William Wollaston; son, Ebenezer Wollaston; son, Joshua Wollaston; dau., Susannah Wollaston; grandson, Joseph Ogden, the son of dau. Lebiah and David Ogden. Exc. sons, Ebenezer Wollaston, Joshua Wollaston.

Thomas Land. Yeoman. Mar. 3, 1747. Mar. 14, 1749. G. 382. Brother, Samuel Land; brother, John Land; sister, Mary. Exc. Samuel Land (brother), John Land (brother).

Mary Jones. Widow. (Nunc.) St. Geo. Hd. Mar. 12, 1749. Mar. 20, 1749. C. 388. Son-in-law, John Jones; son, Evan Jones; Mary Paterson, dau. of Charles Paterson, and Mary, his wife. Attested by James Vance and David Floyd.

Jane Kenner. Pen. Hd. Mar. 18, 1749. Mar. 22, 1749. G. 383. Rachel Evans; Ealinor Porter; Sarah Muldro; Agnes Porter; Mary McCloarn. Exc. Hugh Muldro., John Crawford.

Griffith John. Yeoman. Pen. Hd. Dec. 21, 1748. April 4, 1749. G. 295. Dau., Ann; dau., Elizabeth, wife of John Pierce; dau., Sarah; granddau., Susannah, the dau. of John Lewis; granddau., Ann, the dau. of John Lewis; grandson, David, son of John Lewis; son, David. Exc. David John (son).

Archibald McDonald. Mill Crk. Hd. Apr. 12, 1749. Apr. 18, 1749. G. 302. Wife, Abigail; sons, John McDonald, William McDonald, Thomas McDonald and Archibald McDonald; my sister-in-law; dau., Elinor Moore, alias McDonald, wife to James Moore; son-in-law, James Moore; dau., Abigail McDonald, Mary McDonald. Exc. Thomas McDonald.

James Campion. Mill Crk. Hd. Apr. 21, 1749. May 3, 1749. G. 314. Brother, John Campion's eldest son; brother, John Campion; brother-in-law, James Robinson's four children; namely, Mary, Rachel, Rebecca and Elizabeth Robinson. Exc. James Robinson.

Benjamin Elder. Yeoman. Apr. 23, 1749. May 17, 1749. G. 311. Wife, Mary Elder; son, John Elder; son, Alexander Elder; dau., Hannah Elder; dau., Margaret Elder. Exc. Mary Elder (wife), John Elder (son).

James Hamilton. Mill Crk. Hd. Apr. 22, 1749. May 17, 1749. G. 312. Alexander Montgomery (miller), wife, Mary. Exc. James Guthery; wife, Mary.

John Reynolds. May 29, 1749. June 12, 1749. G. 316. Wife, Ann; children; three eldest sons of my three brothers. Exc. Ann Reynolds (wife), William Reynolds (brother).

Samuel Bickley. City of Philadelphia, Penn. May 15, 1749. June 17, 1749. G. 318. Wife, Margaret; sons, Abraham and William; dau., Mary. Exc. wife, Margaret; son, Abraham; James Polegren.

Thomas Lewis. Pen. Hd. June 13, 1749. June 27, 1749. G. 323. Eldest son, Evan Lewis; son, David Lewis; 2nd son, Alexander Lewis; 3rd son, James Lewis; 4th son, David; son-in-law, Reec Thomas and my dau., Elizabeth, his wife. Exc. son-in-law, Reec Thomas.

Abraham Golden, Senior. Yeoman. St. Geo. Hd. Aug. 26, 1748. July 7, 1749. G. 320. Wife, Ann; son, Abram Golden; son, Anthony; granddau, Mary Marteen, the daughter of Jacob Marteen, dec.; son, Jacob Golden; son, William; grandson, John Golden, son of Joseph, dec.; dau., Ann Gilder; dau., Mary McConnell; dau., Catherine Golden. Exc. sons, Abram, William, Anthony.

Roger Shannon. June 7, 1749. Aug. 14, 1749. G. 325. Mother; sister's son, John Fitzpatrick; George Lawson. Exc. George Lawson.

Caleb Perkins. Blacksmith. B'wine Hd. July 12, 1749. Aug. 28, 1749. G. 330. Son, Caleb Perkins; wife, Ann Perkins; dau., Martha Perkins. Exc. Ann Perkins (wife), John Beson.

John Morris. Pen. Hd. Aug. 6, 1749. Aug. 29, 1749. G. 331. Wife,

Elizabeth Morris; brothers, John David and David David; sisters, Elizabeth and Jannet; cousin, Rachel Davies; cousins, David Davies and Evan Davies. Exc. David Davies, Evan Davies.

John Yarnall. Edgemount. Chester Co., Penn. 30th d. of 5th m., 1747. Sept. 4, 1749. G. 346. Wife, Abigail Yarnall; dau., Mary Pennell; son, Thomas Yarnall; dau., Ann Yarnall; son, Isaac Yarnall; dau., Abigail Yarnall; dau., Hannah Yarnall. Exc. Abigail Yarnall (wife), Phillip Yarnall (brother), Nathan Yarnall (brother).

Robert Farres. Blacksmith. Pen. Hd. Aug. 26, 1748. Sept. 11, 1749. G. 333. Sons, William, John, Arthur, James and Robert; three daus., Agnes, Jean and Mary. Exc. sons, John Farris, William Farris.

Rachel Hyatt, widow of Thomas Hyatt. (Nunc.) Sept. 27, 1749. Misc. 1. 201. Son, Peter Hyatt; sons' wives; son's-in-law wives; step-son, Thomas; his dau., Rachel; granddau., Rachel, dau. of David Hyatt. Attested by Agnes Hook, Mary Vandike.

Joseph Mendinhall. Carpenter. Wil. Sept. 21, 1749. Oct. 31, 1749. G. 348. Wife, Rachel; dau., Sarah. Exc. Rachel Mendinhall (wife).

Thomas Broom. Yeoman. Wil. Nov. 23, 1749. Dec. 3, 1749. G. 352. Grandchildren, David and Thomas Bush; son, John Broom; son, James Broom; son, Robert Broom; children, William and Mary Stuart; dau., Elizabeth Broom; children, Peter and Hannah Ganthony. Exc. James Broom (son), Peter Gathony (son-in-law).

Elias Naudain. Appo. Hd. Nov. 13, 1749. Dec. 6, 1749. G. 350. Wife, Mary; son, Andrew Naudain; son, Cornelius Naudain; son, Arnold; dau., Lydia Naudain; sons, Robert and Charles; two daughters-in-law. Exc. son, Andrew; wife, Mary.

Mary Woodell. Aug. 12, 1749. Dec. 26, 1749. G. 354. "Children." Exc. Paul Alfree.

William Bracken. Yeoman. Mill Crk. Hd. April 8, 1749. Dec. 28, 1749. G. 359. Son, Thomas Bracken; son, John Bracken; son Henry Bracken; dau., Hannah, wife to James Jordan; dau., Margaret, wife to Alex. Moore; dau., Martha Ball, widow of John Ball, Jr.; John Gilliham was married to dau. Susannah, now deceased.; grandson, William Gilliham; granddau., Elizabeth Gilliham; granddau, Martha Jordan; grandson, William Bracken. Exc. Henry Bracken (son), William Brackon (grandson).

Francis Nowell. Weaver. B'wine Hd. Aug. 11, 1750. Jan. 3, 1750. G. 451. Kinsman, Nicholas Moore; Rebecca Bird, dau. of Thomas Bird, late of Brandywine Hd. Exc. Nicholas Moore.

Nases Degon. Blacksmith. N. C. May 11, 1743. Jan. 17, 1750. G. 452. Dau., Oraena; wife, Catherine; grandson, James Polhill (son of Oreana). Exc. Catherine Degon (wife).

John Shannon. Chris. Hd. Sept. 27, 1745. Jan. 25, 1750. G. 473. Dau., Mary Shannon. Exc. Richard Malone, Samuel Adams, Walter Dewison, Lawrance Hahan, in Jamaica; John Kinsey, Dr. Reese Jones, in New Castle.

Cathrine Griffith. Widow. Sept. 10, 1750. (O. S.) Feb. 27, 1750. G. 459. Grandson, David John; grandson, Thomas John; granddau., Cathrine Thomas; three granddaus., Mary John, Sarah John and Dinah John; dau., Mary John. Exc. dau., Mary John.

John Richardson. N. C. Hd. Mar. 15, 1749-50. Mar. 27, 1750. G. 392. Wife, Mary; son, Robert; dau., Mary; dau., Hannah; dau., Sarah; granddau., Hannah, dau. of son, Benjamin, dec.; granddau., Hannah, dau. of son, Stephen, dec.; dau., Hannah Richardson, Joseph Scot, son of my dau., Mary; William Scott (weaver). Exc. wife, Mary; son, Robert.

Andrew Bryan. St. Geo. Hd. Mar. 2, 1749. Mar. 29, 1750. G. 390. Sons, Alexander Bryan, John, Andrew, Nathaniel; daus., Catrina Boyce, Mary Bryan, Agness; son, James. Exc. sons, Alexander Bryan, John Bryan.

James Morris. Newport. Nov. 28, 1748. Mar. 31, 1750. G. 389. Wife, Hannah. Exc. wife, Hannah Morris.

William Taylor. Yeoman. Appo. Hd. Dec. 4, 1749. Ap. 13, 1750. G. 394. Wife, Hester; son, John; son, William Tailer; dau., Hester; Ann Tailer. Exc. wife, Hester; son, John.

Peter Anderson. Yeoman. Red Yyon Hd. April 6, 1750. May 2, 1750. G. 405. Cousin, Mary Montgomery; cousins, John Taylor and James Anderson. Exc. friend, Jacob Vandebar; cousin, John Taylor.

James Hanna. Yeoman. Mill Crk. Hd. April 1, 1750. May 10, 1750. G. 403. Wife, Agnes; uncle, Hugh McWhorter; brothers and sisters in Ireland. Exc. wife, Agnes; Hugh McWhorter.

John Goforth. Farmer. Red Lion Hd. April 26, 1750. May 15, 1750. G. 401. Dau., Elizabeth Cochran; dau., Margaret Cannon; wife, Lydia; son, John; dau., Lydia Goforth; son, William. Exc. wife, Lydia; son, William.

Archibald Murphy. Hamilton Ban Township, Co. of York, Penna. Dec. 28, 1749. June 7, 1750. G. 450. Son-in-law, John Withorow; dau., Elizabeth Withorow; dau., Mary Lockry; son, William Murphy. Exc. son, William Murphy.

Catharine Cox. Red Lion Hd. May 1, 1750. June 13, 1750. G. 407. Mother; brothers, John, Isaac and William Truax; father-in-law; sister, Elizabeth. Exc. sister, Elizabeth; Isaac Trenax (brother).

Philip Vandivere. Yeoman. B'wine Hd. Mar. 1, 1747-8. Aug. 15, 1750. G. 414. Wife, Breta; sons, John and Peter; dau., Susannah; son-in-law, Joseph Jackson. Exc. sons, John Vandivere, Peter Vandivere.

Sarah Daws. Spinster. Wil. 2nd d. of 5th mo., 1750. Aug. 23, 1750.

G. 417. Son, Edward Daws; son, Abram Daws; dau., Mary Way; grandfather; granddau., Hannah Daws.

Miriam Andrews. (Widow to William). Wil. 6th mon. 20th, 1750. Sept. 12, 1750. G. 419. Cousin, Jane Hartley, wife of Thomas Hartley; sons, Ezekial and John Andrews; daus., Hannah West, Ruth Andrews.

John Patterson. N. C. Aug. 16, 1750. Sept. 12, 1750 G. 421. Wife, Mary Patterson (from Ireland); sister, Jv .n Welsh. Exc. Thomas Cooch.

Hester Bishop. Wil. Feb. 2, 1748. Sept. 22, 1750. G. 426. Brother, William Little of Bermuda; Benjamin Smith, brother of my dec. husband, John Smith; Sarah Stapler, John Stapler. Exc. John Stapler.

Robert Guthery. Yeoman. St. Geo. Hd. Sept. 4, 1750. Oct. 13, 1750. G. 427. Mother, Mary Guthery. Exc. mother, Mary.

Ellis Lewis. Wil. 12th mo. called Feb. 1747-8. Oct. 29, 1750. G. 430. Wife, Mary Lewis; sons, Robert Lewis, Nathaniel Lewis and Ellis Lewis; son-in-law, Joshua Pusey; dau., Mary, now marryed to Joshua Pusey; children of brother, Robert Roberts, namely: Mary, Deborah, Lydia, Hannah, Abigail and Martha Roberts; cousins, Elizabeth and Catherine Ellis. Exc. sons, Robert, Nathaniel and Ellis; Joshua Pusey.

Leonard Vandegrift. St. Geo. Hd. Oct. 16, 1750. Nov. 3, 1750. G. 432. My widow, Sarah; eldest son, Christopher Vandegrift; four sons, Leonard, Lewis, Abraham and Isaac; two daus., Mary and Sarah. Exc. wife, Sarah; son, Christopher.

William Scott. Taylor. Aug. 7, 1750. Nov. 8, 1750. G. 438. Wife, Catherine; three children, Joseph, William and Jean. Exc. Catherine Scott, (wife); John Thomason.

Owen Ryan. Appo. Hd. Oct. 26, 1750. Nov. 20, 1750. G. 444. Son, John Ryan. Exc. wife; George Stephenson.

Charles Patterson. Innkeeper. Mar. 9, 1746-7. Nov. 29, 1750. G. 458. Wife, Mary Paterson and her youngest daughter, not yet christened. Exc. wife, Mary Patterson; brother-in-law, John Jones.

Sapiens Harris. Appo. Hd. Nov. 21, 1750. Dec. 15, 1750. G. 442. Wife, Catran. Exc. wife, Catran; sons, Joseph and Jacob Harris.

Peter Hastings. Mill Crk. Hd. Apr. 20, 1748. Dec. 17, 1750. G. 440. Son, John; granddau., Patience Shannon; eldest son, Peter; dau., Isabel and her two children; dau., Jane; dau., Mary; dau. Grace; son, Isaac. Exc. John Hastings (son), Capt. William McCrea.

Isabel Norman, relict of Thomas Norman. Feb. 27, 1748. Dec. 29, 1750. G. 449. Youngest child of Patrick Flynn, Mary Flynn; her brothers, Thomas and John Flynn. Exc. Patrick Flynn.

David Porter. N. C. Jan. 28, 1751. Feb. 5, 1751. G. 456. Sons,

Alexander, David, Patrick; daus., Elinor, Jane; wife, Anguish. Exc. sons, Alexander and David.

Alice Gray. Dec. 23, 1750. Apr. 4, 1751. G. 466. Three children, William, Elizabeth and Alice Gray. Exc. Capt. Alexander Porter.

Robert Nevin. W. Clay Crk. Hd. Mar. 7, 1751. Apr. 11, 1751. G. 467. Wife, Margaret Nevin; two sons; dau., Mary. Exc. Margaret Nevin (wife), Robert Nevin, James McMechen (uncle).

James Bayley. Mill Crk. Hd. Apr. 15, 1751. Apr. 30, 1751. G. 469. John McDougall. Exc. John McDougall.

James Steel. W. Clay Crk. Hd. Apr. 20, 1751. May 1, 1751. G. 468. Wife, Mary; dau.-in-law, Hannah McClean; son, John Steel; son, Moses Steel; son, James Steel; dau., Mary, and her husband, James Alexander; son-in-law, Dan Johnson; son, Alexander Steel; son, William Steel; son, Oron Steel; son, Isaac; brother, Joseph Steel. Exc. Mary Steel (wife), Alexander Steel (son).

Ephraim Logue. Chris. Hd. May 28, 1750. June 1, 1751. G. 474. Wife, Margaret Logue; dau., Margaret Robinson; dau., Catherine Allen; son, David Logue; son, John Logue. Exc. son, John Logue.

John Stalcop. Yeoman. Chris. Hd. Oct. 1, 1748. July 1, 1751. Wife, Mary; sons, John and Andrew Stalcop; dau., Ann Evans; son, Peter Stalcop; son, Emick Stalcop; son, Israll Stalcop; son, Errick Stalcop. Exc. Mary Stalcop (wife), Peter Stalcop (son).

Martha Short, widow of Adam Short. N. C. Dec. 19, 1748. July 20, 1751. G. 481. Two grandchildren, namely: Hester and Mary Buss. Exc. dau., Miriam Daly.

Thomas Babb, Senr. B'wine H'd. Aug. 17, 1748. Aug. 13, 1751. G. 484. Sons. Peter Babb, Thomas Babb, Phillip Babb; daus., Mary, Rebecca, Lydia; grandson, John Gregory; granddau., Rebecca Gregory; granddau., Lydia Gregory. Exc. Peter Babb.

Samuel Silsbee. N. C. July 8, 1751. Aug. 17, 1751. G. 485. Wife, Mary; sons, John and Joseph; dau., Mary. Exc. Mary Sillsbee (wife), Peter Jaquet, wife's brother.

John Ferris. Tanner. Wil. 10th d. of 7th m. 1751. Oct. 3, 1751. G. 493. Wife, Abigail; eight children, namely: Nathan, Ziba, Mathew, Rachell, Rosannah, Elizabeth, Abigail and Deborah. Exc. David Ferris (brother), Zechariah Ferris (brother).

Margaret McMullan. Widow. B'wine Hd. Oct. 6, 1751. Oct. 16, 1751. Misc. 1.360. Son. John McMullan; daus., Jane and Barbery. Exc. son-in-law, John Huston; dau., Barbery.

John Parkinson. Yeoman. Nov. 21, 1751. Nov. 5, 1751. Misc. 1.394. Wife, Jean; son, William. Exc. wife, Jean.

Mary Crawford (Crafort). Town of Whetcreek. Feb. 21, 1752. Feb. 27, 1752. Misc. 1.45. Son-in-law, Robert Heuston; dau., Jean; granddau., Mary Huston; grandson, George; Alexander Robason and my dau., Catreen; brother, Robert Parnet; dau., Marey. Exc. brother, Robert Parnet.

Eliz. Gerritson. Appo. Hd. Dec. 18, 1750. Mar. 30, 1752. Misc. 1.122. Sons, Halliwell and Adam Gerritson; husband, Edmond Garritson, dec.; father, Andrew Peterson; children: Andrew, Henry, Elizabeth, Lydia, Edmund, Mary and Sarah Garritson. Exc. brother, Adam Peterson.

Christian Brimberg. Yeoman. Chris. Hd. Mar. 25, 1752. Apr. 3, 1752. Misc. 2.18. Sons, Peter, Swain Matthias; daus., Mary, Hannah, Elizabeth; son-in-law, Philip Stalcop; John Richardson. Exc. Swain Brimberg, Philip Stalcop.

Issachar Green. —— 11, 1752. May 20, 1752. Misc. 1.121. Wife, Sarah Green; three daus., all minor, namely: Margaret, Hannah and Sarah; sons, John and Job. Exc. wife, Sarah; son, John. Guardian, Olliver Canby (miller).

Richard Griffith. Yeoman. July 21, 1751. June 18, 1752. Misc. 1.124. Wife, Ann Griffith; son, Richard (minor); son, Edward; daus., Susannah, Hannah, Mary (minor). Exc. wife, Ann; son, Edward. Guardians, Rev. Mr. John Rogers, James James; Nathaniel Williams.

Will Kelly. Tailor. St. Geo. Hd. Nov. 1, 1747. Dec. 7, 1752. Misc. 1.260. Daus., Alice, Mary, Sarah and Katharine; "wife." Exc. John Towland, senior; James McDonough.

Albert Vansandt. Farmer. St. Geo. Hd. Dec. 10, 1751. Jan. 11, 1753. N. 141. Son, James Vansandt; wife, Sarah; son, Hermanus Vansandt; his brother, Garrett; his sisters, Christian Dushane and Rebeckah Marteen; son, John Vansandt; dau., Elizabeth Zondon; dau., Ann Borom. Exc. wife, Sarah; oldest son, Hermanus. Trustee, John Vance.

John Jaquet. Yeoman. Swanwick. Feb. 3, 1753. M. 337. Wife, Christiana; three daus., Elizabeth Jaquet, Anna Jaquet, Ingebur Jaquet. Exc. wife, Christiana; brother, Peter Jaquet, brother-in-law, Peter Stidham.

Peter Parker. Farmer. St. Geo. Hd. June 22, 1752. Feb. 24, 1753. Misc. 1.396. Wife, Elizabeth; dau., Hannah Vance; "each of my second wife's children"; son, George Parker. Exc. son, George.

Francis King. Yeoman, St. Geo. Hd. Aug. 31, 1745. May 7, 1753. Misc. 1.263. Wife, Christian; sons, Francis and Leonard. Exc. wife, Christian; sons, Francis and Leonard.

Hugh Watson. Wil. July 23, 1753. July 28, 1753. Misc. 2.12. Friend, Mabell McCall, wife of John McCall. Exc. Zachariah Ferriss.

Richard Thomas. Yeoman. Aug. 7, 1753. Misc. 1.457. Son, Richard; dau., Rachel Griffith; dau., Ann Bush; dau., Sarah Mc-

Mechen; dau., Mary Thomas; son, Lewis; "wife." Exc. son, Lewis.

Zachariah Kettle. July 25, 1753. Sept. 4, 1753. Misc. 1.261. Son, Magnus; father, Cornelius Kettle, dec.; son, John; daus., Mary, Catherine, Ann and Susannah. Exc. friends, Nonce Justis, Cornelius Kettle.

John Toland. July 29, 1753. Sept. 8, 1753. Misc. 1.455. Wife, Mary; Wm. McNichol, Edward McGonnigal, dau., Ann Toland; daus., Mary and Sarah Toland; son, Edmund Toland; son, Patrick Toland. Exc. wife, Mary; Edward McGuire.

David Griffin. Kent Co. Aug. 27, 1753. Sept. 8, 1753. Misc. 1.126. Uncle, Robert Griffin of New Castle Co. Exc. uncle, Robert.

Thomas Hollingsworth. Chris. Hd. June 19, 1752. Oct. 1, 1753. Misc. 1.202. Mother; wife; daus., Susanna. Rachel, Judith; sons, Thomas, Isaac, Nathaniel, Emor and Christopher. Exc. sons, Thomas and Isaac.

William Buchanan. Chapman. Mill Crk. Hd. Oct. 6, 1753. Oct. 16, 1753. Misc. 1.20. Children of Samuel Young, namely: Jane, Elizabeth, Rebecca, Sarah, and Margaret; cousin, Alexander Buchanan; brother, George Buchanan; sister, Francis; John Culbert. Exc. Col. Andrew Lewis, Capt. James Lockhart, Samuel Young.

Zehu Curtis. Nov. 10, 1753. ————. Misc. 1.46. Wife, Mary; two grandsons, Curtis and Robert Clay; dau., Ann Clay; "dau., Ann Clay's other children." Exc. wife, Mary; dau., Ann Clay; son-in-law, Slator Clay.

David James. Cordwainer. Penn. Hd. July 14, 1753. Dec., 1753. Misc. 1.247. Brother, Thomas James; Jannet James, dau. of brother Thomas; Ann James, dau., of brother, Thomas; John James, son of brother, Thomas; cousin, Rachel Bradley; sisters, Sarah and Dinah. Exc. brother, Thomas.

John McDugall. Yeoman. Nov. 22, 1753. Dec. 4, 1753. Misc. 1.362. Wife; children. Exc. wife; Alexander Montgomery.

John Springer, Jr. Chris. Hd. ——— 11, 1753. Dec. 20, 1753. Misc. 1.438. Wife, Sarah; two son, Peter and John; brother, Peter; "my father." Exc. wife, Sarah; Christopher Springer.

Evan Lewis. Yeoman. N. C. Hd. Nov. 18, 1753. Dec. 26, 1753. Misc. 1.313. Nephew, Griffith, son of John Griffith; niece, Hannah Griffith; friend, Rachel Evans; brother, Thomas Lewis; three nephews, David Griffith, Thomas Griffith and John Griffith; niece, Mary, dau. of John Griffith, now wife of Roger Williams; nieces, Sarah Griffith and Elizabeth Griffith; nieces, Hannah Lewis and Amy Lewis, the daus. of my brother, David Lewis; nephew, John, son of my brother, David, dec.; nephew, Joel, son of my brother, David, dec.; nephew, Jehu and Isaac, sons of brother, Thomas Lewis. Exc. brother, Thomas Lewis and his son, Isaac Lewis.

Jacob Vandegrift. April 12, 1750. Jan. 16, 1754. Misc. 1.495. Sons, Leonard and Jacob Vandegrift; dau., Christian Alkinson; daus., Ann and Elizabeth; two sons and six daughters. Exc. sons, Jacob and Leonard.

Dennis O'Bryan. Laborer. (Nunc.) N. C. Dec. 16, 1753. Jan. 27, 1754. Misc. 1.379. Brothers and sisters named: Richard O'Bryan, Mary O'Bryan and Edward O'Bryan. Living in Racannon, about 24 miles from Cork, Ireland. Attested by George Monro.

John Bird. B'wine Hd. Sept. 1, 1753. Feb. 8, 1754. Misc. 1.22. Wife, Margaret; dau., Ann Biddle; son, John; nephew, John Bird, son of brother, Thomas Bird; dau., Ann Bird. Exc. wife, Margaret; Empson Bird.

Abraham Gooding. Gentleman. St. Geo. Hd. Jan. 29, 1754. Feb. 21, 1754. Misc. 1.127. Son, Jacob Gooding; granddau., Elinor Dushane; my three children, namely: son, Jacob; dau., Garterick, wife of Garred Rothwell; dau., Mary, the wife of Cornelius Carty; heirs of James Belvaird. Exc. son, Jacob; friend, Jacob Von Bebber.

Robert Owens. Appo. Hd. Mar. 10, 1754. ———, 1754. Misc. 1.380. Wife, Jannat; four eldest sons, namely: William, Edward, Owen and Evan; three youngest children, namely: Sarah Owen, Robert and Ammon. Exc. brother, Edward Owen.

Hans Hanson. Gent. St. Geo. Hd. Jan. 5, 1753. Apr. 16, 1754. Filed. Sons, Philip and John; granddau., Catherine King; son-in-law, John King; dau., Elizabeth; dau., Gartry. Exc. sons, Philip and John.

Timothy Webster. Carpenter. Appo. Hd. June 17, 1754. Misc. 2.11. Dau., Judith; dau., Elizabeth; brother, Nicholas Hedrah; son, Evan; son, Methuselah. Exc. Thomas Brown.

William Shipley. Wil. 3rd d. of 9th mo. called Sept., 1754. H. & L. 241. Oldest son, Thomas Shipley; eldest dau., Ann Maris; dau., Elizabeth Canby; dau., Sarah Richardson; son, William Shipley; wife, Elizabeth Shipley. Exc. wife, Elizabeth.

John Lewdon. Yeoman. N. C. Hd. Sept. 15, 1754. Sept. 25, 1754. Misc. 1.316. Benjamin Swett; wife, Hannah Lewdon; son, Joseph; daus., Elizabeth, Hannah, Margaret, Mary, Rebecca and Ruth. Exc. brother, Joseph Lewdon; son, Joseph Lewdon.

James Crafford. Yeoman. Jan. 23, 1753. Oct. 1, 1754. Misc. 1.47. Son, John Crafford; son, James Crafford; dau., Rebecca Moore; dau., Anne Fflin; son, William Crafford. Overseers, Alexander Porter, Thomas James. Exc. son-in-law, Patrick Fflin.

Richard Gregg. Yeoman. Chris. Hd. 17th d. of 9th mo., 1754. Oct. 21, 1754. Misc. 1.128. Wife, Ann; children; three sons; five daughters. Exc. wife, Ann. Trustees, couzens, Samuel and Harmen Gregg.

Jacob Harris. Appo. Hd. Sept. 21, 1754. Nov. 1, 1754. Misc. 1.204.

Wife, Anne Harris; dau., Mary Harris. Exc. brother, Joseph Harris; wife, Ann Harris.

John Clark. Marrener. City of New York. Aug. 6, 1743. Dec. 19, 1754. Misc. 1.50. Wife, Mary Clark; four children; son, John Clark; daus., Sarah Clark, Mary Littlejea and Ruth Ann (or Rebeckeh). Exc. son, John Clark; wife.

James Lattimore. Pen. Hd. Nov. 23, 1753. Dec. 26, 1754. Misc. 1.318. Daughter, Mary. Exc. friend, Henry Rowland.

John Vanlewveneigh. Shopkeeper. N. C. Jan. 11, 1753. Dec. 31, 1754. Misc. 1.494. Wife; sons, John, Zachariah and Samuel. Exc. son, Samuel.

James Barber. Weaver. N. C. Jan. 21, 1750. Feb. 11, 1755. Misc. 1.23. Wife; son, John; daus., Agness and Martha. Exc. wife.

Garret Garretson. Chris. Hd. Jan. 21, 1755. Feb. 17, 1755. Misc. 1.130. Wife, Mary; son, John; sons, Henry, George, Garret and Jacob; two daus., Ann and Rebecca; dau., Eleanora. Exc. son, John; wife, Mary. Overseer, William Armstrong.

Daniel Corbit. Appo. Hd. 12th mo. 20th, 1755. Feb. 27, 1755. O. 563. Son, Daniel Corbit, his son Daniel; son, Israel Corbit; sons, John, William, and Jonathan; son-in-law, Jacob Duehattaway; dau. Rachel, wife of Jacob Duehattaway; grandson, John McCool; father, Samuel McCool; granddau., Rachel Ludin, the dau. of Mary Ludin; grandson, John Ludin. Exc. son, Daniel Corbit; son-in-law, Jacob Duehattaway.

Nicholas Van Dike. St. Geo. Hd. Jan. 16, 1755. Apr. 4, 1755. Misc. 1.496. Sons, Nicholas and Abraham; dau., Mary Van Dike; dau., Rachel. Exc. wife; son, Nicholas. Appraisers, David Stewart and John Van Dike.

Thomas Phillips. Chris. Hd. April 26, 1755. Misc. 1.400. Wife, Mary; step-son, Nathan Scothorn; nephew, Thomas Phillips; grandson, John Scothorn. Exc. wife, Mary; step-son, Nathan Scothorn.

William Holliday. Appo. Hd. Jan. 17, 1754. May 21, 1755. Misc. 1.205. Son, John Holliday; son, William Holliday; dau., Anna Holliday; Richard Taylor; dau., Rachel Taylor; Joseph Holliday, Benjamin Holliday. Exc. Anna Holliday, senior; John Holliday.

James Harron. Kent Co. Aug. 21, 1755. Misc. 1.206. James Byrn, Jane Coleman, Clemons Klintham.

Mary King. B'wine Hd. Nov. 20, 1755. Dec. 11, 1755. Misc. 1.265. Son, Frederick King; brother, Jonas Stidham. Exc. Samuel Milner; brother, Jonas Stidham.

Hugh Clark. Yeoman. Mill Crk Hd. Nov. 18, 1755. Dec. 23, 1755. Misc. 1.49. Wife, Martha; dau., Elinor; son, Hugh; brothers, James and William. Exc. wife, Martha; brother-in-law, Wm. Jordaine.

Simon Hadley. Yeoman. Mill Crk. Hd. Nov. 3, 1755. Feb. 17, 1756.

Misc. 1.218. Wife, Phebe Hadley; grandson, Simon Hadley, son of my son, Joshua Hadley; grandson, Jeremiah, son of said Joshua; grandson, Simon Johnson, son of Robert Johnson; grandson, John Hadley, son of my son, Joseph Hadley; grandson, Simon Gregg, son of Richard Gregg, deceased., and my dau., Ann, his wife; dau., Deborah Howel, wife to Jacob Howel; daughter, Hannah Stanfield, widow to John Stanfield; dau., Ruth Linly, wife to Thomas Linly; dau., Katheren Johnson, wife to Robert Johnson; my grandchildren, children of my son, Joseph, namely: Elizabeth Thomson, wife to James Thomson; Deborah Earle, wife to John Earle, and Hannah Earle, wife to Samuel Earle. (This name is either Earle or Carl.) My grandchildren, children of my son, Joshua, namely: Ruth Marshill, wife to John Marshill; Thomas Hadley; Sarah Fred, wife to Joseph Fred; Mary Hadley, Jeremiah Hadley, Joshua Hadley, Jr., Joseph Hadley, Jr., Deborah Hadley, Hannah Hadley and Catheren Hadley. My grandchildren, children of my dau., Hannah, widow of John Stanfield, namely: Simon Dixson; Rebecca, wife of William Marshall; Ruth Dixson, John Stanfield, Jr., Thomas Stanfield, and Samuel Stanfield. My grandchildren, children of my dau., Ruth, wife to Thomas Linly, namely: Catheren, James, Simon, Ruth, Jr., Thomas, Jr., Linly, and John Linly. My grandchildren, children of my dau., Anne, widow of Richard Gregg, namely: Sarah Smith, alias Gregg, Jacob, William, Miriam, Deborah, and Phoebe. Nephew, Thomas Keran; said wife's children, John Buffington, Richard Buffington, Phoebe Wall, Peter Buffington, Isaac Buffington, Joseph Buffington. Exc. grandson-in-law, James Thomson; friend, Daniel Nickols. Overseers, Benjamin Swett, Samuel Gregg.

Thomas Hyatt. Yeoman. St. Geo. Hd. Feb. 16, 1756. Mar. 5, 1756. Misc. 1.209. Sons, John Hyatt, Thomas Hyatt, Valentine Hyatt, Isaac Hyatt, Abraham Hyatt, and Ephraim Hyatt; wife, Catherine; dau., Catherine Cannon; daus., Mary Hyatt, Rachel Davis, Sarah McGraugh, Anne Griffin, Rebecca Hyatt, Eleanor Hyatt, and Susannah Hyatt; granddau., Catherine Hill. Exc. sons, John and Thomas.

Andrew Hendrickson. Chris Hd. Feb. 23, 1749. Mar. 6, 1756. Misc. 1.207. Wife, Christiana; son, John. Exc. wife, Christiana; friend, William Anderson.

John Griffith. Weaver. Pen. Hd. Nov. 27, 1753. Mar. 16, 1756. Misc. 1.134. Sons, David, Thomas, John and Griffith; dau., Mary, wife of Roger Williams; daus., Sarah, Elizabeth and Hannah. Exc. son, Griffith; brother-in-law, Thomas Lewis.

Robert Richardson. Yeoman. Dec. 15, 1756. Feb. 8, 1757. Misc. 1.413. Wife, Hannah; two sons, John and Robert; wife's father, John Lewden, dec. Exc. wife, Hannah; Joseph Lewden, Senior.

John Rothwell. Appo. Hd. Jan. 20, 1757. Feb. 17, 1757. N. 166.

Wife, Elizabeth. Exc. Elizabeth Rothwell (wife), Thomas Rothwell (brother).

William Brittain. ————. Mar. 18, 1757. Misc. 2.25. Son, John Brittain. Exc. John Brittain.

Mathias Shrick. Cooper. Red Lion Hd. Feb. 2, 1754. May 14, 1757. Misc. 1.440. Dau., Ann Schreek; granddau., Mary Schreek, the dau. of my son, John. Exc. dau., Ann. Guardian, Andrew Zobart.

James Gano. Appo. Hd. Jan. 22, 1757. July 24, 1757. Misc. 1.134. Wife, Mary; three sons, Lewis Ganno; Jeames Ganno and John Ganno; grandson, John Ganno (at sea). Exc. sons, Lewis Ganno and Jeames Ganno.

John Garrett. Chris. Hd. July 14, 1749. Sept. 4, 1757. N. 267. Wife, Margaret; son, Thomas; son, John; daus., Elizabeth, Ann, Sarah and Margaret. Exc. son. Thomas.

Rebecca Kenney. Mill Crk. Hd. Sept. 24, 1757. Oct. 24, 1757. Misc. 1.266. "My children." Exc. son, Moses Kenney; Hugh Royandels.

Mary Smith. 20th of 9th mo., 1757. Oct. 27, 1757. Misc. 1.441. Mother, Margaret Smith; brother, Thomas Smith; brother, William Smith; uncle. William Buah; sister, Hollingsworth; sister, Sarah Johnson; brother, John Smith; sister, Hannah Smith; sister, Margaret Smith; sister, Rachel Smith. Exc. mother, Margaret Smith.

John Burnet. Mill Crk. Hd. Nov. 5, 1757. Nov. 17, 1757. Misc. 1.24. Son, William Burnet; son, John Burnet; son, Henry Burnet. Exc son, John Burnet.

William Crawford. Dec. 12, 1757. ————. Misc. 1.54. John Crawford; John Crawford's son, John Crawford; John Crawford's 2nd son, David Crawford; John Crawford's 3rd son, Alexander Crawford; John Crawford's two daus., A—— and Martha; his sister, Ann Crawford; his 3rd sister. Lydia Crawford; his 4th sister, Elinor Crawford; my sister, Ann; my sister, Rebecca's dau., Rebecca; my brother's daughter; my sister Rebecca's sons, namely: James and William Moore; James Moore and Milcha, his wife. Exc. brother-in-law, Francis Moore.

Derrick See. St. Geo. Hd. Dec. 15, 1757. Jan. 2, 1758. Misc. 1.442. Eldest and youngest sons, namely: Peter and Abraham; sons, Richard and William; grandson, William Burgess; brother, James See.

Garret Garretson. Yeoman. N. C. Hd. Jan. 20, 1754. Jan. 6, 1758. Misc. 1.139. Son, John; daus., Anna, Rebecca, Huldah, Mary and Sarah; dau., Elizabeth; grandsons, James and John, sons of my son, Cornelius Garretson, dec.; sons, Eliakim and Jedediah. Exc. sons, Eliakim and Jedediah.

Henry Souder (Sowden). Yeoman. N. C. Apr. 24, 1757. Feb. 22,

1758. Misc. 1.443. Son, Henry; dau., Margaret; son, John. Exc. son, John Souder.

Abraham Lakerman. Yeoman. Shrewsbury Plantation, Appo. Hd. May 18, 1747. Mar. 17, 1758. Misc. 1.319. Son, Garret Lakerman; son, Abraham Lakerman. Exc. sons, Garret and Abraham.

John Grubb. Yeoman. B'wine Hd. Mar. 10, 1758. Mar. 21, 1758. Misc. 1.138. Father, John Grubb; son, William Grubb; Ralph Withers; son, John Grubb; Solomon Chapen; son, Samuel Grubb; son, Richard Grubb; son, Richard's four children, namely: Rachel, Hannah, George and Richard; son, Adam Grubb; Emanuel Grubb; dau., Rachel Pedrick; Hannah Flower, Richard Beaver, Adam Buckley; dau., Mary Moulder. Exc. sons, William, Samuel and Adam.

William Lamply. Marriner. Sloop of war "Prince Edward." Aug. 19, 1757. Apr. 3, 1758. Misc. 1.322. Wife, Rachel Lamply. Exc. wife, Rachel.

David Lewis. Mill Crk. Hd. Nov. 8, 1757. Apr. 22, 1758. Misc. 1.323. Son, James Lewis' son, David Lewis; dau.-in-law, Elizabeth Lewis, wife of son, James Lewis; son, William Lewis; son, William Lewis' son, Benjamin; dau., Mary Lewis. Exc. dau.-in-law, Elizabeth Lewis.

Philip Grimes. Yeoman. Pen. Hd. May 2, 1758. May 15, 1758. Misc. 1.140. Dau., Rosanna Grimes; dau., Mary; dau., Ann; dau., Dorrothea; sons, Edward, James and John Grimes. Exc. brother-in-law, John Read; brother, James Grimes.

Henry Griffith. Yeoman. B'wine Hd. May 14, 1758. May 22, 1758. Misc. 1.137. Son, Evan Griffith; dau., Mary Dougherty. Exc. friends, Samuel Grubb and Richard Moor.

Andrew Hendrickson. Yeoman. Chris. Hd. June 26, 1758. Sept. 2, 1758. Misc. 1.211. Wife, Mary; sons, John, Jonas, Tobias; dau., Mary Kambo; dau., Susannah Justice; daus., Cathrin, Lydia and Sarah. Exc. wife, Mary; son, John.

Peter Ganthony, of Brigantine "Bleakney," commanded by Mr. Moses Minshall. Chris. Hd. Nov. 29, 1757. Nov. —, 1758. Misc. 1.136. Dau., Ann Ganthony. Exc. coz., Margaret Smith.

Ezemy Kelly, widow. (Nunc.) Mill Crk. Hd. Aug. 3, 1757. Dec. 21, 1758. Misc. 1.266. Son, Thomas Kelley; son, James; dau., Mary Kelly; daus., Margaret and Elizabeth Kelly; sons, William, Samuel and John. Exc. son, William.

David Kirkpatrick. Chris. Hd. June 8, 1758. Jan. 1, 1759. Misc. 1.268. Sister, Margaret Kirkpatrick. Exc. sister, Margaret.

Thomas Cartmill. B'wine Hd. Feb. 12, 1759. Mar. 14, 1759. Misc. 1.51. Son, William Cartmill; grandson, Thomas Cartmill; his two sisters, Ann and Hannah; dau., Sarah Breek; dau., H(J)annah Killam; grandsons; Thomas Cartmill's mother's husband, George Robinson. Exc. son, William Cartmill; son-in-law, John Killam.

Anthony Dushane. Red Lion Hd. July 13, 1759. Aug. 1, 1759. Misc. 1.71. Wife, Rachel; son, Michael Dushane; dau., Susannah Britt; Charles Cannon; dau., Mary Robinson. Exc. son, Michael Dushane.

Benjamin Underwood. Farmer. Pen. Hd. Nov. 24, 1759. Dec. —, 1759. Misc. 1.469. Wife, Sarah; son, John; dau., Fabey; son, Benjamin; dau., Sarah; sons, Solomon and Nathan; dau., Ann; Joseph, Elizabeth and Samuel. Exc. Francis Moore, Alexander Porter.

Henry Stidham. Brd'y Hd. June 24, 1757. Dec. 16, 1759. Misc. 1.444. Wife, Margery Stidham; sons, Jacob, Adam and Henry; daus., Margaret, Sarah, Ann, Susannah and Mary. Exc. son, Jacob Stidham, John Allmond.

John Vandike. St. Geo. Hd. Dec. 5, 1759. Dec. 26, 1759. Misc, 2.1. Brother, Isaac Vandike; wife, Margaret; dau., Ann Vandike; brothers, James and David; three sisters, Jemima, Mary, Elizabeth. Exc. wife, Margaret; brother, Isaac; brother-in-law, Jacob Peterson.

Samuel Vanleuveneigh. Shop Keeper. Town of New Castle. June 28, 1759. Dec. 27, 1759. Misc. 1.497. Nieces, Rebecca and Mary Vanleuveneigh; the daus. of my brother, Zachariah; nieces, Catherine and Elizabeth Vanleuveneigh, the daus. of my brother, John, dec.; Eliakim Garretson. Exc. brother, Zachariah.

George Gillespie. Minister. Nov. 25, 1758. Jan. 30, 1760. Misc. 1.142. Son, Samuel Gillespie; wife; daus., Hannah, Elizabeth, Agness Gillespie; son, George Gillespie; grandson, George Wallace; granddau., Mary Armitage; grandchild, George Gillespie; granddau., Rebekah Armitage; son-in law, Joseph Wallace, and Mary; son-in-law, Samuel Armitage, and his spouse, Martha; two granddaus., Rebekah and Elizabeth Blair. Exc. wife, Rebekah Gillespie; son, Samuel Gillespie.

John Kinkead. Pen. Hd. Dec. 9, 1750. Feb. 21, 1760. Misc. 1,269. Brother, James; mother, Sarah; father, William Kinkead. Exc. father, William.

David Graham. Weaver. N. C. July 16, 1757. Apr. 3, 1760. Misc. 1.146. Wife, Mary; "child or children." Exc. wife, Mary Graham.

William Vandike. Appo. Hd. Mar. 3, 1760. Apr. 4, 1760. Misc. 1.499. Wife, Agnes; three children. Exc. wife, Agnes.

John Smith. Dec. 10, 1751. Apr. 13, 1760. Misc. 1.437. Wife, Margaret; three sons, William, John and Thomas. Exc. William Smith.

Jane Clement. St. Geo. Hd. Feb. 11, 1760. Apr. 15, 1760. Misc. 1.59. Brothers, David and Benjamin Clements; father, Samuel Clement; sister, Mary, wife of Evan Thomas; sister-in-law, Hannah, wife of brother, David. Exc. brother, David Clements.

Jacob Taylor. "Nayler." Wil. Dec. 1, 1759. May 20, 1760. Misc. 1.459. Friend, Esther Broom; friend, Jacob Broom; friend, Isaac Broom; friend, Abraham Broom. Exc. James Broom, David Bush, Jr.

Edmund Liston. Appo. Hd. Sept. 6, 1757. June 7, 1760. Misc. 1.342. Wife, Sarah; sons, Thomas Liston, Ebenezer Liston; son, Abraham Liston; son, Joseph Liston; dau., Sarah Liston; son, Edmnud Liston. Exc. wife; sons, Thomas and Abraham Liston.

John Lattimer. Feb. 16, 1759. Aug. —, 1760. Misc. 1.327. Brother, William Lattimer. Exc. brother, William Lattimer.

Robert Barr. Yeoman. Mill Crk. Hd. ———. Aug. 6, 1760. Misc. 1.27. Wife, Rachel; son, Robert; William Fort, Rachel Fort; her grandmother, Rachel Barr. Exc. wife, Rachel; son, Robert.

George Hill. May 31, 1760. Aug. 7, 1760. Misc. 1.213. Wife, Susanna. Exc. wife, Susanna.

Jacob Grantham. Farmer. N. C. Hd. June 14, 1760. Aug. 9, 1760. Misc. 1.137. Son, Isaac; dau., Dorcas Jaquet; John Story; wife, Margaret; George Grantham, son of my brother, Charles Grantham. Exc. son, Isaac; Benjamin Chew, Thomas Jaquet.

Adam Buckley. B'wine Hd. Sept. 24, 1760. Wife, Ann Buckley; son, John Buckley; dau., Elizabeth Williamson; Edward Whitaker and wife, Elizabeth; grandson, Adam Williamson; his father, John Williamson; granddau., Ann Price; Adam Clayton; William Grubb, son of John Grubb; Susannah Jackson. Exc. John Buckley (son), John Williamson (son-in-law).

Thomas Rodgers. Merchant. Dinwiddie Co. May 13, 1757. Oct. 13, 1760. Misc. 1.415. Wife, Martha; niece, Johanna Rodgers; her brother, Thomas Rodgers. Adm. John Butler.

Alexander Bryan. St. Geo. Hd. Nov. 21, 1760. Dec. 15, 1760. Misc. 1.28. Brother, James Bryan; sister, Cathrine Boice; brothers, John and Andrew Bryan; sisters, Mary and Agnes. Exc. brothers, John and Andrew.

Christian Brown. Sept. 1, 1757. Dec. 27, 1760. Misc. 1.26. Son, Abraham Brown; sons, Samuel and Peter. Exc. Peter Vandever, senior.

George Houston. Red Lion Hd. Feb. 10, 1761. Feb. 19, 1761. Misc. 1.213. Wife, Margret; two sons, James and Jacob; Margaret Porter, Ann Clark, Mary Houston; son, James Houston, William Reynolds. Exc. son, James; son-in-law, David Porter.

Samuel Moore. Yeoman. Appo. Hd. Mar. 4, 1761. ———. H. & I. 25. Dau., Agnes Holliday; dau., Jane Moore. Exc. dau., Jane Moore.

Josiah Lewis. Red Lion Hd. Apr. 2, 1761. Apr. 11, 1761. Misc. 1.328. Wife, Mary; brother, Philip Lewis; my sister's children; cousin, Peter Stout; cousin, Josiah David and Sarah David;

cousin, John Moor; cousin, Sarah West; cousin, Immanuel Stout. Exc. brother, Philip Lewis; wife, Mary.

Anne Griffith. Widow. Feb. 17, 1761. Apr. 21, 1761. Misc. 1.150. Dau., Hannah Butcher, wife of Thomas Butcher; granddau., Ann Butcher, dau. of Thomas Butcher; dau., Mary Griffith; son, Richard Griffith. Exc. son, Richard. Guardian, John Jones, Esq.

Eliakim Garretson. N. C. Hd. 3rd mo. 5th, 1761. April 30, 1761. Misc. 1.151. Wife, Lydia; son, James; son, Joseph; dau., Elizabeth. Exc. friends, John Pyle, Aaron Mustgrove.

George Burch. Farmer. June 6, 1761. July 2, 1761. Misc. 1.29. Daus., Rachel, Lydia; sons, Joseph and George; dau., Mary; son, Christopher. Exc. wife, Jane Burch; son, Joseph Burch.

Ann Gilder. St. Geo. Hd. June 4, 1760. July 4, 1761. Misc. 1.149. Dau., Mary Pierce; dau., Ann Gilder; dau., Elizabeth Gibbs; dau., Sarah Gilder. Exc. son, Joseph Pierce.

Edward Robinson. ———. July 13, 1761. H. & I. 543. Grandsons, Edward and Joseph Robinson, sons of Jonass Robinson, dec.; grandson, Richard Robinson, son of Richard Robinson; dau., Elizabeth Armstrong, wife of Robert Armstrong; grandson, Jacob Robinson, son of Richard Robinson, dec.; wife, Isabel; son, Isral Robinson. Exc. William Armstrong, Thomas Duff.

William McCausland. Farmer. Pen. Hd. Aug. 31, 1761. Sons, Andrew, James and John; dau., Catharine. Exc. son, Andrew; dau., Catharine.

Marmiduck Jemison. Aug. 30, 1761. Sept. 3, 1761. H. & I. 544. Father, John Jenison; brothers, Andrew, Samuel and John Jenison; sisters, Margaret and Mary Jenison; sisters, Iheen and Rosy Jenison. Exc. Thomas McCrakin, John Hendry.

Nicholas Bennet. Yeoman. St. Geo. Hd. Aug. 1, 1761. Sept. 5, 1761. Misc. 1.30. Son, William; brother, William Bennet. Exc. brother, William Bennet.

Peter Hendrickson. Yeoman. Chris. Hd. Aug. 7, 1761. Oct. 1, 1761. Misc. 1.215. Wife, Anna; sons, John, Peter, David, and Edward Hendrickson; daus., Catheren, Sarah, Anna, and Rebecca. Exc. wife, Anna; son, David.

William David. Yeoman. May 20, 1761. Oct. 5, 1761. H. & I. 545. Sons, Isaac and John David; daus., Mary and Ann David. Exc. brother, John David.

John Allmon. (Nunc.) B'wine Hd. Nov. 11, 1761. Nov. 13, 1761. H. & I. 528. Three children; one son; two daus.; brother, William Allmon. Attested by William Stedham, Susanna Stedham, John Peterson.

John Harding. B'wine Hd. Mar. 6, 1759. Nov. 17, 1761. H. & I. 549. Wife, Mary Harding; son, Isaac. Exc. wife, Mary; Adam Grubb.

Henry Vandike. Yeoman. St. Geo. Hd. Dec. 28, 1761. Feb. 4, 1762.

Misc. 2.2. Son, Jacob; wife, Elizabeth; dau., Mary, wife of Alexander Montgomery; granddau., Elizabeth Montgomery. Exc. son, Jacob.

Joseph Thomas. Yeoman. Pen. Hd. June 15, 1762. H. & I. 253. Wife, Jane; grandson, Joseph Thomas, son of my son, Benjamin; grandsons, David Howell, and Enos Howell, sons of my dau., Dinah Howell, wife of David Howell; son-in-law, James James; five children, Benjamin Thomas, Joseph Thomas, John Thomas, Elinor, wife of Joseph Jacobs, and Pricilla, wife of William Bochannen.

Joseph Louchran. Yeoman. Appo. Hd. Oct. 15, 1762. Aug. 17, 1762. Misc. 1.329. Wife, Martha; children, Joseph, Katherine, Mary and James. Exc. wife, Martha.

David Rees. Pen. Hd. June 17, 1760. Nov. 19, 1762. K. 53. Sons, Jehu and David; daus., Margaret, Charity and Mary. Exc. Moris Williams; son, Jehu Rees.

John Porter. Farmer. Red Lyon Hd. Nov. 14, 1763. Dec. 2, 1763. Misc. 1.401. Wife, Katriane; sons, Robert and Samuel; daus., Jean and Sarah. Exc. wife, Katriane; son, Samuel.

James Grimes. Yeoman. Pen. Hd. Nov. 29, 1762. Dec. 6, 1762. Misc. 1.152. Wife, Margret Grimes; daus., Ann, Mary, Ruth, Rosanah and Isabela; son, William; mother; brother-in-law, Daniel Grimes; brother, Philip. Exc. wife, Margret; John Reed.

Joseph Hill. Appo. Hd. Apr. 5, 1762. Dec. 23, 1762. H. & I. 31. Two children of Thomas Hill, the son of my brother, John Hill; Joseph Hill, son of brother, John Hill; children of said Joseph Hill; Lyddya, dau. of my said brother, John Hill; children of said Lyddya, by her former husband; widow of Joseph Buxon, who was son of my sister, Elizabeth Hill; Mary Janvier, dau. of Philip Janvier; wife, Mary. Exc. wife, Mary; Peter Alrichs, Daniel Corbit.

Adam Peterson. St. Geo. Hd. Jan. 23, 1763. ———. H. & I. 32. Cousins, Richard Cantwell and Lydia Cantwell; Dr. Jacob Peterson; wife, Veronica. Exc. Veronica Peterson (wife), Matthew Reah.

William Hay. Innholder. Wil. Jan. 1, 1763. Mar. 1, 1763. Misc. 1.217. Son, Jehu Hay; son, David Hay; dau., Elizabeth Hay. Exc. brother-in-law, Isaac Weaver; John Hanby.

William Carson. Gent. Pen. Hd. Jan. 23, 1762. Mar. 18, 1763. Misc. 1.60. Wife, Mary; daus., Jenat, Agness and Mary Carson. Exc. wife, Mary; Henry Carson.

Elias Humphries. St. Geo. Hd. Mar. 9, 1763. Apr. 20, 1763. Misc. 1.236. Wife, Lyddia; sons, Joseph and Abraham; dau., Mary. Exc. James Piper.

Samuel Bradford. Red Lion Hd. Dec. 31, 1763. H. & I. 190. Wife,

Margret; son, William Bradford; daus., Sara, Martha; grandson, Samuel Bradford. Exc. son, William Bradford.

Swain Walraven. Chris. Hd. Dec. 20, 1763. Feb. 21, 1764. Misc. 2.10. Wife, Catheran; sons, Isaac and Peter; dau., Ann; daus., Christiana, Lydia and Cathrian. Exc. Cathrian Walraven; John Hendrixson.

Martha Loughran. (Nunc.) Feb. 12, 1764. Feb. 22, 1764. Misc. 1.331. Children to be taken by Wm. Finne; husband, Joseph Loughran, dec.; step-son, James Loughran. Attested by Pheby Offley, Magdalen Thompson.

John Lockhart. Mill Crk. Hd. Aug. 31, 1757. Sept. 13, 1764. Misc. 1.332. Son, Matthew Lockhard; son, Arthur Lockhard; grandson, John Lockhard, son of my son, Matthew. Exc. friend, Evan Rice.

Patrick Lyons. Yeoman. Appo. Hd. Nov. 7, 1763. Oct. 8, 1764. Misc. 1.333. Dau., Cathrine; son, Patrick Lyons; daus., Sarah and Ann Lyons. Exc. friend, Dr. Hugh Matthews.

Ann Catharin Tranberg. Widow. Wil. Aug. 4, 1764. Oct. 11, 1764. Misc. 1.460. Dau., Rebecah Bonzell; dau., Elizabeth Springer; sister, Magdalen Robinson, and my niece, her dau.; son-in-law, Gabriel Springer; Mr. Henry Elves; granddau., Honour Bonzell; granddau., Cathrine Parlen.

Robert Bryan. Yeoman. Sept. 21, 1764. Codicil, Oct. 5, 1764. Oct. 12, 1764. Misc. 1.31. Wife, Hannah; unborn child; son, Robert; brothers, Nathaniel and Charles; brother Charles' son, Robert; cousin, Robert Bryan, son of brother James, dec.; brothers, William and Andrew. Exc. brother, Nathaniel Bryan; brother, Charles Bryan.

Mary Littler. Widow. Wil. Oct. 18, 1764. Misc. 1.335. My sister, Bettrige's son, Thomas Christy; friend, William Nails. Exc. John Hobson or John Kendall.

Patrick Keran. Sept. 24, 1764. Nov. 5, 1764. Misc. 1 270. Wife, Bridget; son, Patrick; dau., Catherine. Exc. Patrick Keran, Jr.

Peter Sigfredus Alrick. N. C. Hd. Sept. 19, 1764. Nov. 28, 1764. N. 230. Wife, Susannah Alricks; sons, Fredus and Lucas Alricks; dau., Susannah; brother-in-law, Jonas Stidham; nephew, Peter Jaquet. Exc. Susannah Alricks, Fredus Alricks, Lucas Alricks.

John Walraven. Farmer. Appo. Hd. Sept. 13, 1764. Dec. 7, 1764. Misc. 2.7. Wife, Susannah Margat; dau., Susannah Walraven; son, John Walraven; sons, Elias and William Walraven; dau., Margret Walraven; dau., Rachel Truax. Exc. wife, Susannah Margat Walraven.

William Hedges. Wil. Jan. 26, 1765. Mar. 7, 1765. Misc. 1.238. Wife, Rebecca Hedges; her brother, Hon. Daniel Delany of Annapolis; estate in Great Britain; grandfather, William Hedges.

Cornelius Garretson. N. C. Hd. Jan. 21, 1765. Mar. 9, 1765. Misc. 1.155. Cousin, William Garretson of Canawango; cousin, Jediah Garretson of Newport; Mary Jaquet, dau. of Anthony Jaquet; brother Casperons's two sons, namely: John and William Garretson; said cousin William's brother, Joseph; cousin John Garretson's son, Cullender; cousin, Ann Hussey; cousin, Huldah Lembro; cousin, Mary Scot; cousin, James Garretson, son of Cornelius; cousin, Sarah Garretson, dau. of Garretson; cousin, Elizabeth Garretson; friend, Anthony Jaquet. Exc. cousin, Jediah Garretson, Anthony Jaquet.

Vincent Lowe. Gentleman. Talbot Co., Md. Dec. 14, 1691. Mar. 27, 1765. N. 55. Father-in-law, Seth Foster, and his eldest dau., Elizabeth Lowe; wife, Elizabeth Lowe; Foster Turbut; Mary Turbut, dau. of Michell Turbut; brother, Nicholas Lowe, Ralph. Exc. James Murphy, Michell Turbut.

James Harriss. Yeoman. W. Clay Crk. Hd. June 8, 1765. Sept. 3, 1765. L. 215. Wife; cousin, Samuel Brafort; cousin, Thomas Harriss, son of my brother, Joseph Harriss; cousin, James Holliday; my sister's son; my brother, John Harriss's dau., Patience Harriss; cousin, Judith Harriss, dau. of brother Joseph Harriss; cousin, Mary Harriss, dau. of David Harriss; cousin, James Harriss, son of brother, Joseph Harriss; " Mother." Exc. William Welsh.

William Spencer. Innholder. N. C. Sept. 12, 1765. Sept. 26, 1765. Misc. 1.446. Sons, Richard, William and Stephen Spencer; dau., Elizabeth Robinson; wife, Bridget. Exc. brother-in-law, Richard W. Williams; wife, Bridget Spencer.

John Leaugue. Weaver. Appo. Hd. Oct. 11, 1763. Jan. 20, 1766. Misc. 1.337. Dau., Jane Sylvan; her mother; son, Samuel League. Exc. son-in-law, David Sylvan and his wife, Jane.

Patrick Porter. Yeoman. Red Lyon Hd. Nov. 15, 1765. Mar. 4, 1766. Misc. 1.402. Daus., Mary and Jannet; son, David. Exc. David Porter.

Jeremiah Sullivan. Baker. Chris. Hd. Apr. 1, 1766. Apr. 9, 1766. Misc. 1.447. Uncle, Timothy Morris—in Ireland; Patrick Fitzsimmons; brother, Daniel Sullivan; sister, Margaret Sullivan— in Ireland. Exc. Philemon McLaughlin; Cornelius Hoolohen.

Hugh Kelly. Nov. 15, 1760. May 30, 1766. Misc. 1.271. Brother, John Kelly; sister, Elizabeth Kerney, wife of John Kerney; sister, Grace Kerney, wife of William Kerney; mother Mary Kelly. Exc. Robert Bogg.

John Houston. ———. June 13, 1766. H. & I. 141. William Clever, nigh of kin to testator. Exc. Mary Houston, widow; Arthur Moore.

Adam Peterson. St. Geo. Hd. Jan. 23, 1763. June 13, 1766. H. & I. 32. Wife, Veronica Peterson; cousins, Richard Cantwell and

Lyddia Cantwell. Exc. wife, Verosica Peterson; friend, Matthew Reah.

William Weldon. Mar. 30, 1766. June 21, 1766. H. & I. 144. "Wife"; son, Isaac Weldon; daus. Exc. wife.

Haley Pell. Innkeeper. Appo. Hd. Mar. 1766. June 21, 1766. Misc. 1.404. Wife, Rachel; son, Thomas; son, Haley. Exc. son, Thomas.

Hance Peterson. Chris. Hd. May 2, 1765. July 26, 1766. H. & I. 146. Sons, James and Peter Peterson; dau., Elinor Justice, wife of Magniss Justice; dau., Elizabeth Hains, wife of Cornelius Hains; grandson, Hezekiah Peterson, son of my son, Andrew; son, Andrew Peterson. Exc. sons, ――― and Andrew.

Charles Naudain. Appo. Hd. July 30, 1766. Aug. 19, 1766. Misc. 1.364. Wife, Ann; sons, Henry, Cornelius, Larroux and Charles. Exc. Arnold Naudain, Henry Peckard, Senior.

Abraham Golden. Aug. 31, 1766. Sept. 8, 1766. H. & I. 152. Son, John; three daus., Elinor, Anne, Elizabeth; James Vandegrift, son of Jacob the carpenter. Exc. son, John.

John Sherer. Yeoman. B'wine Hd. Sept. 8, 1766. Sept. 11, 1766. H. & I. 153. Wife, Rebecca; son, Archibald Sherer; other children, Jane, Mary, William, Eleanor, Ann, Sarah; sons, James and John. Exc. son Archibald; neighbor, John Bogan.

Job Harvey. Fuller. Pen. Hd. Sept. 6, 1766. Sept. 20, 1766. H. & I. 154. Wife, Elizabeth Harvey; son, Job Harvey; children, Josiah, Susannah and Elizabeth Harvey; Joseph, Samuel and William; daus., Jemima and Keziah Harvey. Exc. wife, Elizabeth Harvey.

Margaret Kelly. N. C. Sept. 8, 1766. Sept. 26, 1766. Misc. 1.272. Son, Tobyas; grandson, Thomas Dennison; dau., Jane Dennison, mother of Thomas; James Dennison. Exc. dau., Jane Dennison.

David Clark. Yeoman. Appo. Hd. Aug. 18, 1766. Sept. 30, 1766. Misc. 1.62. Sons, John and William; dau., Rachel; wife, Eleanor. Exc. wife, Eleanor; son, William; Nicholas Vandike.

Samuel Gillespie. W. Clay Crk. Hd. Aug. 20, 1766. Oct. 1, 1766. Misc. 1.160. Brother, George; sisters, Elizabeth and Agnes; sister, Martha Armitage; Rebecca Elliot; sister, Hannah Bryan; brother George's son, George Gillespie, Jr.; mother. Exc. brother, George; Joseph Wallace.

Judiah Garretson. Farmer. Sept. 5, 1766. Oct. 22, 1766. Misc. 1.162. Son, Eliakim; James Garretson, son of Cornelius; sisters, Huldah Gooding and Mary Scott; sisters, Sarah and Elizabeth Garretson; sister's dau., Hannah Heney. Exc. William Sant Clair; sister, Huldah Gooding.

Thomas Gilpin. Wil. Sept. 20, 1766. Oct. 28, 1766. Misc. 1.156. Brother, Joseph; his son, Thomas; wife; Joseph, brother of said Thomas; Caleb Seal; brother Samuel's son-in-law, George Evans;

sister Rachel's son, Joseph Peirce; Joseph Shallcross; sister
Ann's son, Thomas Hallet of Long Island; said Thomas' father,
Richard Hallet; said Thomas' sister, Lydia; sister, Esther;
brother, Moses. Exc. cousin, Thomas Gilpin of Philadelphia.

Benjamin Larnder. Appo. Hd. Nov. 12, 1764. Oct. 28, 1766. Misc.
1.338. Daus., Jane and Mary Lardner. Exc. friend, Isaac Hazell.

Jacob Truax or Trevax. ———, 1760. Dec. 20, 1766. Misc. 1.463.
Sons, Cornelius and Peter; my two daughters; wife; brother,
Philip Trevax. Exc. wife; Thomas Tobin.

James Gillespie. Late of Lancaster Co., now of Newark. Jan. 8,
1767. Jan. 14, 1767. Misc. 1.166. Wife, Jane; nephew, James
Gillespie, son of my brother, Allin Gillespie; James Gillespie's
brothers and sisters; brother Robert's children in Carolina;
brother-in-law, John Evans and Sarah. Exc. wife, Jane; brother,
Allin Gillespie; John Singleton.

Mary Gooding, alias Whittett. Feb. 16, 1753. Jan. 22, 1767. Misc.
1.163. Son, William Whittett; grandchildren, Mary and Jannett
Belvaird; Susannah Gooding, John Gooding; grandchildren, William Gooding; grandchildren, Mary and William Hyatt; husband,
Abraham Gooding.

John Corry (or Corney). W. Clay Crk. Hd. Jan. 29, 1767. Feb.
2, 1767. Misc. 1.64. Dau., Mary Martin; wife, Mary Correy (or
Corney). Exc. wife, Mary; Samuel McAntier.

Agnus Huston. B'wine Hd. Jan. 15, 1767. Apr. 4, 1767. H. & I.
190. Three daus., Agneus, Margaret and Martha; son, James.
Exc. son, James.

Samuel Bradford. Red Lyon Hd. Dec. 31, 1763. Apr. 20, 1767. H.
& I. 190. Wife, Margret; son, Wm. Bradford; daus., Sarah and
Martha; grandson, Samuel Bradford, son of Wm. Bradford. Exc.
son, Wm. Bradford.

Jacob Kreig. N. C. Hd. Mar. 29, 1767. Apr. 29, 1767. H. & I. 193.
Wife, Roosenna; three children. Exc. Jonas Stidham, Peter
Jaquet, Jr.

Ann James. N. C. July 28, 1766. May 7, 1767. H. & I. 194. Dau.,
Catherine Bradford; sons, Abraham and William Golden, the
heirs of Ann Gilder; deceased and last husband, Simon James;
grandson, John Golden, son of Joseph Golden. Exc. John Golden,
son of Abraham Golden.

Samuel Gregg. Yeoman. Chris. Hd. 9th d. of 10th Mo., 1767. May
11, 1767. H. & I. 195. Wife, Ann Gregg; sons, Samuel and John;
sons, Joseph and Thomas; four daus., Betty, Sarah, Hannah,
Mary. Exc. wife, Ann; son, Joseph. Trustees, brother-in-law,
George Robinson; nephew, Harmon Gregg.

John McCool. St. Geo. Hd. May 14, 1767. May 21, 1767. H. & I.
199. Mother, Sarah McCool; brothers, Thomas and George Mc-
Cool; sister, Margaret McCool; sister, Elizabeth. Exc. brother,
Thomas McCool; John Merriss.

Michael Offly. N. C. May 16, 1767. May 28, 1767. Misc. 1.381. Wife; only son, Michael; five daus., Elizabeth, Mary, Anne, Liddy and Phoebe. Exc. wife, Phoebe; son.

William Whittet. Gentleman. St. Geo. Hd. June 29, 1767. July 29, 1767. H. & I. 201. Cozen, Wm. Whittet Price; friend, Isabelle Hyatt, wife of Thomas Hyatt; friend, William Golden; cozens, Jannet Benson, Susannah Latimer, William Gooding, Rebecca Price. Exc. Richard Cantwell, William Golden.

Margaret Poulson. B'wine Hd. July 24, 1767. Aug. 4, 1767. H. & I. 203. Dau., Mary Pierce; six daus., Elizabeth, Mary, Margaret, Christian, Catheraine and Lydia; sons, William and Jasper.

David Rowland. Pen. Hd. Oct. 24, 1766. Aug. 4, 1767. Misc. 2.27. Wife, Jean. Exc. wife, Jean.

John Campbell. B'wine Hd. Aug. 3, 1767. Aug. 18, 1767. H. & I. 204. Mother; brothers, George and James Campbell; sisters, Isable Campbell, Ann Cords; sister, Carso. Exc. friend, James Stevenson.

Emanuel Grubb. Yeoman. B'wine Hd. May 5, 1764. Aug. 19, 1767. Misc. 2.25. Heirs of son, Joseph, deceased.; son, Thomas; heirs of son, Nicholas; heirs of son, John; son, Benjamin; heirs of son, Peter; dau., Edith Thatcher; dau., Ann Black; son, Emanuel; wife, Ann. Exc. son, Emanuel.

Hannah Thompson. Sept 9, 1767. Sept. 17, 1767. Misc. 1.465. Cousin, Joseph Fox, son of William Fox. Exc. John Hobson, Thomas Littler.

Timothy Stidham. Wil. July 6, 1767. Dec. 10, 1767. M. 279. Cornelius Crips, eldest son of granddau., Elizabeth; Simon Crips, 2nd son of granddau., Elizabeth; Matthew Crips and Elizabeth, his wife; granddau, Elizabeth Stidham; granddau., Elizabeth Crips; grandson, Joseph Stidham. Exc. Joseph Stidham.

Joseph Newlin. Husbandman. Chris. Hd. 1768. H. & I. 237. Wife, Phebe; sons, Ellis and Nathaniel; daus., Elizabeth and Edith.

Peter Hanson (or Hance). Red Lion Hd. Feb. 9, 1768. Mar. 3, 1768. Misc. 1.243. Wife; dau., Elizabeth; brother, Nathaniel; brother's son, Jacob. Exc. wife and her brother, Joseph Ogle.

John White. Wil. Jan. 5, 1766. Apr. 8, 1768. H. & I. 191. Wife; son, William; dau., Lydia. Exc. wife and stepson, John Stapler.

Jacob Vn Bebber. Red Lion Hd. Apr. 20, 1768. Apr. 28, 1768. Misc. 2.4. Wife, Mary Vn Bebber; son, William Vn Bebber; dau., Sarah Vn Bebber. Exc. son, William; dau., Sarah.

John Hendrickson. Mariner. Wil. Apr. 27, 1768. May 18, 1768. Misc. 1.241. Sister, Mary Hendrickson; sister, Rachel Peterson. Exc. stepfather, Peter Peterson.

William Gregg. Farmer. Mill Crk. Hd. Aug. 26, 1768. Oct. 13, 1768. Mis. 1.167. Wife, Ann Gregg; dau., Hannah; sons, Daniel,

Isaac, Harmon. Exc. Ann Gregg. Trustees, brother, Harmon Gregg; friend, Samuel Dixson.

Samuel Kirkpatrick. Yeoman. Red Lion Hd. Oct. 14. 1768. Oct. 24, 1768. Misc. 1.276. Wife, Elizabeth; dau., Jane Kirkpatrick; son in-law, Benjamin Eder; dau.-in-law, Margaret Eder; dau. in law, Elizabeth; dau., Sarah Kirkpatrick. Exc. wife, Elizabeth.

John Isaac. ———. Dec. 21, 1768. H. & I. 240. Exc. Rachel Isaac.

John Lynam. Chris. Hd. Dec. 12, 1768. Dec. 21, 1768. Misc. 1.340. Sons, Andrew and John Lynam; dau., Cathrin Lynam; wife, Chatrian Lynam; my oldest brother's son, Andrew Lynam. Exc. son, Andrew Lynam; friend, Robert Robinson.

William Ford. Farmer. Chris. Hd. Feb. 2, 1769. Mar. 3, 1769. Misc. 1.71. Wife, Ann Ford; youngest dau., Abby Ford; three sons, Joseph, Abram, and Benjamin; six daus., Sarah, Mary, Hannah, Phebe, Rachel, Abby. Exc. wife, Ann; son, Abram.

William Shipley. Yeoman. Bor. Wil. Chris. Hd. Sept. 9, 1754. Mar. 17, 1769. H. & I. 241. Wife, Elizabeth; son, Thomas Shipley; daus., Ann Maris, Elizabeth Canby, Sarah Richardson; son, William Shipley. Exc. Elizabeth Shipley.

William Wattson. B'wine Hd. June 12, 1767. Mar. 21. 1767. H. & I. 250. William Anderson; wife, Margaret Wattson; sister-in-law, Jane Neeley. Exc. wife, Margaret Wattson; John Neely.

Robert McKnight. ———. Apr. 7, 1769. H. & I. 252. Son, Alexander McKnight; grandchild, Isabella Nevins; grandson, William Nevins; son, Moses McKnight. Exc. son, Moses McKnight; wife, Isabella McKnight.

Joseph Thomas. Yeoman. Pen. Hd. June 18, 1762. Apr. 15, 1769. N. 265. Wife, Jane; grandchildren; Joseph Thomas, son of my son, Benjamin Thomas; David and Enos Howell, sons of my dau., Dinah Howell, wife of David Howell; son-in-law, James James; five children, Benjamin, John, Joseph, Elinor, wife of Joseph Jacobs, and Precilla, wife of William Buchannen. Exc. wife, Jane Thomas; David Howell.

William Harraway. St. Geo. Hd. April 4, 1769. April 18, 1769. Misc. 1.244. Son, John Bermingham Harraway; dau., Ann McClann; dau., Veronica. Exc. Richard Hambly; son, John Bermingham.

Edmund Liston. Appo. Hd. July 1, 1769. July 24, 1769. Misc. 1.342. Sons, William and Edmond Liston; dau., Sarah Townsend; wife; daus., Ann and Rachel Liston; father, Edmund Liston, dec. Exc. son, William Liston, Sarah Townsend, Ann Liston.

Francis Clark. Kennet Township, Chester Co., Penn. Aug. 6, 1769. Aug. 26, 1769. M. 213. Brother, Thomas Clark's wife and children; nephew, John Clark; brother John Clerk's four youngest children, one named William. Exc. nephew, John Clerk.

Henry Gunniss. N. C. Hd. Sept. 10, 1769. Sept. 15, 1769. Misc.

I.170. Brother, John; Christopher; wife, Mary Gunniss. Exc. wife, Mary; John Bryson.

Robert Johnson. Yeoman. Wil. 26th d. 7th mo., 1769. Sept. 25, 1769. M. 288. Wife, Catherine Johnson; son, Hadley Johnson; sons, Simon and Caleb Johnson, grandfather of Caleb Johnson, namely: Simon Hadley; sons, Jonathon, Isaac and Stephen; dau., Hannah, wife of Wm. Baily; dau., Lydia, wife of Thomas Baldwin; dau., Phebe. Exc. sons, Simon and Caleb.

Leonard Vandegrift. Aug. 29, 1769. Oct. 2, 1769. Misc. 2.5. Wife; daus., Lydia, Susanna and Phebe; son, Jacob; two youngest sons, Jesse and Ebenezer. Exc. wife, Lydia; son, Jacob.

Ann Chandler. Widow. 11th d. of 6th mo., 1768. Nov. 6, 1769. H. & I. 280. Son-in-law, Jonathon Grave. Exc. Jonathon Grave.

Lawrence Summers. St. Geo. Hd. Apr. 20, 1769. Nov. 13, 1769. Misc. 1.449. Wife, Lydia Summers; son, Andrew Summers; Jacob Moore, guardian for Andrew. Exc. wife, Lydia; Jacob Moore.

John Garreson. Gentleman. Chris. Hd. Mar. 27, 1770. Apr. 28, 1770. Misc. 1.171. Friend, Henry Garrison, son of Peter.

James Craig, Senior. Mill Crk. Hd. Nov. 14, 1769. May 17, 1770. Misc. 1.65. Dau., Mary, wife of Samuel Henry; dau., Ann, wife of Arthur McCluer; grandson, William Creage; dau. and son of Samuel Woods, namely: Andrew, Rebecca and Isabell; son, James Creage. Exc. son, James Creage.

Robert Knotts. Appo. Hd. No dates. Misc. 1.272. Wife, Mary; brother, Edward John Knott.

Daniel Oborn. Yeoman. Pen. Hd. Feb. 17, 1769. June 5, 1770. Misc. 1.382. Son, Joseph Oborn; daus., Rachel Fairis, Mary Brown; grandchildren, Elizabeth Davis and Susanna Davis; dau., Sarah Oborn; son, James Oborn. Exc. son, James.

William Blackburn. N. C. Apr. 29, 1770. June 12, 1770. K. 75. Wife, Ingabor; son, Richard; dau. (not named). Exc. wife, Ingabor.

David Howell. Pen. Hd. Feb. 17, 1770. June 30, 1770. Misc. 1.245. Wife, Ann Howel; sons, David and Amos Howel; granddau., Diana; Jacob Gooding. Exc. David Howell, Enos Howell.

George Hilles, Senior. Dec. 31, 1770. Jan. 9, 1771. N. 427. Son, George; dau., Elizabeth Adams, wife of George Adams; five grandchildren, Nancy, Salley, Lucy, Elizabeth and Deborah Adams; Ann Raney. Exc. William Patterson, Samuel Patterson, son, George.

Andrew Lynam. Chris. Hd. Dec. 31, 1768. Jan. 21, 1771. Misc. 1.344. Grandson, Andrew Lynam, son of my eldest son, George; rest of said George's children; heirs of second son, Andrew; heirs and children of son John, dec.; dau., Katherina and Peter, her husband; dau., Mary, and Jacob, her husband; son-in-law,

James Anderson; grandsons, William and Andrew Anderson, the sons of my dau., Bridget, and her husband, James Anderson. Exc. grandsons, William Anderson and Andrew Anderson.

Margaret Pusey. N. C. Dec. 20, 1769. Mar. 14, 1771. Misc. 1.405. Three children, Thomas, Prudence and Elizabeth. Exc. three children, Thomas, Prudence and Elizabeth.

Charles Newel. Apr. 6, 1770. Apr. 10, 1771. Misc. 1.363. Wife, Catherine, in Ireland; sisters, Sarah, Margaret and Ann; mother, Ann; two brothers, Allen and John Newel—all in Ireland. Exc. cousin, Wm. Shaw.

Edward Knott. Practitioner in Physic. Appo. Hd. Nov. 1, 1770. May 21, 1771. Misc. 1.278. Wife, Frances; daus., Margaret and Eleanor; son, Edward John Knott; dau., Dorcas; son, Robert. Exc. wife, Frances.

John Gyles. Merchant. Wil. Apr. 3, 1771. May 24, 1771. Misc. 1.131. Wife; son, James; dau., Elizabeth; cousin, William Moore, merchant in Ireland; mother; two sisters, Elizabeth and Jean. Exc. wife. Guardian, John McKinley.

Lewis Reece. Mill Crk. Hd. June 4, 1771. June 17, 1771. Misc. 1.422. Wife, Sarah; sons, John, Thomas, George, Lewis; daus., Cathar, Mary and Elizabeth Reece; uncle, John Donnel. Exc. wife, Sarah; son, John Reece; John Reece (millwright).

Andrew Turner. (Nunc.) July 19, 1771. Misc. 1.466. Wife, Mary; dau., Margret; two step-daus., Mary and Elizabeth Vernon, William Stevenson. Attested by Jane Clark, wife of William Clark, Jr.

William Griffin. Farmer. Appo. Hd. Aug. 2, 1769. Aug. 21, 1771. Misc. 1.172. Sons, Charles, William and David Griffin; dau. Mary Stout; granddaus., Mary Leech and Sarah Stout; dau. Martha Ashford; two granddaus., Mary and Elizabeth Jones; granddau., Martha Ashford; granddau., Eleanor Griffin. Exc. sons, Charles, William and David Griffin.

Matthias Morton, Sr. Yeoman. N. C. Hd. Oct. 1, 1769. Oct. 3, 1771. M. 336. Son, Jacob Morton; dau., Mary Walraven; son, Thomas Morton; son, Morton Morton. Exc. son, Jacob Morton.

Samuel League. Appo. Hd. Aug. 23, 1771. Dec. 20, 1771. Misc. 1.346. Wife, Mary League; " brother-by-law," David Solivan; mother, Jane League; cousins, Mary and David Solivan; Jonas Edinfield; Wm. Loan, James Wilkinson. Exc. wife, Mary League.

Thomas Ogle. W. Clay Crk. Hd. Jan. 27, 1768. Dec. 31, 1771. Misc. 1.384. Sons, Thomas and George Ogle; dau., Catherine; sons, Joseph and Benjamin Ogle; son-in-law, Peter Hanson and his wife, Mary; dau., Anne; wife, Catherine; son, James; sister, Judah Harris; John Evans, Jr. Exc. sons, Joseph and James; wife, Catherine.

William Tussey. Husbandman. B'wine Hd. Feb. 6, 1766. Jan. 6, 1772. K. 1. Wife, Mary; sons, William and Isaac; daus., Mary, Rebecca, Christian and Sarah. Exc. wife, Mary Tussey; son, William Tussey.

David Bigs. (Nunc.) Jan. 14, 1772. Misc 1.34. Dau., Dorcas Walen; dau., Sarah Bigs; two sons, Jonathan Bigs and Levi Bigs. Attested by Charles Moore, Allen Congelton.

Magdelane Butcher. Feb. 24, 1770. Jan. 25, 1772. K. 3. Grandson, Cornelius Truax. Exc. Cornelius Truax.

Isaac Janvier. N. C. May 29, 1760. Feb. 5, 1772. K. 2. Mother, Mary Janvier; brothers, Samuel and Phillip Janvier; sisters, Mary and Sarah Janvier. Exc. brother, Samuel Janvier.

Francis Graham. Yeoman. Mill Crk. Hd. Apr. 10, 1761. Feb. 19, 1772. K. 5. Wife, Jeane; daus., Elizabeth, Mary and Agnes; four sons, William, Robert, Francis and John. Exc. wife, Jane; friend, Evan Reid.

Jacob Van Dike. Farmer. St. Geo. Hd. July, 1765. Mar. 10, 1772. K. 8. Sister, Mary, wife of Henry Foster; four cousins, Nicholas, Abraham, Mary and Rachel Van Dike, all children of my uncle, Nicholas Van Dike, dec., and Rachel, his wife; uncle, Thomas Van Dike, his four children, Thomas, James, Elizabeth and Daniel. Exc. Henry Foster, Nicholas Van Dike.

Benjamin de Vou. Husbandman. N. C. Hd. Jan. 29, 1772. Mar. 14, 1772. K. 9. Son, Frederick de Vou; dau., Mary, wife of Isaac Cannon; grandsons, Benjamin, Isaac, David, Daniel and Jasper de Vou; wife, Catherine. Exc. wife, Catherine; son, Frederic; John Yeates.

Samuel Stewart, Jr. Feb. 22, 1772. Mar. 16, 1772. K. 11. Brothers, James and John; sister, Eleanor. Exc. brother, James.

Nicklos Donnocho. Pen. Hd. Feb. 10, 1772. Mar. 17, 1772. K. 12. John Reed, only son of John Reed; Robert McCreary, Junior. Exc. Robert McCreary, Senior.

Elizabeth Gillespie. W. Clay Crk. Hd. Nov. 19, 1771. Apr. 8, 1772. K. 14. Sister, Agnes; brother, George; sisters, Mary and Hannah; sister, Martha, wife of Samuel Armitage; children of sister Martha; niece, Rebecca, wife of Samuel Elliott; their children; niece, Elizabeth Blair; sister, Hannah Bryans, widow. Exc. brother, George; sister, Agnes.

William Pettigrew. Yeoman. W. Clay Crk. Hd. Mar. 31, 1772. Apr. 13, 1772. K. 18. Mother; Andrew Hood, son of John Hood; Mary Hood; brother, Thomas Pettigrew; sister, Jane Pettigrew; Margaret Delap, dau. of Jacob and Elizabeth Delap. Exc. Joseph Rotheram, Jr., John Hood.

Elizabeth Kershey (Hershey). Mill Crk. Hd. Feb. 20, 1772. Apr. 21, 1772. K. 20. Dau., Rachel; sons, Isaac and Solomon; granddau., Solomon Hershey's dau. Catherine; grandson, Isaac; dau.

Rachel's dau., Elizabeth; granddau., Elizabeth, dau. of son, Benjamin. Exc. sons, Solomon and Isaac.

John Phillips, Senior. Yeoman. Mill Crk. Hd. 11th d. of 2nd mo., 1771. April 23, 1772. K. 21. Three grandchildren, namely: my son William's son, James Phillips; my dau. Esther's son, James Dixson; my dau. Sarah's son, James Young; dau., Elizabeth Pryor; grandchild, Hannah Pryor. Exc. son, William Phillips.

Nathaniel Silsbee. Bricklayer. N. C. Dec. 1, 1769. Apr. 29, 1772. K. 23. Son, Nathaniel; daus., Ann, Mary. Exc. daus., Ann and Mary; " my brother-in-law, Peter Jaquet."

Patrick Connelly. Wil. Apr. 4, 1772. May 9, 1772. K. 25. Friend, William Cummings, Sr. Exc. William Cummings, Senior.

John David, Senior. St. Geo. Hd. Dec. 22, 1770. May 19, 1772. K. 26. Brother David David, living in Wales; his children; sister Elizabeth Gondy, living in Maryland; her children; cousin, Isaac David's (dec.) five children; cousin, John David, son of my brother, Wm. David, dec.; cousins, Nathaniel and Thomas David, sons of brother James, dec.; James David and sister Sarah, children of brother James, dec.; cousin, Ann Bird, wife of William Bird. Exc. Ann Bird.

John Kellam. Yeoman. B'wine Hd. Mar. 17, 1772. May 20, 1772. K. 29. Wife, Hannah; sister-in-law, Sarah Brooks, widow; nephew, David Kellam, son of brother Richard; nieces, Margaret and Mary; brother, Moses Kellam. Exc. wife, Hannah.

William Hickland (Kirkland). B'wine Hd. Apr. 4, 1772. May 20, 1772. K. 27. Son, William Hickland; daus., Nanney, Mary, Dinah, Rachel and Betty; wife, Dinah Hickland. Exc. wife; son, Wm. Hickland.

Thomas Rothwell. Apr. 26, 1772. May 21, 1772. K. 31. Wife, Mary Rothwell; mother, Gartrude Conway; brothers; Gartrude Rothwell; sons, John and Thomas. Exc. Mary Rothwell, Peter Hyatt, James Matthews.

Joshua Baker. Chris. Hd. June 2, 1772. June 6, 1772. K. 33. Wife, Alice Baker; sons, Samuel, Peter and Joshua Baker; mother, Margery Baker; dau, Margery Harlan. Exc. son, Samuel Baker; friend, John Merriss.

John Springer. Chris. Hd. ———. June 15, 1772. K. 35. Wife; sons, Charles and William Springer; daus., Mary and Rebecca Springer; sons, Israel and John Springer; son-in-law, John Agustis; dau., Elizabeth Agustis. Exc. William Fillips, Alexander Moore.

Thomas Murphy. Appo. Hd. June, 1767. June 23, 1772. K. 37. Wife, Sarah Murphy; son, James Murphy; cousin, Thomas Murphy, the son of brother, John Murphy. Exc. Sarah Murphy (wife).

John Dickey. Wil. June 22, 1772. July 24, 1772. K. 38. Wife, Eliza-

beth Dickey; sons, James, Thomas, John and William; grand-
dau., Martha Dickey, dau. of son, Robert, dec., niece of John
Foster; dau., Margaret Cowpland; grandsons, Thomas and Philip
Cowpland; dau., Mary McComsey. Exc. James Adams, Caleb
Sheward.

Alexander McComsey. Carpenter. B'wine Hd. June 23, 1771. Aug.
19, 1772. K. 40. Wife, Jane; three youngest children. Exc.
Jane McComsey, wife.

John Stewart. Sept. 3, 1772. Oct. 1772. K. 42. Wife, Margaret;
son, James; brother, James Stewart; sister, Elinor Stewart. Exc.
wife, Margaret Stewart; brother, James Stewart. Guardian,
Samuel Patterson.

Alexander McAntire. W. Clay Crk. Hd. Sept. 30, 1772. Oct. 14,
1772. K. 44. Wife, Jean McAntier; sons, William, Samuel and
Alexander McAntier; dau., Sarah McAntier; dau., Mary McAntier. Exc. brother, Andrew McAntier; Samuel McAntier, Robert
McAntier.

David Thomas. Farmer. St. Geo. Hd. Sept. 5, 1770. Oct. 3, 1772.
K. 46. Wife, Margaret Thomas; sons, Nathan, Enoch, James,
Edward and Isaac; dau. Mary Anderson's children; dau., Rebecca
McWhorter; granddaus., Mary and Rebecca Anderson; grand-
sons, David and Robert McWhorter; granddau., Jane McWhor-
ter. Exc. Margaret Thomas, wife; Isaac Thomas, son; James
Thomas, son.

Mary Hedges. Mill Crk. Hd. July 30, 1772. Nov. 14, 1772. K. 63.
Granddau., Rebeckah Mullan; son, Tobias Hedges. Exc. Alexander McMullan.

Jeremiah Wollaston. Yeoman. Mill Crk. Hd. 11th d. of 2nd mo.,
1772. Nov. 14, 1772. K. 51. Grandson, Jacob Wollaston, his
brother, Joseph; son, George Wollaston; grandson, Wollaston,
brother of Jacob and Joseph; son, Thomas Wollaston; daus.,
Ann, Lydia and Catherine; friend, John Stapler. Exc. sons,
George and Thomas.

David Rees. Yeoman. Pen. Hd. June 17, 1760. Nov. 19, 1772. K.
53. Sons, Jehu and David; daus., Margaret, Charity, Mary. Exc.
friend, Moris Williams; son, John Rees.

John Greave. Chris. Hd. 12th m. 25, 1772. Jan. 8, 1773. K. 56.
Wife, Jane Greave; sons, Thomas Greave, William Greave; daus.,
Ann Hayes, Sarah Allen; daus., Mary Dowd, Jane Hicklin and
Hannah Greave; son, Samuel; father, Samuel Greave, dec. Exc.
son, Samuel Greave.

Alexander Chance. Yeoman. Appo. Hd. Dec. 23, 1772. Jan. 12,
1773. K. 57. Wife, Elizabeth; dau., Rebecca; sons, Edmund and
John; dau., Mary Allfoard; grandson, John Chance; grandson,
Thomas Allfoard; granddau., Elizabeth Fields.

William Steel. Mill Crk. Hd. Dec. 15, 1772. Feb. 16, 1773. K. 60.

Sister, Margaret Rankin; sister, Jane Alexander; niece, Margaret Donnell, brother-in-law, Jacob Moore, and his wife, Hannah. Exc. brother-in-law, Jacob Moore.

Elizabeth Crumey. St. Geo. Hd. Apr. 23, 1772. Feb. 17, 1773. K. 61. Grandson, Samuel Crummy. Exc. Robert Porter, Merchant.

John Allen. W. Clay Crk. Hd. Mar. 13, 1773. Mar. 24, 1773. K. 66. Wife, Elizabeth; sons, Robert Allen and John Allen; brother, Andrew Allen's son, John Allen. Exc. wife, Elizabeth; William Eakin.

Deborah Ferriss. Wil. 2nd M., 18th, 1773. Mar. 24, 1773. K. 64. Father, David Ferriss; mother, Mary Ferriss; sisters, Sarah Andrews and Mary Lightfoot; brothers-in-law, John Andrews and Wm. Lightfoot; cousins, Samuel Andrews and Isaac Andrews; nieces, Susanna, Mary and Deborah Lightfoot; cousins, Samuel Lightfoot, Hannah Townsend, Elizabeth Ferriss, Elizabeth Newlin. Exc. David Ferriss, Sarah Andrews.

Mary Hammons. Widow of William Hammons of Kent Co. 15th d. of 5th m., 1771. Mar. 29, 1773. K. 67. Son, Joshua Pottex; dau., Lydia Goodwin. Exc. son-in-law, Richard Goodwin.

John Davis. W. Clay Crk. Hd. Apr. 13, 1770. Apr. 20, 1773. K. 69. Sister, Margaret Davis. Exc. sister, Margaret Davis.

Samuel Kerr. W. Clay Crk. Hd. Apr. 6, 1772. May 25, 1773. K. 74. Wife, Mary; sons, Andrew and Nathaniel; James Kerr; sons, John and Samuel; daus., Margaret Kerr, Isbell, Mary, Ruth and Elizabeth; son, James. Exc. son, Andrew.

Sarah Kinkead. Pen. Hd Mar. 18, 1773. June 7, 1773. K. 70. Sons, James, Thomas and Joseph Kinkead; Rebecca Osten, Anne McGaughey, Sarah Williams; dau., Jane Kinkead. Exc. dau., Jane.

William Nesbit. N. C. Dec. 16, 1772. June 23, 1773. K. 71. Father, Thomas Nesbit, Doure Co., Ireland; son, Thomas; wife, Mary; dau., Sarah. Exc. wife, Mary; Alexander Montgomery.

Joshua Curtis. Tanner. St. Geo. Hd. May 28, 1773. July 28, 1773. K. 77. Brother, Richard Curtis; said brother's eldest son, John; Sarah Rob, wife of John Rob; Rebecca Tarney, dau. of said Sarah Rob; brother Richard's four children, namely: Hannah, Joshua, Rebecca and Martha. Exc. William Hall.

Samuel Enos. Yeoman. N. C. Hd. July 28, 1773. Aug. 5, 1773. K. 78. Wife, Margaret; five children, Susanna, Hanna, Samuel, Richard and Barbara. Exc. wife, Margaret; brother, Joseph Enos, John Clark.

John Mercer. St. Geo. Hd. July 16, 1773. Aug. 13, 1773. K. 85. Son, John Mercer; dau., Susannah, wife of Robert Porter; dau., Elizabeth, wife of George Ferress; wife, Sarah Mercer; sons, Perregrine, Edward and William; daus., Ann, Hannah and Rebecca. Exc. wife, Sarah Mercer.

Samuel Stewart. Farmer. B'wine Hd. July 31, 1773. Aug. 19, 1773.

K. 80. Wife, Margaret; Mary, the dau. of Nicholas Robinson; niece, Elizabeth Baldwin; Samuel, son to brother James. Exc. brother, James Stewart; Nicholas Robinson.

Peter Aldricks. St. Geo. Hd. Sept. 16, 1772. Aug. 21, 1773. K. 82. Wife, Mary; son, Wessell; grandsons, Wessell and William, sons of son, Wessell; granddau., Rebecca; son, Harmanus' four daughters, Mary, Martha, Hester and Hannah; dau., Mary, wife of John Peterson; other three daughters; grandchildren, John and Peter Peterson and a girl; sons, Peter and John. Exc. wife, Mary; sons, Hermanus and John.

Margaret Houston. Red Lion Hd. Aug. 5, 1773. Sept. 20, 1773. K. 86. Cousin and friend, Wm. Blair, son of Rev. Samuel Blair, dec.; Rev. Dr. John Rogers of New York; cousins, William Clark and Rev. Robert Smith; Jacob Tobin, son of Thomas Tobin; cousin, William King; sister, Sarah Purvians, in Ireland; children of John and William King, in Ireland. Exc. Robt. Porter, merchant of Red Lion.

Henry Gregg. Chris. Hd. Aug. 17, 1773. Oct. 1, 1773. K. 90. Mother, Mary Gregg, widow. Exc. mother, Mary Gregg. Guardian, cousin, Joseph Gregg.

Joseph Griffith. Pen. Hd. Sept. 7, 1773. Oct. 5, 1773. K. 90. Wife, Mary Griffith; sons, John and James; Samuel Griffith, dec.; three daus., Catherine, Susanna, and Rebecca Griffith. Exc. wife, Mary, and her brother, Enoch Jones. Guardians, brother, Benjamin Griffith; Andrew Fisher.

Robert Watt. St. Geo. Hd. Apr. 30, 1773. Oct. 26, 1773. K. 93. Wife, Mary; sons, James and Robert Watt. Exc. son, Robert.

Robert McCreary. Pen. Hd. Mar. 13, 1773. Nov. 19, 1773. K. 96. Wife, Elinor; son, Robert; dau., Rachel. Exc. Elinor McCreary, wife; William Armstrong.

Adam Peterson. St. Geo. Hd. Nov. 8, 1773. Nov. 26, 1773. K. 97. Wife, Rachel. Exc. Rachel Peterson.

Griffith John. Sept. 15, 1766. Dec. 22, 1773. K. 100. Eldest dau., Ann; dau., Haun; wife, Persus John; youngest children, Martha, Mary and Rachel. Exc. Rees Rees.

Malcomb McCombs. Yeoman. W. Clay Crk. Hd. July 29, 1773. Jan. 3, 1774. K. 102. Son, William; wife, Margaret; three daus., Hannah, Margaret, and Mary; sons, Robert, John, Malcomb and Thomas. Exc. Margaret McCoombs, wife; William McCoombs, son.

William Lee. N .C. Hd. Jan. 10, 1774. Jan. 17, 1774. K. 104. Wife, Janet; unborn child or children; two brothers, George and Alexander Lee.

Moses Leadley. Weaver. N. C. Nov. 24, 1773. Feb. 2, 1774. K. 106. Wife, Mary; son, Isaac Leadley; Mary James, youngest dau. of Thomas James. Exc. wife, Mary.

Jacob Stilly. Yeoman. Chris. Hd. Sept. 14, 1771. Feb. 6, 1774. K. 114. Son, Andrew Stilly; two sons-in-law, Charles Hedge and John Bird; dau.-in-law, Mary Stilley; children, Andrew, John, Elizabeth Stilley, alias Pollard; Margaret Stilley, alias Merridith, and Catharine Stilley. Exc. son, Andrew Stilly.

Benjamin Ford. Yeoman. B'wine Hd. Mar. 23, 1771. Feb. 9, 1774. K. 107. Widow; six children, Benjamin, and David and Elizabeth Howell, Mary Deriskson, Hannah Perkins and Jane Golden; three youngest sons, William, Philip and Joseph Ford; four youngest daus., Prudence, Jemima, Ann and Sarah. Exc. son-in-law, Thomas Perkins; Thomas Babb.

Benjamin Rhodes. N. C. Hd. Dec. 6, 1773. Feb. 15, 1774. K. 110. Cousins, Benjamin and Samuel Rhodes. Exc. cousin, Richard Rhodes.

John Way. Yeoman. Mill Crk. Hd. Feb. 9, 1774. Feb. 18, 1774. K. 111. Wife, Ruth; son, Jacob; his sisters, Sarah and Lidia; unborn child. Exc. brother, Joseph Way.

John McClay. N. C. Hd. Feb. 8, 1774. Mar. 1, 1774. K. 115. Wife, Rachel McClay; eldest son, James; two daus., Nancy and Mary; youngest son, John; brother, William McClay; brothers-in-law, James Moody, William Moody and Isaac Moody. Exc. William McClay (brother), Isaac Moody (brother-in-law).

Mouns Justis. Yeoman. Sept. 19, 1766. Mar. 9, 1774. K. 122. Son, Magnus; dau., Sarah; wife, Chatorin; dau., Amela Springer; son, Justa Justis; daus., Mary, Chatorin, and Elenor. Exc. Chatorin Justis (wife), Magnus Justis (son).

John Weldin. Mar. 31, 1767. Mar. 25, 1774. K. 124. Son, James Wheldon; sons, John and Joseph Wheldon; grandson, William Shaw. Exc. son, James; dau., Mary.

John Redman. Appo. Hd. Feb. 22, 1774. Mar. 28, 1774. K. 125. Wife, Mary; eldest son, John Redman; son, David; dau., Elizabeth Liston. Exc. wife, Mary Redman; son, David Redman.

Mary Truax. Jan. 19, 1761. Apr. 6, 1774. K. 126. Two children, Mary and Peter Trevax; Jervaine or Jerome Dushane.

Daniel Corbit, Senior. Mar. 25, 1774. Apr. 18, 1774. K. 128. Son, Daniel; son, John (dec.); sons, Isaac and Jonathan; dau., Mary Wilson; dau.-in-law, Lydia Corbit; wife, Mary. Exc. David Wilson, Jonathon Corbit.

John Finney. Doctor. N. C. Sept. 6, 1770. Codicil, Mar. 21, 1774. Apr. 8, 1774. K. 129. Wife, Sarah Finney; daus., Elizabeth and Ann Dorothea; sons, David and Robert; brother, Robert Finney. Codicil: grandson, John French Finney; granddaus., Elizabeth and Ann. Exc. wife, Sarah Finney; son, David Finney.

Isaac Buckingham. Blacksmith. Wil. 24th of 4th mo. 1774. May 11, 1774. K. 132. Brother, Thomas Buckingham; sisters, Margaret and Sarah; dec. sister, Hannah's son, namely: John Pennock;

mother; brother, Jos. Shallcross; brother-in-law, David Mercer. Exc. brother, Jos. Shallcross or Vincent Gilpin.

Ann Gregg. Chris. Hd. April 5, 1774. May 18, 1774. K. 134. Sons, Joseph, Samuel, John and Thomas Gregg; four daus., Betty, Sarah, Hannah, Mary. Exc. son, Joseph.

John Hanson. Farmer. St. Geo. Hd. Mar. 25, 1774. May 20, 1774. K. 135. Wife, Rachel Hanson; son, Larrance; son, John Hanson; dau., Mary King; dau., Sophia Van Dyke; dau., Rachel Miles; dau., Elizabeth Hanson. Exc. wife, Rachel Hanson; son, John Hanson; son-in-law, James Miles.

James Stewart. Farmer. St. Geo. Hd. May 23, 1774. May 27, 1774. K. 137. Father; sister-in-law, Margrate Stewart; sister, Jane Magill; sister, Mary Stewart. Exc. Mary Stewart, sister; Benjamin Bunker.

David English. Mill Crk. Hd. Sept. 2, 1773. May 27, 1774. K. 139. Wife, Jannat; daus., Agnes and Elizabeth; daus., Sarah, Rebecca and Jane. Exc. wife, Jannat; daus., Sarah and Rebecca.

Abigail Curry. May 15, 1774. May 27, 1774. K. 138. Sister, Amelia Beddle; cousins, Martha and Amelia Bunker; cousins, Abigail Bunker and John Bunker; cousins, Jere Bunker and Elizabeth Bunker; brother, William Paul. Exc. Benjamin Bunker.

Edward Dawes, Esquire. Wil. 5th m., 21, 1774. June 6, 1774. K. 142. Wife; son, Cephas, (stepson of present wife); son, Jonathon; dau., Sarah; son, Rumford; son, Abija (children of second wife); grandson, Jonathan Dawes; son-in-law, Job Harvey. Exc. Job Harvey; Griffith Minshall.

Jonathan Greave. Yeoman. Chris. Hd. 7th d. of 5th mo., 1774. June 11, 1774. K. 100. Son, Jacob Greave; father, Samuel Greave; son, Jonathan Greave; son, David Greave. Exc. sons, Jacob and Jonathan.

Jane Bartlett, widow of John Bartlett. Appo. Hd. Apr. 28, 1774. June 14, 1774. K. 141. Sons, John, Thomas and Isaac; daus., Mary and Elizabeth. Exc. John Jetton.

Aaron Borom. St. Geo. Hd. Feb. 19, 1774. June 20, 1774. K. 146. Wife, Elizabeth Borom. Exc. wife, Elizabeth.

Lydia Dunning. Widow. N. C. Hd. Feb 1, 1774. June 27, 1774. K. 147. Dau., Lydia Dunning; dau., Sarah Aldridge; dau., Mary, wife of Thomas Scully; dau., Elizabeth Aldridge. Exc. Mr. Peter Turner.

Catherine Kittle. N. C. Hd. June 17, 1774. June 29, 1774. K. 149. Cousin, Mary Janvier; niece, Mary Glenn; brother, John Kittle; nephew, Thomas Glenn; cousin, Cornelius Kittle.

Arthur Carr. Yeoman. W. Clay Crk. Hd. Dec. 17, 1772. July 19, 1774. K. 152. Mother, Jane Carr; brothers, David and William Carr; brothers-in-law, Matthew Hilles and Charles Campbell;

sister, Martha Breslin's son, Joseph. Exc. David and William Carr.

Joseph Ford. B'wine Hd. Sept. 10, 1772. July 21, 1774. K. 153. Sons, William, Thomas and James Ford; granddau., Mary Ford; grandson, Joseph Ford, son of son William; wife, Mary Ford. Exc. James Ford.

Richard Bell. Blacksmith. July 15, ——. July 22, 1774. K. 155. Wife, Margaret Bell; John McCall; James McCall, son of John. Exc. John McCall.

Peter Jeton.. Yeoman. St. Geo. Hd. Feb. 22, 1774. July 30, 1774. K. 150. Son, Peter; dau., Mary, wife of Abraham See; granddau., Catharin, wife of William Burgess; granddau., Mary; grandson, Peter; dau., Esther, wife of Morris Williams; dau., Rachel, wife of William See; dau., Sarah, wife of Richard See; grandson, Abraham Eves, son of James Eves. Exc. Peter Jeton, son.

Simon Ernester. Red Lion Hd. Aug. 14, 1774. K. 169. Eldest son, John; second son, Isiah; sons, John and Eliazer; wife, Elizabeth. Exc. wife, Elizabeth; son, Eliazer.

Robert Kerr. Southwark, Pa. July 25, 1774. Aug. 4, 1774. K. 157. Wife, Mary Kerr; brother, Samuel Kerr; Hugh Ferguson. Exc. Samuel Moore (Brewer), Joseph Hunter.

John Martin. Farmer. N. C. Hd. Aug. 9, 1774. Aug. 18, 1774. K. 159. Wife, Margaret; children. Exc. Margaret Martin, wife; William Pemock.

Rees Rees. Red Lion Hd. July 2, 1770. Aug. 19, 1774. K. 160. Son, Daniel Rees; sons, Thomas and Oliver Rees; daus., Mary and Sarah. Exc. sons, Thomas and Oliver.

Thomas Thomas. Yeoman. Pen. Hd. May 17, 1773. Aug. 23, 1774. K. 161. Granddau., Priscilla Cowen; granddau., Ann Haughey; dau., Sarah Haughey and her son, William Haughey; dau., Mary Thomas, and her son, Richard Thomas; grandson, Thomas Haughey; granddaus., Mary and Jane Thomas; grandson, Lewis Thomas; son, Caleb; grandson, Theodore Thomas. Exc. William Thomas, son.

Samuel Bradford. W. Clay Crk. Hd. Aug. 22, 1774. Sept. 16, 1774. K. 166. Wife, Catran; daus., Eliz. and Mary; son, James; grandmother, Juda herris. Exc. Catran Bradford, William Gallaher.

Mary Hart. Widow. St. Geo. Hd. Aug. 25, 1774. Sept. 16. 1774. K. 165. Dau., Grace; children, Grace, George, John and Joseph. Exc. brother, Jacob Houston.

Jane David. Pen. Hd. Jan. 4, 1774. Sept. 27, 1774. K. 168. Son, John David; grandson, Joshua David; dau., Margarate. Exc. son, John David.

Samuel Nichols. Farmer. Mill Crk. Hd. 21st of 8th mo., 1774. Oct. 1, 1774. K. 170. Wife, Elizabeth Nichols; son, Ellis; dau.,

Susanna; daus., Mary, Martha, Elizabeth and Edith. Exc. wife, Elizabeth Nichols; brother, Daniel Nichols.

Mary Jaquett. Long Hook. Aug. 15, 1774. Oct. 5, 1774. K. 172. Brother, Samuel Jaquett; sisters Dorcas and Rebecca Jaquett. Exc. mother Elizabeth Jaquett.

John Butcher. Yeoman. St. Geo. Hd. Sept. 17, 1774. Oct. 8, 1774. K. 174. Wife, Jane Butcher; Thomas Butcher, Senior; Thomas Butcher, Junior. Exc. Jane Butcher.

Niels Justis. Mill Crk. Hd. Aug. 19, 1774. Oct. 10, 1774. K. 175. Dau., Mary Justis; wife, Mary Justis; sons, Jacob, Andrew and Enoch Justis; dau., Steena Justis; dau., Susannah Justis; dau., Margaret Willson; son, Seven Justis. Exc. Jacob Justis, son; Justa Walraven.

William Armstrong. Yeoman. Chris. Hd. Aug. 6, 1774. Oct. 14, 1774. K. 181. Wife, Ann; nephew, William Armor; nephew, John Armstrong; Robert Armstrong, William Armstrong. Exc. wife, Ann.

Adam Kirk. Chris. Hd. 24th d. of 9th mo., 1774. Oct. 5, 1774. K. 178. Four daus., Lydia, Hannah, Abigail and Phebe; wife, Phebe Kirk; eldest son, Adam Kirk; sons, Caleb, William and Joshua Kirk. Exc. wife, Phebe Kirk; son, Caleb Kirk.

William Black. N. C. Hd. Sept. 7, 1774. Oct. 2, 1774. K. 183. Wife, Esther; dau., Ann; brother, Richard; nephew, John Black, son of Richard. Exc. wife, Esther Black.

Robert McCalley. Farmer. Terkernaghan, in the parish of Donaghedy, and county of Tyrone. Sept. 14, 1772. Nov. 9, 1774. K. 186. Brother's oldest son, Robert McCalley; brother's dau., Isabella M'Calley, now married to Charles McGlaughlin, parish of Badony. Exc. nephew, Robert McCalley.

Robert Chambers. W. Clay Crk. Hd. 4th m. 24, 1773. Nov. 19, 1774. K. 189. Son, John Chambers; dau., Mary, wife of James Buckingham; dau., Sarah, wife of Benjamin Gregg; dau., Martha, wife of James Thompson; son, Benjamin Chambers. Exc. son, John Chambers; son, Samuel Chambers; cousin, William Miller.

Ann Packard. Oct. 25, 1774. Nov. 19, 1774. K. 185. Daus., Ann Armstrong, Janet Packard, Catherine Packard. Adm. son-in-law, George Armstrong.

Henry Packard, Senior. Appo. Hd. June 13, 1771. Nov. 22, 1774. K. 191. Sons, Peter and Henry Packard; wife, Ann; daus., Janet and Catharine; dau., Ann Armstrong; grandsons, Thomas Packard and John Mercer Packard; granddaus., Elizabeth, Anna, Susanna and Mary Packard. Exc. son, Peter Packard.

Joshua Littler. Wil. 11th m. 18th, 1774. Dec. 3, 1774. K. 196. Son, Thomas Littler; grandsons, Thomas and Joshua Canby; son, John Littler; daus., Susanna, Sarah, Hannah and Mary; my apprentice girl, Leah Claypole. Exc. dau., Mary; friend, Vincent Bonsall.

William Van Bibber. Yeoman. Red Lion Hd. July 30, 1769. Dec. 5, 1774. K. 193. Unkle, Henry Van Bebber; sister, Sarah, alias Hyatt Van Bebber; nephew, Thomas Belew. Exc. unkle, Henry Van Bebber.

Christopher Stoop. N. C. Hd. Dec. 8, 1774. Jan. 4, 1775. K. 199. Wife, Sarah Stoop; dau., Mary Stoop; dau., Lydia Stoop; dau., Judith Stoop; 3 sons, Ephraim, Benjamin and Morgan. Exc. wife, Sarah Stoop; son, Ephraim Stoop.

Benjamin Swett. N. C. Dec. 4, 1774. Jan. 9, 1775. K. 201. Wife, Susanna; cousin, Mary Janvier, widow of John Janvier, and her four children, viz: Richard, Thomas, Sarah and Lydia; cousins, the six children of Richard Price and Sarah, his wife, viz; John, Hyland, Rebecca, Mary Ann, Sarah and Lydia; Rebecca James, dau. of Abel James of Phila.; son-in-law, Henry Drinker; nephew, Benjamin Swett of Burlington. Exc. wife, Susanna Swett; Henry Drinker, George Read.

Benjamin Kellam. B. Wine Hd. Jan. 23, 1775. Feb 3, 1775. K. 203. Wife, Mary Kellam; brother, Moses Kellam; nephew, John Kellam. Exc. wife, Mary Kellam.

Pheby Newlin. Widow of Joseph Newlin. Chris. Hd. 25th of 1st month, 1775. Feb. 11, 1775. K. 207. Sons, Ellis Newlin and Nathaniel Newlin; dau., Elizabeth Yarnell; dau., Edith Jones. Exc. John Yarnall, Phillip Jones.

William Guthery, (Guttery). Mill Crk. Hd. Dec. 30, 1774. Feb. 11, 1775. K. 205. Wife, ———; sons, Alexander, William, James and Adam; dau., Mary; dau., Margaret. Exc. son, Alexander.

William Grubb. Yeoman. B'wine Hd. 8th of 11th m., 1774. Feb. 22nd, 1775. K. 208. Sons, William, John, Jehn, Robert, Aaron and Moses; dau., Mary Robinson, dec'd.; dau., Lydia Grubb; dau., Deborah Grubb; son-in-law, Charles Robinson. Exc. son, Moses Grubb.

William Milner. Chris. Hd. Aug. 15, 1769. Mar. 2, 1775. K. 211. Brothers, John Milner and Samuel Milner; sisters, Sarah and Elizabeth, mother ———. Exc. brother, John Milner.

John Dushane. Red Lion Hd. Feb. 12, 1775. Mch. 7, 1775. K. 213. Wife, Sarah; son, John Clark Dushane. Exc. wife, Sarah Dushane.

Thomas Hill. Yeoman. Late of New London, Chester co., Pa. May 16, 1757. Mch. 21, 1775. K. 215. James Hill's sons in Ireland, Matthew Sodgwick's sons in Ireland, Kathyrn May, alias Hill, friend, John Wollih, John Hill and Joseph, Sedgwick James, son of Richard James. Exc. Richard James.

William Donally. Farmer. N. C. Hd. Feb. 28, 1772. Mch. 25, 1775.

Wife, Margaret; dau. Elizabeth's two eldest children; dau. Christiana's two eldest children. Exc. wife, ·Margaret, William Clark.

William Haithorn. St. Geo. Hd. Mch. 9th, 1775. Apr. 18, 1775. K. 218. Sisters, Elizabeth Haithorn, Mary Lee and Ruth Haithorn. Exc. John Jones, Esq.

Jerome Dushane. Yeoman. Red Lion Hd. Mch. 29, 1775. Apr. 18, 1775. K. 219. Sons, Jesse, Anthony and Thomas, dau. Hannah, dau. Mary, dau. Katharine, dau. Elizabeth and dau. Margaret, dau. Jaminia. Wife, Hannah; dau., Francina and her husband Jacob Martin. Exc. sons, Thomas Dushane and Anthony Dushane.

John Vail. St. Geo. Hd. Mch. 7, 1753. Apr. 22, 1775. K. 222. Wife, Jane. Exc. David Stewart. Letters of adm. granted to James Matthews.

George Taylor. Cordwainer. B'wine Hd. May 12, 1775. May 17, 1775. K. 228. Wife, Sarah Taylor; son, George Taylor; dau., Hannah Lepuse; dau., Sarah James; dau., Mary Cartmill; dau., Rebecca Rickey; granddaughters, Nancy, Hannah and Rachel Kellam.

Archibald Armstrong. Gentleman. Chris. Hd. Aug. 21, 1767. May 18, 1775. K. 229. Wife, Ann Armstrong; sons, William and John; mentions title and interest in land in Ireland; son-in-law, Col. John Armstrong and dau. Rebecca Armstrong his wife; son-in-law, Rev. George Duffield and Margaret my dau. his wife; grandson Archibold Armstrong, son of my son John; his brother, my grandson, James Armstrong. Exc. son William, son John.

Jacob Vanleuvenigh. St. Geo. Hd. May 24, 1775. May 30, 1775. K. 234. Couzen John Burgess. Exc. John Burgess.

Margaret McDonnally. N. C. Hd. May 24, 1775. June 3, 1775. K. 235. Granddaughters, Margaret Moody and Margaret Kirkpatri;ck; dau., Margaret Moody. Exc. son, James Kirkpatrick.

John Elliott. Innholder. B'wine Hd. June 27, 1774. June 16, 1775. K. 237. Wife ——, and son, Edward; daughters, Margaret, Susannah. Exc. wife, Chloe, brother Thomas Elliott.

John Burgin. Yeoman. Appo. Hd. Apr. 8, 1775. June 20, 1775. K. 240. Son, John Burgin; wife, Catharine. Exc. wife, Catharine Burgin, son-in-law James Happy.

Amy Griffith. Pen. Hd. Apr. 7, 1773. June 24, 1775. K. 242. Husband, John Griffith; sons, Isaac, Jesse, Josiah and David; grandson, David Rees; granddau., Rebeckka Rees. Exc. son, Josiah, David Howel.

James Nixon. Yoeman. B'wine Hd. May 16, 1773. June 26, 1775. K. 244. Wife, Mary; James McCorkle; sons, George Nixon, James Nixon; son-in-law, James Hannah and Elizabeth his wife; son-in-law, John Latta and Mary his wife; son-in-law, Samuel

Donnald and Catharine his wife; dau., Jean Nixon. Exc. wife. Mary, son George.

Rachel Tobin. Red Lion Hd. June 20, 1775. July 15, 1775. K. 246. Sons, Thomas, John, Peter and Jacob Tobin; dau., Nelly Rankin; granddaughter, Rachel Truax. Exc. John Clark of Dragon Neck.

George Adams. Shallop man. W. Clay Crk. Hd. May 6, 1775. Aug. 15, 1775. K. 248. Wife, Elizabeth; daughters, Sarah, Elizabeth, Deborah, Lucy, Mary and Ann; son, Levi; dau. Rachel, now married to John Clark; dau. Ruth, now married to Jacob Hollingsworth. Exc. wife, Elizabeth Adams, sons-in-law, Jacob Hollingsworth and John Clark.

John Tomlinson. Chris. Hd. July 23, 1775. Aug. 21, 1775. K. 251. Wife, ——, five children, viz: Rachel, John, Sarah, Joseph and Elizabeth. Exc. wife, Elizabeth; son, John Tomlinson.

Arthur Allston. Yeoman. Appo. Hd. July 19, 1775. Sept. 5, 1775. K. 255. Wife, Sarah; sons, Jonathon Allston and Thomas Allston; dau., Rachel, two more younger children, ——. Exc. wife, Sarah.

Elizabeth McLaughlan. Town of N. C. Aug. 5, 1775. Sept. 7, 1775. K. 253. Father-in-law, Daniel McLonen; Miss Elizabeth Reynolds of Phila.; mother; sister Mary, wife of Isaac Grantham; Agnes McLonen; three children of late husband, James McLaughlan. Exc. Nicholas Van Dyke.

John Corrans. White Clay Crk. Hd. June 10, 1775. Oct. 2, 1775. K. 257. Wife, Margaret; brother, Timothy; father and mother in Ireland. Exc. wife, Margaret, George Reynolds.

Thomas Reynolds. Farmer. White Clay Crk. Hd. Jan. 14, 1772. Oct. 2, 1775. K. 259. Dau., Margaret; dau., Ann Platt; granddau., Dinah Platt; grandsons, Samuel Platt and John Platt; dau. Mary Eaton's children, viz: Ezekiel, Ann, George, John and Thomas; son, George; granddau., Margaret Platt, alias McCrea; dau., Elizabeth Rodgers; grandson, Thomas Rodgers; granddau., Margaret Rodgers; granddau., Ann Rodgers; dau., Martha McComb; granddau., Ann Reynolds. Exc. son-in-law, Samuel Platt, son George Reynolds.

Charles Cannon. Farmer. N. C. Hd. Oct. 9, 1775. Oct. 17, 1775 K. 263. Sons, Abraham Cannon and Isaac Cannon; dau., Lydia, wife of Isaac Cannon; dau., Ruth Cannon; dau., Ellinor Cannon. Exc. eldest son Abraham Cannon.

Samuel Johnston. Town of N. C. Jan. 9, 1775. Oct. 25, 1775. K. 265. Wife, Frances Johnston; consin, Robert Orr, and his daughters Jean and Isabella McCloy; James Kinnear, Mary McKetrick. Exc. wife, Frances, John Clark.

John Anderson. Yeoman. Town of N. C. Sept. 18, 1775. Oct. 31st, 1775. K. 266. Son, James Anderson; nephew, James Anderson, son of my brother James Anderson. Exc. Daniel McLonen.

William Cummings. Yeoman. Wil. Jan. 3, 1773. Nov. 4, 1775. K. 268. Daughters, Mary and Martha, eldest son William, son Joseph, wife Martha. Exc. wife, Martha.

Caleb Chandler. Farmer. Chris. Hd. Oct. 5, 1775, Nov. 15, 1775. K. 270. Brother Abraham Chandler, father and mother, Isaac Chandler and Caleb Chandler, sisters Ann and Ruth. Exc. brother Abraham Chandler.

Richard Thompson, Sr. Cecil Co., Md. Apr. 17, 1775. Nov. 23, 1775. K. 273. Sons, Ephraim Thompson, Robert Thompson and Richard Thompson; daughters, Sarah Young, Tabitha, Mary Bird and Susanna Scott; grandsons, Augustine Bryon, John Bryon, Noble Hamm, Thompson Bird and Samuel Thompson, son of John; granddau., Araminta Hamm. Exc. son Ephraim.

William Armstrong. Goldsmith. Chris. Hd. Aug. 17, 1775. Dec. 18, 1775. . K. 271. Brothers, Robert, John and Edmund, (dec'd); uncle, William Armstrong (dec'd.); aunt, Ann Armstrong (dec'd.); sisters, Margaret Welsh and Elinor Armstrong. Exc. brother, Robert.

Mary Nesbit. N. C. Hd. Dec. 1, 1775. Dec. 20, 1775. K. 275. Daughters, Ann Ruth and Sarah Nesbit; son, Thomas Nesbit. Exc. daughter, Sarah Nesbit.

John Kettle. Husbandman. Oct. 29, 1775. Dec. 27, 1775. K. 276. Wife, Mary Kettle; nephew, Thomas Glenn; cousin, Mary Janvier; niece, Mary Glenn.

Mary Jacobs. Oct. 5, 1769. Jan. 15, 1776. K. 279. Granddau., Mary Skeer. Exc. son-in-law, Nath'l Word. Letters of adm. granted to son-in-law of Nath'l Word (dec'd.).

Isabel Speer. Red Lion Hd. Oct. 7, 1766. Jan. 16, 1776. K. 280. Children, viz: James, John, Isabel Speer, Ann Speer, Elizabeth Speer and Robert Speer; deceased husband, James Speer. Exc. son, Robert.

Margaret Stewart, widow of John Stewart. White Clay Crk. Hd. Feb. 6, 1776. Feb. 14, 1776. K. 283. Son, James Stewart; brother Samuel Allen's children, John Allen's children, sister Mary Stewart's daughter, Jane Stewart; husband's mother, Elenor Eakin. Exc. Thomas McGee.

Sarah Janvier. Widow. Town of N. C. Nov. 11, 1775. Feb. 15, 1776. K. 285. Kinswoman, Mary Morgan; children, viz: Francis, John, Philip and Sarah; grandchildren, viz: Sarah Tatlow, Susanna Tatlow, Rachel Tatlow, John Tatlow and Francis Dehaven Janvier. Exc. sons, Francis Janvier, John Janvier and Phillip Janvier, dau., Sarah Janvier.

James Sykes. Feltmaker. N. C. Aug. 6, 1727. Feb. 16, 1776. Misc. 427. Wife, Mary; sons, Stephen and James. Exc. Mary Sykes.

Elizabeth Vandyke. St. Geo. Hd. June 25, 1773. Feb. 22, 1776. K. 292. Sister Jemima (dec'd.); brothers, David and James Vandyke; three nieces, daughters of brother Isaac (dec'd.); niece, Sarah Vandyke, dau. of brother Thomas; niece, Elizabeth Boyer, dau. of (dec'd.) sister Mary and intermarried with Thomas Boyer; niece, Ann, dau. of (dec'd.) bro. John; sister, Grace Peterson; brother-in-law, Dr. Jacob Peterson; two nieces, Mary and Hester Peterson; dec'd bro. Isaac's son John. Exc. Nicholas Vandyke.

Zacharias Derrickson. Farmer, Chris. Hd. Jan. 3, 1776. Mch. 7, 1776. K. 289. Wife, Sarah; sons, William, Jacob, Zacharias, Peter, Cornelius, David and Joseph; daughters, Martha Dixon, Elizabeth Derrickson and Christiana Derrickson. Exc. sons, Jacob and Zacharias.

John Hill. Blacksmith. Pen. Hd. Mch. 4, 1775. Apr. 17, 1776. K. 295. Wife, Sarah; son, Thomas; three grandchildren, Kesia Kelley, Nathen Kelley and Elias Kelley. Guardian, Daniel Rees. Exc. son, Thomas Hill.

Isaac See. Feb. 10, 1772. May 10, 1776. K. 297. Son, Isaak. Renunciation of widow, Hester See.

William Clark. Town of N. C. Jan. 22, 1774. June 1, 1776. K. 298. Wife, Ma'rtha; sons, William and John; dau., Margaret. Exc. sons, William and John.

Thomas Johnston. Yeoman. Appo. Hd. Feb. 18, 1776. Aug. 22, 1776. K. 301. Wife, Jean; sons, John, Thomas, Robert and William; daughters, Mary and Margaret. Exc. son, William Johnston.

Solomon Springer. Innholder, Chris. Hd. Aug. 19, 1776. Sept. 6, 1776. K. 303. Wife, Liddy; four children, viz: Nancy, Jehu, Susannah and Solomon. Exc. wife, Liddy Springer, Leven Justis.

William Brobson. Barber. Borough of Wil. Aug. 12, 1776. Sept. 20, 1776. K. 304. Sons, Joseph and James; sister, Jane Meholland of Ireland, widow; wife, Judith; niece, Mary Brobson, dau. of brother Joseph. Exc. wife, Judith, Nicholas Robinson.

Jonas Stedham. Yeoman. Chris. Hd. Aug. 21, 1776. Sept. 20, 1776. K. 307. Wife, Elenor Stedham; sons, Cornelius, John and Jonas; daughters, Stenah Stedham, Ingebor Stedham and Elenor Stedham. Exc. sons, Jonas and John.

Thomas Owens. Weaver. Jan. 6, 1776. Oct. 21, 1776. K. 311. James Conway. Exc. James Conway.

David Thomas. Pen. Hd. Nov. 10, 1776. Nov. 16, 1776. K. 314. Wife, Elizabeth; William Barnes. Exc. wife, Elizabeth Thomas.

Margaret Watson. B'wine Hd. Apr. 3, 1775. Nov. 20, 1776. K. 316. Sister, Jane Neeley; niece, Margaret Anderson, her eldest son and other children; Rebecca Anderson and her sister Margaret Anderson, Ruth Webster, Margaret Stuart. Exc. James Stuart.

Susannah Piper. St. Geo. Hd. Nov. 11, 1776. Nov. 26, 1776. K.

317. Son, John Piper; daughters, Mary Piper, Hannah Piper and Margaret Piper. Exc. John Golden.

Mary Hill, widow of Joseph Hill. Appo. Hd. Oct. 24, 1776. Nov. 28, 1776. K. 319. L. 100. Catharine Bradford, dau. of Susannah Bradford of Phila.; Valentine Read, son of Rev. Thomas Read; Joseph Hill, son of husband's nephew, John Hill; nephews, John and William Glenn, sons of sister Ann Glenn; daughter of niece Charlotte McCall (dec'd.); Mary Shaffly, dau. of sister Martha Griffith, dec'd; niece, Ann Griffith; Harmanus Alrich, son of brother Harmanus Alrich, dec'd.; Wessell Alrich, son of nephew Wessell Alrich; Rebekah Alrich, sister to Wessell Alrich; West, James, William and Nancy, children of Harmanus Alrich; Harmanus Alrich, Mary Parker, Martha Stockton, Hester Humphries and Hannah Alrich, children of brother Peter Alrich, dec'd. Exc. nephew, William Alrich, niece, Ann Griffith.

John Bird, Jr. Farmer. B'wine Hd. Jan. 26, 1776. Dec. 24, 1776. K. 322. Two sons, John and Benoni; two daughters, Anna Mary and Sarah; sister Ann with exc. to act as guardians. Exc. brother-in-law, John Bird, Thomas Babb.

David Stewart. Yeoman. St. Geo. Hd. Nov. 13, 1776. Dec. 24, 1776. K. 324. Children of dec'd daughter, Mary Dushane; children of daughter, Ann Craven; children of daughter, Margaret Wilds; sons, Samuel and David. Valentine Dushane, John Craven, Richard Wilds.

Lawrence Skeer. St. Geo. Hd. Dec. 15, 1776. Dec. 28, 1776. K. 331. Three sisters, viz: Grace Aldridge, Mary Aspril and Eleanor Skeer. Exc. brothers, Harmans Aldridge, Joseph Aspril.

Alexander Miller. Newport. May 15, 1775. Jan. 3, 1777. K. 333. L. 152. Wife, Beata; son, John; son-in-law, William Robinson; grandson, Alexander Robinson. Exc. wife, Beata Miller, son-in-law William Robinson, Justa Walraven.

Robert Bailie, of Del. Battalion. Jan. 4, 1777. Jan. 9, 1777. K. 338. Capt. Henry Darby, William White. Exc. Thomas Sharpe, William Sharpe.

James Manson. St. Geo. Hd. Dec. 3, 1776. Jan. 9, 1777. K. 336. Wife, Sarah; daughters, Mary Kean, Rebecca Standly and Margaret Whitehead; nephews, John Byman, William Manson and Thomas Manson. Exc. wife, Sarah Manson.

Hannah Dixson. Chris. Hd. Jan. 6, 1777. Jan. 18, 1777. K. 340. Daughters, Ann Wilson and Elizabeth Underwood; son, William; granddaughters, Hannah Dixson and Elizabeth Jemison, son-in-law, Nathaniel Smith; dau.-in-law, Elinor Dixson, grandson, Thomas Dixson. Exc. son-in-law, Thomas Wilson.

William Forwood. B'wine Hd. Aug. 13, 1771. Jan. 18, 1777. K. 342. Wife, Mary; sons, William, John, James, Joseph, Jacob and Samuel; three daughters, Margaret Dunning, wife of Simon Dunning; Mary Almond, widow of William Almond; Rebecca Brierly, wife of Hugh Brierly; grandsons, John Brierly, Michel Dunning, William Forwood, son of Samuel; granddau., Hannah Almond. Exc. sons, John and Samuel.

Mary Jones. Pen. Hd. Jan. 31, 1777. Feb. 4, 1777. K. 347. Daughters, Rachel and Jennet; stepdau., Sarah Jones; brother-in-law, Robert Jones. Exc. Hugh Glasford.

William Anderson. Chris. Hd. Dec. 12, 1776. Feb. 10, 1777. K. 350. Wife, Sarah; sons, Josiah, Charles and William; mother, Bridget Anderson; daughters, Martha, Mary and Ann. Exc. wife, Sarah Anderson, John Hendrickson, Theopilus Evans, Oliver Evans.

Leonard Humphries. Yeoman. St. Geo. Hd. Jan. 29, 1777. Feb. 12, 1777. K. 353. Wife, Catharine; dau., Sarah; two sister's children in Carolina. Exc. wife, Catharine Humphries, William Woodland.

Hannah Cobb, in the 4th regiment of Virginia Troops. Village of Newark. Feb. 15, 1777. Feb. 18, 1777. K. 354. Daughters, Mary Cobb and Sarah Jones; son, William Cobb. Exc. Samuel Woodbridge.

Samuel Faries. Red Lion Hd. Sept. 7, 1776. Feb. 19, 1777. K. 356. Brother, Jacob Faries; wife, Mary; sister, Margaret Black; nieces, Margaret and Jean Faries, daughters of Jacob Faries; niece, Margaret Black. Exc. wife, Mary, Isaac Alexander, Jacob Faries.

Elizabeth Beaty. Chris. Hd. Feb. 28, 1768. Feb. 27, 1777. K. 349. Dau., Jane Sutherland; granddau., Elizabeth Sutherland; son-in-law, William Armstrong and Ann his wife; son-in-law, Thomas Sutherland and Jane his wife. Exc. son, John Beaty.

James Matthews. Mar. 18, 1776. Mar. 4, 1777. K. 360. Wife, Ann; son, Thomas; two daughters, Lydia and Hester. Exc. wife, Ann Matthews, David Howel.

Mary Henderson. St. Geo. Hd. Feb. 9, 1777. Mar. 4, 1777. K. 361. Son, John Henderson; brother, Benjamin Aul. Exc. John Vail.

John McCallmont. Newport. Jan. 16, 1777. Mch. 5, 1777. K. 372. Wife, Sarah; sons, David, John, George, Arthur and James; daughters, Elenora, Susanna, Margaret and Sarah. Exc. wife, Sarah McCallmont, sons David and James McCallmont, George Latimer.

John Henderson. St. Geo. Hd. Feb. 6, 1777. Mch. 6, 1777. K. 363. Wife, Jane. Exc. wife, Jane Henderson.

James Conaway. Pen. Hd. Feb. 25, 1777. Mch. 10, 1777. K. 364. Wife, Sarah; stepson, Peter Dawson. Exc. wife, Sarah Conaway, Maj. John Aiken.

Onery Finel. Pen. Hd. Jan. 4, 1777. Mch. 19, 1777. K. 366. Eleanor, Mary and Dinah Thomas, daughters of Joseph Thomas and Margaret, his wife; Mary Brown, dau. of John Brown; William Brown, son of John Brown. Exc. Joseph Thomas.

Thomas Scott. Appo. Hd. Nov. 14, 1771. Mch. 24, 1777. K. 368.
Wife, Sarah. Exc. wife, Sarah Scott.

William Bunker Paul. Labourer. Mar. 8, 1777. Mar. 24, 1777. K.
370. Sister Amelia, Sarah Bunker, youngest dau. of Henry
Bunker. Exc. uncle, William Weir.

James Floyd, Jr. Bricklayer. Red. Lion Hd. —— 1777. Mar. 27,
1777. K. 376. Friend William Norris and Charity, his wife, my
Rev. father James Floyd. Letters of adm. granted to brother-in-
law, Thomas Pierce and Eleanor Pierce.

Perry Robeson, of Sussex Co. Port Penn. St. Geo. Hd. Feb. 8,
1777. Apr. 2, 1777. K. 377. Cousin Hannah Robeson, dau. of
my uncle, Cornelius Robeson; two sons of uncle; Parker Robeson, and Daniel Robeson. Exc. cousin, Simon Collick.

Lydia Rothwell St. Geo. Hd. Mar. 28, 1777. Apr. 7, 1777. K. 378.
Five surviving daughters; dau., Patty; sons, Thomas, William and
Ebenezer. Exc. Cornelius Armstrong, James Moody, son Eben-
ezer.

Patrick Conner. Bombay Hook. Appo. Hd. Jan. 16, 1777. Apr. 9,
1777. K. 379. Wife, Mary; five unmarried children; daughters,
Elizabeth Norton and Jane Taylor; son, Patrick Conner. Exc.
son, John Conner, wife, Mary Conner.

David Lewis. Yeoman. Bedford Co., Pa. Mar. 28, 1777. Apr. 11,
1777. K. 380. Wife, Elizabeth. Exc. wife, Elizabeth Lewis,
brother-in-law, Thomas Watson.

John King, on board privateer brig "General Mifflin," Capt. John
Hamilton. Newport. Sept. 19, 1776. Apr. 12, 1777. K. 381. Son,
John King; sisters to wit, Ann Dixson, Jean Clark and Ketrin
Pope. Exc. wife, Mary King, James Latimer.

John Matthess. St. Geo. Hd. Aug. 30, 1774. Apr. 18, 1777. K. 382.
Granddau., Mary Gill, dau. of John Gill, dec'd., and Margaret, his
wife; sons, James, Robert and Samuel; dau., Jane, wife of John
Evans. Exc. Samuel and Robert, sons.

Hugh Steel. Husbandman. Red. Lion Hd. Feb. 19, 1774. Apr. 19,
1777. K. 384. Wife, ——; son, John Steel; father-in-law, John
Jacquet. Exc. Alexander Porter, Jr.

Peter Stidham. Mar. 3, 1777. Apr. 25, 1777. K. 385. Wife, Sarah;
eldest son, William; youngest son, Peter; son, Lucas; two daughters, Mary and Sarah; Rev. Joseph Smith, Jacob Colesberry,
Lucas Alricks, Robert Furness, Robert Robertson. Exc. wife,
Sarah Stidman; sons, William and Lucas.

Jacobus Haines. Yeoman. N. C. Hd. Nov. 1, 1775. May 12, 1777.
K. 389. Wife, Margaret; sons, Jacobus, Henry and Cornelius;
dau. Elizabeth Peterson's children, grandson Jacob Powell. Exc.
sons, Henry and Jacobus.

Dinah James. Aug. 11, 1771. May 14, 1777. K. 391. Niece, Sarah
Torrence; Jannet James, wife of Alexander Faries; Ann James,

wife of Henry Clark; Mary James, Jr. Letters of adm. granted to nephew, John Torrence.

James Lattomus. Appo. Hd. May 13, 1777. May 24, 1777. K. 392. Dau., Dinah Lattomus; sons, John and James Lattomus. Exc. William Allfree, Esq.

Rebecca Jones, widow of William Jones. Borough of Wil. 2nd day of 4th m., 1777. May 26, 1777. K. 394. Sons, Phillip, William and Joseph. Exc. sons, Phillip and Williams Jones.

Jacob Kruson. Farmer. Appo. Hd. May 21, 1777. May 31, 1777. K. 396. Wife, Ann; children ——. Exc. wife, Ann Kruson; brother, Garrett Kruson.

George Gilpin. Borough of Wil. May 4th, 1777. June 2, 1777. K. 398. Brother, Isaac Gilpin; sister, Betty Gilpin; cousin, Vincent Gilpin. Exc. Vincent Gilpin, Elizabeth Gilpin.

Rachel Isaac. Widow. B'wine Hd. Feb. 9, 1777. June 4, 1777. K. 399. Friend, Phebe Mast; sister Hannah and her children; sister, Barbery; nephew, Samuel Hollingsworth and his dau. Rachel; nephew, Jacob Hollingsworth; John Elliott, grandson of late husband. Exc. John Stapler.

Michael Kelley. (Nunc.) Dragon's Neck. Red. Lion Hd. May 11, 1777. June 7, 1777. K. 401. Hugh Marin, Patrick McCue; testator declared he had no wife or relation in America or any other part of the world. Attested by Henry White, Philip Truax.

Peter Connor (Conar). Appo. Hd. Mar. 3, 1774. June 10, 1777. K. 402. Wife, Catren; son, Peter; John Calahan. Exc. wife, Catren.

William Reynolds. Yeoman. Mill Creek, Hd. Oct. 20, 1774. Aug. 7, 1777. Misc. 417. Dau., Eleanor Ross, widow of James Ross; son, Thomas; dau., Ann Read, wife of William Read; dau., Martha Carson, wife of Umphrey Carson; children of dau. Eleanor, viz.: Thomas Ross, Margaret and Ann. Exc. son, Alexander.

William Marshall. Innholder. Borough of Wil. Feb. 23, 1774. Aug. 11, 1777. L. 86. Wife, Elinor; daughters Sarah and Mary, wife of John Higgins; friend, Dr. John McKinley. Exc. wife, Elinor Marshall and dau. Sarah Marshall.

Mary Ryland. Cecil Co., Md. Apr. 7, 1775. Aug. 12, 1777. Misc. I. 421. Daughters, Rebecca Ryland, Mary Ryland and Mary Ann Pearce; Stephen Ryland. Exc. son-in-law, Henry Pearce.

Thomas Black. W. Clay Crk. Hd. Feb. 17, 1777. Aug. 18, 1777. Misc. II. 35. Sons, John Black and James Black; daughters, Rebecah Black and Ann Black; brother, Charles Black. Exc. sons, John and James.

David Tweedy. Mill Crk. Hd. May 11, 1768. Aug. 20, 1777. L. 91. Wife, Jane; children, Catherine, Simon, John and David; apprentice, John McCormick. Exc. wife, Jane Tweedy, brother-in-law, ——.

Francis Anderson. Cordwainer. Aug. 13, 1776. Aug. 25, 1777. Misc. I. 1. Exc. friend, John Anderson of York Co., Pa.

Joseph Harris. Yeoman. Appo. Hd. Aug. 8, 1777. Aug. 26, 1777. L. 89. Three sons, James, Joseph and Jacob Harris; two daughters, Elizabeth Ball and Catharine Harris. Exc. sons James and Joseph.

Robert Hunt. Yeoman and Innholder. Appo. Hd. May 5, 1777. Nov. 13, 1777. L. 3. Adopted son, Charles Hunt; nephew, Robert Hunt; Elizabeth Bostick, dau. of late wife; in Ireland, three sisters, viz.: Anne Nixon, Mary McMichael, and Elizabeth Gardiner; Anne Martin, Sarah Bullock, Mary Hunt, dau. of Mary Wilson, now or late of County Tyrone, Ireland. Exc. William Alfree, Philip Reading.

Andrew Bryan. Aug. 26, 1777. Dec. 1, 1777. L. 5. Sons, Nathaniel and Andrew; daughters, Mary, Rebecca, Lydia and Agnes. Exc. son, Nathaniel, John Crawford.

John Ozier. St. Geo. Hd. Nov. 27, 1777. Dec. 15, 1777. L. 51. Wife Elizabeth's father, Richard Hutchinson; dau., Mary; children, viz: Rachel, wife of Andrew Zelephone, Jacob, John, Perry, Rebecca, Joseph, Sarah and William. Exc. son, Jacob Ozier.

Henry Van Bebber. Yeoman. St. Geo. Hd. Jan. 5, 1778. Mar. 30, 1778. L. 8. Wife, Hester; two sons, Andrew and James Van Bebber. Exc. wife, Hester Van Bebber; brothers, Isaac and Abraham Van Bebber.

Daniel Worms. W. Clay Crk. Hd. Mar. 12, 1778. Apr. 9, 1778. L. 10. Wife, Mary; daughters, Margaret, Ann, Mary, Magleanah and Elizabeth; son, Peter. Letters of adm. granted to Mary Worms, widow.

Peter Leonard. (Nunc.) Mar. 26, 1778. Apr. 11, 1778. L. 11. Exc. Andrew Rainy. Attested by Barbary Fifer, James McCormick.

Elizabeth Vanhorn. Widow. Jan. 14, 1778. Apr. 17, 1778. L. 13. Sons, Nicholas, Abraham, Jacob and Isaac; daughters, Sarah Weldrum, Hannah Sappington and Rachel Vanhorn. Exc. son, Jacob Vanhorn.

Peter Stalcup. N. C. Hd. Feb. 24, 1778. Apr. 20, 1778. L. 14. Natural dau., Sarah; brother, Samuel Price; sisters, Sarah Price and Hannah Moore. Exc. brother, Samuel Price; Alexander Porter.

Robert Watt. Red Lion Hd. Apr. 16, 1778. Apr. 21, 1778. L. 16. Wife, Dorcas; mother, Mary; dau., Anne; brother, James; Margaret Kirkpatrick. Exc. Robert Porter, Anthony Dushane.

John Taylor. St. Geo. Hd. Apr. 23, 1778. Apr. 28, 1778. L. 20. Wife, Elizabeth Taylor; cousin, James Anderson; friends, Francis Taylor, Samuel Taylor, Susanna Taylor, Elizabeth Taylor and Mary Taylor. Exc. Robert Porter, James Armstrong.

Nicholas Wood. Mar. 17, 1778. Apr. 24, 1778. L. 18. Wife, Ann; Catharine Diven; Sally, dau. of Hester Watts; Amalia, dau. of

Elizabeth Harper; John, son of Susannah Bird; Nicholas and Ann Wood, children of brother William Wood. Exc. brother, William Wood; Richard Ellis.

Mary Allfree. Appo. Hd. Oct. 6, 1777. May 4, 1778. L. 24. Dau., Catharine Lyons; grandchildren, Catharine Hart, James Hart, Allfree Hart, William Hart and Garrett Hart. Exc. son, William Allfree.

Richard Caulk. (Single man). Late of Appo. Hd. Apr. 20, 1778. May 4, 1778. L. 22. Sister, Mary Pennington. Exc. brothers, Benjamin Caulk and Jacob Caulk.

Mary King, widow of John King. Yeoman. Chris. Hd. May 28, 1777. May 8, 1778. L. 26. Niece, Margaret Robeson, daughter of William Robeson; son, John King; sister, Elizabeth Robeson; brother, John Miller; mother, Beata Miller. Exc. George Latimer, brother-in-law, William Robeson.

Bridget Colegate. Widow. Appo. Hd. Sept. 6, 1775. May 18, 1778. L. 29. Son, John Colegate; dau., Mary Dale, widow. Grandchildren, Richard Colegate Dale and Nancy Dale. Exc. dau., Mary Dale; cousin, Richard Cantwell, Esq.

Thomas Lewis. Yeoman. Pen. Hd. Mar. 5, 1778. May 22, 1778. L. 32. Grandchildren, David Thompson Lewis, Margaret Lewis (dau. of Jehu Lewis), Thomas Lewis James, Esther James, Susanna James, Mary James, Sarah Lewis and Susanna Lewis. dau. Susanna, Barbara Curry, son-in-law, John James. Exc. son, Isaac Lewis.

Mary Twiggs. (Nunc.) Widow. Newport. May 7, 1778. May 28, 1778. L. 34. Attested by Robert and Elenor Furniss. Granddau., Elinor Scotthorn. Grandson, John Scotthorn. Letters of adm. granted to Hanna Scothorn.

Thomas Bird, Sr. Yeoman. B'wine Hd. Dec. 28, 1776. June 2, 1778. L. 35. Wife, Rachel; John Husbands, Peter Woolbough, Joseph Elliott. Son, Thomas; granddau., Rachel Bird, dau. of son Wm., dec'd. Children of dau. Rebekah, viz: William, Rachel, John, Mary, Jane, Rebekah, Isaac, and Harmon Bratten. Dau. Elizabeth, wife of Samuel McClintock; Rachel, wife of William Reynolds; Sarah, wife of Elijah Hooten. Exc. son, John Bird.

Martha Montgomery, wife of Robert Montgomery, Sr. Mill Creek Hd. Mar. 22, 1778. June 13, 1778. L. 38. Children, Sarah McCalley, William Montgomery, Martha Wilson, Robert Montgomery, and Jean Montgomery. Children of dau. Margaret Willson, dec., viz: Martha Willson and Rendall Willson. Exc. dau., Jean Montgomery.

Richard Hambly. St. Geo. Hd. Oct. 14, 1777. June 17, 1778. L. 41. Wife, Hannah. Four children, viz: Richard, Sarah, Sabra and Elizabeth Hambly. Exc. George Barker, Thomas McDonough.

Mary Wynkoop. Appo. Hd. June 19, 1778. June 29, 1778. L. 43.

Son, Nicholas Hammond, of Island of Jersey, British Channel. Father, James Dyre. Mother, Rebecca Dyre. Sons, Abraham and James Wynkoop. Exc. son, James Wynkoop.

William Hazlet. W. Clay Crk. Hd. Jan. 16, 1778. July 27, 1778. L. 46. Brother, James Hazlet; John Black of Sunbury. Exc. brother, James Hazlet, Mary Slater.

Abigail Passmore. Town of N. C. Mar. 21, 1778. July 31, 1778. L. 47. Husband, John Passmore. Grandson, Jacob Grubb. Six youngest grandchildren of son, John Lamplugh, viz: Jacob, Nathaniel, Susanna, and Martha; names of other two unknown to testator. Dau., Martha Levy. Granddau., Susanna Anderson. Exc. Robert Furniss, Jacob Colesberry, William Colesberry.

Mary Pennington. May 15, 1778. Aug. 4, 1778. L. 50. Son, Joseph; dau., Mary Rothwell. Exc. son, Joseph Pennington.

Samuel Carpenter. Yeoman. St. Geo. Hd. Sept. 10, 1776. Aug. 20, 1778. L. 55. Wife, Mary; son, William; nephews, Powell and William Carpenter; nieces, Mary and Abigail Carpenter, daughters of half-brother, William. Exc. half-brother, William Carpenter; cousin, William Carpenter.

Benjamin Stockton. St. Geo. Hd. Oct. 12, 1776. Aug. 22, 1778. L. 58. Wife, Martha; sister, Elizabeth Stockton of Maryland. Exc. wife, Martha Stockton.

Lewis Howell. Practitioner of Physick. Town of Newark. March 8, 1776. Aug. 25, 1778. L. 60. Brother, Richard Howell; mother, Sarah Howell; father, Ebenezer Howell; sister, Susannah Howell. Abel Glasford. Exc. Hugh Glasford; uncle, Elnathar Davis.

William Anderson. Yeoman. B'wine Hd. June 1, 1770. Aug. 28, 1778. L. 62. Wife, Christian; daughters, Bridget Bird, Mary Smith, Sarah Smith and Rebeccah Raulston; sons, James, John, William, Jacob and Erick. John Staples. Exc. sons, William and Jacob.

Elenor Marshall. Widow. Wil. June 15, 1778. Aug. 29, 1778. L. 65. Friend, Elizabeth Ferris; grandchildren, Eleanor, William, Acquilla and Marshall Huggens, children of dau., Mary. Exc. dau., Sarah Marshall, Robert Bryan.

James Cameron. (Nunc.) ———. Aug. 31, 1778. L. 67. Attested by Richard Clayton and Mary Daine. Wife, Ann to adm. estate, assisted by John Meariss, Esq.

Robert Kenny. Mill creed Hd. Dec. 25, 1777. Sept. 9, 1778. L. 69. Sister, Mary Wilson; Jean Kenny, wife of Moses Kenny; Matthew Kenny, Robert Kenny, Rebecka Kenny and Mary Kenny, daughters of said Moses Kenny. Exc. Evan Rice.

William Wilson. Yeoman. W. Clay Crk. Hd. Mar. 26, 1778. Sept. 16, 1778. L. 71. Wife, Jean; Jean Pugh, dau. of 3rd wife; dau., Mary Reynolds wife of John; children, William and Ann. Exc. friend, James Wilson.

Robert Clark. Pen. Hd. Aug. 8, 1778. Sept. 22, 1778. L. 73. Sister, Mary Fornam; sister's son, Robert Cann; sister's dau., Sushanna Tweedy. Exc. David Tweedy.

Jannet McLonen. Sept. 19, 1778. Sept. 28, 1778. L. 75. Sister, Anna McLonen; niece, Mary Grantham; Isaac Grantham and Mary, his wife; heirs of Janat Hamilton of Va.

Bertha Miller. Chris. Hd. June 30, 1778. Oct. 8, 1778. L. 78. Son, John Miller; dau., Elizabeth Robeson; son-in-law, William Robeson; grand-children, Alexander Robeson and Margaret Robeson. Exc. William Robeson and Peter Justis.

Joseph Holliday. Farmer. Appo. Hd. May 23, 1778. Oct. 10, 1778. L. 82. Wife, Jean; father ——; children,——. Younger children, Ann Holliday and Samuel Holliday. Exc. wife, Jean Holliday.

Herbert Burgess. St. Geo. Hd. July 29, 1778. Oct. 10, 1778. L. 80. Brother, Peter Burgess' eldest son, John; brother, Peter Burgess' eldest dau., Rachel; brother, John Burgess, William Burgess. Exc. bro., John Burgess.

Philip Morrow. St. Geo. Hd. Oct. 6, 1778. Oct. 13, 1778. L. 84. Exc. Barnard McDermot of Daniel Massey's Cross Roads in Md.

Hannah Bonham. Mill Creek Hd. Oct. 10, 1767. Oct. 15, 1778. L. 93. Widow of Malakiah Bonham of Kingswood, West New Jersey; dau., Elizabeth John, wife of Jacob John of Mill Crk. Hd. Grandchildren, Enoch John, Heath John, Thomas John, Jacob John and Ann John, children of dau., Elizabeth. Exc. John Evans, Evan Rice.

William West. Cordwainer. Chris. Hd. 8m 1, 1777. Oct. 20, 1778. L. 97. Son-in-law, Jacob Craige and Mary, his wife; son-in-law, George Stern and Sarah, his wife. Exc. George Stern, and Sarah Stern.

John Dougherty. Yeoman. N. C. Feb. 15, 1777. Oct. 27, 1778. L. 103. Exc. Patrick Hughs, shallopman.

John Cazier. Oct. 24, 1778. Nov. 9, 1778. L. 104. Wife, Rachel; two grandchildren, John and Henry Conway; six children, viz: John, Jacob, Henry, Mathias, Sarah and Susannah. Exc. son, Jacob.

Rev. Philip Reading. Appo. Hd. Sept. 6, 1778. Nov. 18, 1778. L. 106. Wife, Hester; son, Philip; daughters, Catharine Ann Reading and Hester Reading. Robert Hunt, dec'd. Exc. wife, Hester Reading; George Read; son, Philip Reading.

William Hartley. Taylor. Feb. 15, 1777. Nov. 18, 1778. L. 109. Exc. Daniel Smith.

John Welsh. Yeoman. B'wine Hd. Oct. 9, 1778. Nov. 27, 1778. L. 110. Daughters, Jean, Ann, Elizabeth, Mary; son, John; dau. Mary, her husband, ——; her children, ——; children of son, James, his wife, Margaret. Friend, Hannah Branton; Peter Vandever, Jr., Jos. Tatnall, Wm. Poole, Jos. Stidham and John Stapler. Exc. Mark Elliot, Jr., kinsman; Isaac Tussy.

Nicholas Bennet. Yeoman. St. Geo. Hd. Aug. 31, 1761. Dec. 12, 1778. L. 116. Son, William Bennet. Exc. brother, William Bennet.

Peter Moore. Farmer. Appo. Hd. Nov. 31, 1778. Dec. 17, 1778. L. 114. Son, John Moore; dau., Mary Moore; son-in-law, Andrew Barnnitt; children of same; little cousin, John Barnnitt. Exc. dau., Mary Moore.

William Barns. Yeoman. Pen. Hd. Nov. 20, 1778. Dec. 22, 1778. L. 117. Mother, Elizabeth Barns; sisters, Ann and Martha. Exc. brothers, Thomas and John Barns.

Daniel Rees. Red Lion Hd. Jan. 15, 1777. Dec. 22, 1778. L. 118. Brother, Thomas Rees; sisters, Mary James and Sarah Howel. Exc. brother, Thomas Rees.

Christian King. St. Geo. Hd. Aug. 16, 1765. Dec. 24, 1778. L. 120. Son, Leonard; dau., Ann; dau. Christian and her three children. Exc. sons, Francis and Leonard.

Robert Montgomery. Yeoman. Mill Creek Hd. June 12, 1775. Feb. 2, 1779. L. 125. Wife, Martha; sons, Robert, William, and Hugh Montgomery; daughters, Jean, Margaret Griffith, Sarah McCullogh, and Martha Willson. Exc. wife, Martha Montgomery; son, Hugh Montgomery.

Michael Mardock. Mill Creek Hd. Jan. 9, 1779. Feb. 2, 1779. L. 129. Wife, Bridget; son, William; three daughters, Mary, Catharine and Elizabeth. Exc. William Tate.

David Lewelin. Yeoman. Jan. 23, 1777. Feb. 3, 1779. L. 134. Wife, ———; Ruth Davis, wife's brother's dau.; Isabel McCay, dau. of James McCay; brothers, Thomas, and William Lewelin; stepmother, Mary Wilson. Exc. wife, ———; Andrew Kerr.

Ann Britahan. Widow. Appo. Hd. Feb. 23, 1778. Feb. 4, 1779. L. 131. Dau., Hannah McClerey; son, Andrew; William Heveran; granddau., Ann. Exc. dau., Hannah McClerey; son, Andrew Britahan.

Christiania Anderson. Widow. B'wine Hd. Jan. 22, 1779. Feb. 5, 1779. L. 133. Sons, Jacob, Erick, James, William and John; daughters, Bridget, Mary, Rebecca and Sarah. Exc. son, John Anderson.

Margaret Kirkpatrick. Widow. Chris. Hd. Jan. 4, 1779. Feb. 11, 1779. L. 137. Two granddaus., Catharine and Elinor Montgomery; granddau. Elenor, dau. of Samuel Campbell; dau., Margaret Campbell. Exc. son-in-law, Samuel Campbell.

Robert Boyce. Weaver. Mill Creek Hd. 4m 18, 1778. Feb. 12, 1779. L. 138. Wife, Mary; sons, Robert, John, Richard and Francis; daughters, Martha and Isabel. Exc. wife, Mary Boyce; son, John Boyce.

Benjamin McCoole. St. Geo. Hd. Sept. 7, 1776. Feb. 16, 1779. L. 140. Brother, William McCoole; nephews, Ashton Hall and Benjamin Meriss Exc. Benjamin Meriss.

William McCoole. St. Geo. Hd. Sept. 7, 1776. Feb. 16, 1779. L. 141. Wife, Elizabeth; her father, John McBride, dec'd; brother, John McCoole, dec'd; brothers and sisters, ———. Exc. John Meriss and John Hall.

Margaret Grantham. June 29, 1776. Feb. 17, 1779. L. 143. Grandsons, Daniel Turner, Andrew Gravenreat Colesbury, and Henry Colesbury; daughters, Catharine Colesbury, and Elizabeth Turner; granddaughters, Margaret Turner, dau. of Peter Turner. Becky ———, Mary Colesbury, Margaret Turner (dau. of Thomas Turner), Ann, Elizabeth and Mary Turner, and Babe, dau. of Thomas Turner. Exc. Peter Turner and Jacob Colesbury.

Rachel Cazier. Mar. 14, 1779. Mar. 23, 1779. L. 146. Son, Andrew Dushane; daughters, Hester Hattery, Rachel McAntire, Lydia Eliason and her two children, and Susannah Cazier; Joseph Hattery's children, namely, James, Andrew, Thomas, Lydia and Rachel. Exc. Jacob Cazier.

Valentine Dushane. Red Lion Hd. Mar. 10, 1779. Mar. 23, 1779. L. 147. Daughters, Susanna Houston, Martha Kettle, Ann Wiles, Elizabeth Dushane and Eastor; sons, Cornelius, Valentine and David. Exc. sons, Cornelius and Valentine.

David Windell. Chris. Hd. Aug 23, 1779. Apr. 17, 1779. L. 149. Wife, Rebecca; daughter, Rebecca; cousin, Joseph Robinson. Exc. Joseph Robinson, wife, Rebecca Windell.

John Elliot, Esq., Capt. of Marines in Continental Navy. Dec. 14, 1778. May 8, 1779. L. 154. Mrs. Elizabeth Hatch, otherways Lehr af Boston; brother, James, of New Jersey; mother, Christian Elliot, widow; sisters, Jean Johnston, otherways Elliott, and Sarah Elliott of Ireland. Exc. brother, James Elliott; cousin, Capt. Samuel Corry of Phila.

Henry Brackin, Sr. Mill Creek Hd. May 16, 1779. May 26, 1779. L. 156. Sons, William Brackin and Henry Brackin; daughters, Hannah, wife of Joseph Ball, Sarah and Elizabeth; son-in-law, James Moore and his wife, Susanna; granddau., Susanna Moore. Exc. son, Henry Brackin; son-in-law, Joseph Ball, and dau., Sarah Brackin.

Erick Anderson. Yeoman. Chris. Hd. May 9, 1779. June 2, 1779. L. 160. William Graham, alias Anderson, son of Catharine Graham, Alexander Anderson, son of brother James; brothers, William, Jacob and John; sisters, Sarah Smith, wife of Isaac, Bretah Bird, wife of Thomas Bird, Rebecca Ralston, wife of Paul. Exc. brother, John Anderson.

Thomas Bennet. Yeoman. Appo. Hd. July 16, 1779. Aug. 5, 1779. L. 164. Wife, Elizabeth; sons, Thomas, Ebenezer, Perry and

John; daughters, Elizabeth Hawkins and Mary Taylor. Exc.
son, Ebenezer Bennet. Capt. Abraham Staats.

Isaac Chandler, Jr. Chris. Hd. July 5, 1779. Aug. 10, 1779. L. 166.
Father and mother, Isaac and Elizabeth Chandler; brother, Abra-
ham; sisters, Ann and Ruth. Exc. father, Isaac Chandler, Caleb
Kirk.

Samuel Morris. Yeoman. Appo. Hd. Mar. 23, 1777. Aug. 10, 1779.
L. 167. Brother, Jonathon Morris; three sisters, Mary Worrell,
Phebe Henry, and Hannah Pierson; half-brother, Morgan James;
Sarah Vernon and her son, Benjamin; Mary Wilson. Exc.
brother, Jonathon Morris.

Peter Wolbough. Farmer. B'wine Hd. ———, 1779. Oct. 11, 1779.
L. 169. Wife, Lydia; John Husbands, Samuel Bowlor's widow
and eldest son; Peter Wolbough; bound girl, Ann Chandler; Ann
and Rebecca Mortonson, daughters of Joseph Mortonson, dec'd.
Exc. wife, Lydia.

Sarah Morgan. Widow. Formerly of Phila. Sept. 28, 1779. Oct.
23, 1779. L. 171. Step-dau., Sarah Evans, widow of William
Evans, and her children, Esther Dickey and Sarah Evans; late
father, Thomas Hood; brother, John Hood. Exc. Joseph Green;
step-dau., Sarah Evans.

Harmanus Alrichs. St. Geo. Hd. Sept. 26, 1779. Oct. 25, 1779. L.
173. Wife, Grace; unborn child; brothers, Peter, John and Wessel
Alrichs. Exc. wife, Grace.

Richard Reynolds. Mar. 16, 1777. Nov. 3, 1779. L. 174. Wife, Mary;
daughter, Bridget; William, Rebecca and Richard, children of
brother, Thomas Reynolds. Exc. wife, Mary Reynolds; nephew,
Richard Reynolds.

Edward Brown. Farmer. Appo. Hd. Sept. 23, 1779. Nov. 5, 1779.
L. 175. Wife, Mary; four children now unmarried; son, Arra
Smyth; sons, John and Isaac; dau., Ann; dau., Rebecca Irons;
five grandchildren, ———. Exc. wife, Mary Brown; son, Arra
Smyth.

Mary Derrickson. Widow. B'wine Hd. Dec. 4, 1779. Dec. 20, 1779.
L. 178. Granddaughters, Mary Perkins, Polly Shearman, and Ann
Shearman; grandson, Jacob Derrickson; daughters, Hetty Per-
kins, Peggy Steadom, Susannah Tryon, and Nellie Shearman;
friend, Ann Garner; daughter-in-law, Ingalea Derrickson. Exc.
Son-in-law, Caleb Perkins.

Thomas James. Jan. 10, 1776. Jan. 18, 1780. L. 180. Wife, Tamer;
"each of my brothers' and sisters' children." Exc. wife, Tamer
James.

David John. Yeoman. Pen. Hd. Aug 29, 1779. Feb. 7, 1780. L.
183. Wife, Mary; son, Jehu; niece, Susanna Wattson, wife of
Thomas Wattson. Exc. friend, Thomas Wattson.

Sarah Noxon. Feb. 18, 1780. Mar. 6, 1780. L. 186. Sister-in-law,

Sarah Frisby; cousin, Mary Pearce; eldest son, Benjamin; son, James. Exc. Henry Ward Pearce.

Martha Ball. Widow of John Ball, blacksmith. Mill Creek Hd. Jan. 22, 1776. Mar. 22, 1780. L. 187. Four daughters, Mary Barkley, Elizabeth McMullan, Martha Brackin, and Hannah Ritchey; children of dau., Milder Griffin, dec'd, and their father, Matthew Griffin; sons, John and Joseph Ball; Ann Ball, present wife of son, John Ball. Exc. John Ball.

James Brattin. B'wine Hd. Oct. 21 1779. Mar. 27, 1780. L. 191. Wife, Barbarow; sons, John, William, Robert, and Jacob; daughters, Barbarow, and Nancy. Exc. Jacob Brattin (son).

John Fulton. Feb. 18, 1780. Apr. 18, 1780. L. 193. Mother, Barbara Fulton; sister, Mary Kirkpatrick's son, George. Exc. mother, Barbara Fulton.

John Edwards (Nunc.) Yeoman. Pen Hd. Nov. 4, 1780. Apr. 25, 1780. L. 194. Dau., Hannah and husband; wife, ——; two youngest daughters. Attested by James James, Mary James. Exc. wife, Hannah Edwards, Isaac Lewis.

William Hudson. Appo. Hd. Apr. 21, 1780. May 5, 1780. L. 195. Brother, Charles Hudson; father, Charles Hudson; aunt, Rebecca Truax. Exc. brother, Charles Hudson.

Elizabeth Warks, Widow. Appo. Hd. Apr. 28, 1779. July 18, 1780. L. 199. Son., William Chevins; sister, Susannah Boyer's 3 daughters, viz: Dolly, Elizabeth and Rachel Boyer. Exc. Arthur Moore.

Abraham Vandegrift. Red Lion Hd. June 18, 1780. July 22, 1780. L. 200. Wife, Elizabeth; only son, Abraham Vandegrift; brother, Christopher Vandegrift's youngest son, Christopher; brother, Lewis Vandegrift's son Leonard Vandegrift. Exc. Francis King.

John Jones, Esq. Apr. 1, 1780. July 29, 1780. L. 201. Son, Cantwell Jones; dau., Sarah Jones; sister, Mary Patterson. Exc. Richard Cantwell and Mary Patterson.

Sigfriedes Alrichs. Husbandman. May 20, 1780. Sept. 5, 1780. L. 205. Brothers, Benjamin, Joseph, Jonas and Lucas; wife, Rachel; sons, David, and Isaac, and Jacob; Rachel's brother, Isaac. Exc. wife, Rachel; brother, Lucas; brother-in-law, Jacob Colesberry.

Margaret Steele. Sept. 23, 1780. Oct. 2, 1780. L. 208. Daughters, Jane Alexander, Margaret Rankin and Hanna Moore; grandson, Andrew ——; granddau., Martha Taylor. Exc. dau., Margaret Rankin; son-in-law, Isaac Alexander.

Cornelius Eliason. July 1, 1775. Oct. 17, 1780. L. 210. Third son, Elias Eliason; sister, Prudence Downing's 2 sons, Thomas and William Downing; sister Martha Harper's children, viz: Elizabeth, James and Thomas Harper. Exc. brothers, Elias and Abraham Eliason.

Isaac Vanhorn. St. Geo. Hd. Apr. 24, 1780. Nov. 20, 1780. L. 212.

Brother, Abraham Vanhorn; sister, Rachel. Exc. brother-in-law, Benjamin Sappington of Cecil Co., Md.

James Shaw. Appo. Hd. Nov. 13, 1780. Nov. 21, 1780. L. 213. Daughters, Mary, Sarah, Martha and Jane; sons, John, William and James Shaw. Exc. son, James Shaw.

James Dougherty. St. Geo. Hd. Apr. 6, 1780. Dec. 1, 1780. L. 214. Housekeeper, Elioner Hendrixon. Exc. friend, Wessell Alrichs.

John Gilpin. Merchant. Winchester, Va. Feb. 24, 1778. ―――― L. 220. Wife, Lydia Gilpin; sons, Joshua Gilpin and Thomas Gilpin; aunt, Ann Gilpin of Wil.; Margaret Heath; uncle, Thomas Gilpin, dec'd.; sisters, Esther Fisher and Sarah Fisher; brothers, Samuel R. Fisher and Jabez Maud Fisher; nephews, Joshua Fisher and Thomas Fisher, son of Miers Fisher; dau., Sarah Gilpin. Exc. wife, Lydia; son, Joshua; brothers, Thomas Fisher, Samuel Rowland Fisher, Miers Fisher, and Jabez Maud Fisher.

John Slater. July 8, 1780. Dec. 5, 1780. L. 228. Wife, Mary; dau., Martha; granddau., Elizabeth. Exc. wife, Mary; cousin, William Robinson and Thomas Rankin.

Josiah Thomas. Pen Hd. Dec. 10, 1780. Jan. 16, 1781. L. 230. Brothers, Isaac, David and Jesse Thomas. Exc. brother, David.

Mary Glenn. N. C. Hd. Jan. 4, 1781. Feb. 5, 1781. L. 231. Brother, Thomas Glenn; uncle, John Kittel (dec'd.); relation, Mary Dushane. Exc. brother, Thomas Glenn.

Margaret Laferty (Nunc.). Widow. N. C. Hd. Jan. 23, 1781. Feb. 7, 1781. L. 232. Two daughters, Catharine and Nancy Laferty; Chambers Hall and Ephraim Stoops, witnesses. Attested by Benjamin Stoop and Cornelia Stoop.

Archibald Little. Taylor. Bor. of Wil. Sept. 11, 1779. Feb. 9, 1781. L. 233. Wife, ――; sons, Archibald and Robert; daughters, Ann Jemimah, Susannah and Sarah; Joseph Warner and Jacob Broom; brother-in-law, James Lea; friend, John Stapler. Exc. Nicholas Robinson and Nathan Wood.

William Wood. Apr. 21, 1780. Feb. 12, 1781. L. 237. Wife, Sarah; sons, Nicholas, Solomon and William; dau., Ann. Exc. wife, Sarah Wood, John Carnan.

John Bayley. Appo Hd. Jan. 10, 1781. Feb. 14, 1781. L. 238. Wife, Frances; sons, Thomas, James, John, Valentine, Robert, Major, and Francis; daughters, Esther, Ann, and Elizabeth. Exc. wife, Frances; son, Thomas.

Mary Williams. Appo. Hd. Oct. 13, 1779. Feb. 24, 1781. L. 239. Daughters, Rachel and Mary; sons, Cornelius and Elijah. Exc. John Crawford. Renunciation of right to adm. this estate of Rachel Vansant, eldest dau. of testator in favor of her brother-in-law, Joseph Wood.

Francis Alexander. Yeoman. Jan. 18, 1781. Apr. 9, 1781. L. 229.

Wife, Elinor; daughters, Fanny, Mary and Susanna; sons, William, Isaac, Benjamin, and Jesse. Exc. Benjamin Alexander; son-in-law, John Aicken.

William Grimes. W. Clay Crk. Hd. Apr. 14, 1781. Apr. 26, 1781. L. 240. Wife, Jean; son, William Grimes, living in Ireland. Exc. James Glasgow.

Flora Witherspoon. St. Geo. Hd. Oct. 20, 1772. May 22, 1781. L. 244. Three granddaughters, Hester Moore, Mary Moore and Susannah Moore, daughters of James Moore; sons, John and Thomas. Exc. Isaac Moody, Andrew Bryan.

Barbara Fulton. May 5, 1781. May 25, 1781. L. 245. Sons, James and John (dec'd); daughters, Mary, and Margaret; Samuel, son of Margaret. Exc. son, James; son-in-law, Samuel Kirkpatrick.

Jesse Bowen. Pen. Hd. May 30, 1780. June 5, 1781. L. 197. Wife, Susannah; dau., Jane; son, Oswell. Exc. William Whan.

Abraham Short. N. C. Hd. Feb. 19, 1781. July 26, 1781. L. 246. Wife, Preacilla; son, Abraham; daughters, Rachel Wattson, Preacilla ——; granddau., Mary Short, dau., of son, John; grandsons, Thomas Short, and John Welsh, son of dau., Preacilla. Exc. son, Abraham.

John Dodds. Town of Newark. July 13, 1781. Aug. 6, 1781. L. 247. Sister, Ann Dodds, alias Ann Rock; nephew, James Dodds, son of brother, Samuel. Exc. cousin, James Anderson; brother-in-law, Oliver Rock.

Eleanor Cannon, Widow of Isaac Cannon. Red Lion Hd. Jan. 7, 1776. Aug. 28, 1781. L. 248. Son, Isaac; his son, Jacob Cannon; dau., Hester Deveau and her husband, Frederic Deveau; dau., Eleanor Baily; granddaughters, Rachel Armstrong, Eleanor Armstrong, Eleanor Deveau, now Eleanor Hill, Mary Deveau, and Mary Scott; grandson, Isaac Deveau. Exc. son, Isaac Cannon; grandson, Jacon Cannon.

Isaac Whitelock. Brewer. Bor. of Wil. 5m. 1, 1779. Sept. 9, 1781. L. 223. Wife, Sarah; sons, Daniel and Charles; daughters, Mary Dawes and Martha Whitelock; Rumford Dawes; former wife; children of son, Charles; children of son, Daniel. Exc. Daniel Byrnes, Abraham Gibbons and Joseph West, and son-in-law, Rumford Dawes, and wife, Sarah Whitelock. Appraisers, John Ferris, Ziba Ferris, John Pemberton, Caleb Seal and John Hayes.

Gabriel Springer. Hatter. Wil. July 31, 1781. Sept. 19, 1781. L. 250. Wife, ——; step-dau., Catharine Parlin. Brothers and Sisters; sister-in-law, Rebaccah Bonzell, widow; nephew, Charles Springer, son of brother Charles Springer; nephew, Gabriel Springer, son of brother Edward Springer; Levi Springer, son of Charles, who is son of uncle, Joseph Springer. Exc. wife, ——; friend, Joseph Stidham.

Isaac Chandler. Chris. Hd. 10m. 14, 1781. Nov. 3, 1781. L. 254. Son, Caleb, dec'd.; sons, Abraham and Isaac; four daughters,

Ann, Ruth, Mary and Rachel; wife, ——; Samuel Nichols, Isaac Hollingsworth. Exc. daughters, Ann and Ruth.

James James. St. Geo. Hd. July 26, 1779. Dec. 17, 1781. L. 255. Wife, Mary; five children, viz: William, John, James, Elisha and Mary. Exc. wife, Mary James; William Akin (Eakin).

Jacob Belew. Red Lion Hd. Mar. 11, 1780. Dec. 21, 1781. L. 253. Wife, Sarah; son, Thomas; daughters, Sarah, Fanny Pryer and Elizabeth; Thomas Reece, widow Kilpatrick, John Pryer. Exc. wife, Sarah Belew, John Hyet (Hyatt).

William McKean. St. Geo. Hd. —— Jan. 2, 1782. L. 258. Son, Thomas B. McKean; dau., Lettitia McKean; "my widow;" brother, Thomas McKean, daughter-in-law ———. Exc. Mary McKean and John Thompson.

Joseph Enos. Husbandman. Oct. 14, 1776. Jan. 8, 1782. L. 259. Wife Jane; Susannah Stewart; sons, Joseph, John, James and Stephen; daughters, Mary, Jane and Susannah Enos. Exc. wife, Jane Enos; sons, John and Joseph; John Thompson, Esq.

Thomas Collins. Farmer. N. C. Hd. Jan. 12, 1782. Feb. 5, 1782. L. 262. Five grandchildren, to wit, Thomas, George, John and Feamer Dayken, Mary, and Cathran Allfree. Exc. wife, Cathran; son, John Collins.

Mary Vanbebber. Widow. July 20, 1774. Feb. 13, 1782. L. 263 and 359. Granddaughters, Mary Clay, Ann Clay, Elizabeth Clay, Sarah Clay; children of grandson, Curtis Clay, viz: Joseph Clay, Robert Clay, Curtis Clay. Seven grandsons, Curtis Clay, Robert Clay, John Clay, Thomas Clay, Slater Clay, William Clay and George Clay. Exc. dau., Ann Clay.

Caleb Way. Bor. of Wil. ———. Feb. 15, 1782. L. 265. Wife, Elizabeth; son, Caleb; daughters, Hannah Pierce, Sarah Wilson, Mary Hanson; grandson, John Pierce. Exc. son, Caleb Way, Benjamin Mendinhall, Caleb Sheward.

John Godlif. Chris. Hd. 10m. 26, 1780. Feb. 18, 1782. L. 267. John and Jonathan Greave, sons of Samuel Greave; Hermon Gregg and John Gregg, sons of Hermon Gregg, dec'd. Exc. John Garrett.

Mary Martin. Widow of William. Appo. Hd. July 17, 1781. Mar. 1, 1782. L. 269. Son, John Guton Moore; brothers, Thomas and Isaac Bartlett; sister, Elizabeth Bartlett; sister-in-law, Margrit Wilson. Exc. Richard Cantwell, Jo. Clever.

John Veal (Nunc.). Yeoman. Mill Crk. Hd. Jan. 21, 1782. Mar. 19, 1782. L. 268. Dau., Edith and dau., who now resides in Jersey. Attested by Sarah McNeil and Margaret McNeil.

Joseph Pierce. B'wine Hd. Feb. 1, 1782. Mar. 25, 1782. L. 357. Wife, Beaula; sons, Henry, John, Timothy, Joseph, Levi and Richard. Exc. sons, Joseph and Richard.

John Hackett. Appo. Hd. Mar. 1, 1782. Apr. 4, 1782. L. 270. Son, Joseph; daughters, Elizabeth Griffin, Catharine Wright and Ann

Hackett; daughters, Sarah and Mary's children; wife, Ann. Exc. son, Joseph.

John Cole. Sept. 9, 1780. Apr. 17, 1782. Misc. 66. Six children, Lambert. Peregrine, Archibald, Isaac, Peter and dau., Mary Reynolds; grandsons, John Reynolds, William Cole, and Archibald Cole. Exc. son, Isaac Cole.

William Tate. Yeoman. Mill Crk. Hd. Apr. 3, 1782. Apr. 27, 1782. L. 274. Wife, Ann; daughters, Hannah (wife of Solomon Trap); Ruth, wife of Philip Dixson; Martha, wife of Jesse Chandler and Mary Tate; sons, William and Levi. Exc. sons of wife, Ann; Thomas and Isaac Dixon.

George Rice. Mar. 25, 1782. May 10, 1782. L. 277. Wife ——; five children, William Rice, Mary Linton, Thomas Rice, Rebecca Rice and Milly Rice. Exc. wife, Sarah Rice; son, William Rice.

John Paulson. Merchant Taylor. Bor. of Wil. Feb. 28, 1782. May 29, 1782. L. 278. Wife, Elenor; daughters, Mary, Elizabeth and Elenor. Exc. brother, Peter Paulson, Robert Armstrong; wife, Elenor.

Thomas Chandler. Chris. Hd. ——, 1780. June 4, 1782. L. 286. Wife ——; sons, Thomas and Jesse Chandler; father, Swithin Chandler, dec'd.; brother, Swithin Chandler and Ann, his wife; cousin, Thomas Chandler; dau., Dinah Gregg and her husband; granddau., Elizabeth Hollingsworth. Exc. sons, Thomas and Jesse.

John Zebley. B'wine Hd. May 22, 1782. June 8, 1782. L. 354. daughters, Rachell, Ann and Dorothy; sons, John, Owen, James and Willliam. Exc. sons, James and John Zebley.

Samuel Lewis. Cordwainer. Bor. of Wil. May 4, 1782. July 8, 1782. L. 292. Sons, Samuel, William, Pierce and Jesse; dau., Joanna, wife of Jonathon Kirk, Jr.; daughters, Ann and Patience. Exc. dau., Ann Lewis.

Hugh Hutchinson. Yeoman. Appo. Hd. Apr. 6, 1780. Aug. 23, 1782. L. 291. Wife, Mary; daughters, Mary Weldon, Martha Thomas, Ann Hutchinson; son, John. Exc. wife, Mary; son, John.

William Bird. Feb. 19, 1780. Sept. 6, 1782. L. 218. Wife, Ann; sons, Thomas and William Bird; daughters, Susanna and Mary Bird; Abraham Anderson, James Benjamin Brinker, David Clement. Exc. wife, Ann Bird; Cornelius Armstrong.

John Hambilton. Yeoman. N. C. Hd. Sept. 13, 1782. Oct. 1, 1782. L. 296. Daughters, Martha, Mary and Susanna Hambilton; sons, James, Robart, David and Charles Hambilton; grandson, John Hambilton, son of Robart and Ann Hambilton. Exc. son, Robart; Thomas Raukin.

Thomas Drugan. (Nunc.) Sept. 3, 1782. Oct. 1, 1782. L. 333. Relation, Hugh Wood; nephew, Patrick Drugan. Attested by Daniel Charles Heath.

James Cochran. St. Geo. Hd. Apr. 24, 1782. Nov. 4, 1782. L. 302. Sons, Moses and John; daughters, Elizabeth, Mary and Rebeccah; grandson, Joseph, son of son John. Exc. sons, Moses and John.

Richard Carson. Cordwainer. Wil. 4m. 7, 1781. Dec. 4, 1782. L. 298. Wife, ——; daughters, Hannah, Jane (her children), Mariam, Dinah and Phoebe, and her husband, Richard Dickinson; John Yarnall, Nathan Wood, Caleb Seal, Joseph West, Edward Hewes. Exc. wife, ——.

Jonathan Rumford. Shopkeeper. Wil. Jan. 24, 1772. Dec. 24, 1782. L. 307. Wife, ——; son and daughter, William and Sarah Shipley; son, Jonathon Rumford; sister, Miriam Dawes. Exc. son, Jonathan.

William Clark. N. C. Hd. Feb. 13, 1783. Feb. 25, 1783. L. 311. Sister, Margaret; Allice, Ann and Elizabeth Clark, daughters of brother, John Clark, dec'd.; Richard, William and John Clark, sons of brother, John Clark, dec'd. Exc. brother-in-law, William Armor.

Jean Veal. Widow. St. Geo. Hd. Apr. 10, 1780. Mar. 10, 1783. L. 318. Sons, Thomas and Isaac Veal; Thomas Culbertson, oldest son of dau., Jean; daughters, Jean Culbertson and Margaret Veal. Letters adm. to sons, Thomas and Isaac.

Thomas Wilson. Chris. Hd. 2m. 21, 1783. Mar. 11, 1783. L. 314. Children, William, Richard, Hannah, Durnal, Esther, George and Thomas. Exc. William Wilson, Thomas Wilson.

Isabella Hutchinson. Widdow. Pen. Hd. Feb. 3, 1783. Mar. 20, 1783. L. 310. Daughters, Ann and Isabel; grandson, John Campbel; granddaughters, Isabel and Eliner Coldbraith. Exc. William Robinson or Andrew Muldroch.

Mary Boyce. Mill Crk. Hd. 1m. 1, 1783. Mar. 22, 1783. L. 316. Widdow of Robert; daughters, Martha and Isabel; sister-in-law, Elizabeth Hobson, wife of Joseph; sons, Francis, Robert, John and Richard Boyce. Exc. son, Francis.

John Hanson. N. C. Hd. Mar. 21, 1783. Apr. 2, 1783. L. 320. Cousin, Elinor Rankin, relict of Capt. Rankin. Exc. Dr. Nathaniel Silsbee.

William Fields. Yeoman. Appo. Hd. Apr. 6, 1783. Apr. 29, 1783. L. 321. Sons, Allen, William, John, Benjamin and Abraham; wife, Sarah; son-in-law, Solomon Attkinson; brother, Abraham Fields. Exc. wife, Sarah; son, Allen.

George Taylor. Waterman. Wil. Jan. 9, 1783. May 23, 1783. L. 356. Wife, Mary; Samuel Shipley, John Jones and Benjamin Canby. Exc. wife, Mary.

Moses Grubb. Yeoman. Bor. of Wil. Apr. 6, 1783. June 2, 1783.

L. 328. Father, William Grubb, dec'd; wife, ———; son, Thomas; dau., Lydia; brothers, Aaron and John Grubb; Deborah Craig, Lydia Gibson. Exc. wife, ———.

Ruth Gest. Bor. of Wil. 4m. 11, 1783. June 2, 1783. L. 363. James Dilworth, son of sister Mary; sister, Jane Gest; brother, Joseph Gest; Daniel Temple, son of Joseph Temple. Exc. uncle, Isaac Mendenhall.

James Thompson. Mill Crk. Hd. Oct. 4, 1779. June 12, 1783. L. 324. Eight children, Greas Pennack, Daniel, James and Joseph Thompson, Sarah and Emmey Chambers, Ann Pennack and Elizabeth Thompson. Exc. son, Daniel Thompson; son-in-law, Joseph Chambers.

John Griffith. Pen. Hd. Aug. 10, 1774. June 29, 1783. L. 289. Wife, Amy; two daughters, Susanna and Rachel; two grandsons, John Williams and David John. Exc. son, David Griffith.

Joseph Laughran. Yeoman. Appo. Hd. Apr. 1, 1778. July 12, 1783. L. 330. Children of William Finney, viz: Archibald Finney, Mary Finney and Catharine Clark; brother, James's children, viz: Rebecca, Elizabeth, John and two younger sisters; Sarah Masin, Solomon Semeter; sister, Catharine Laughran. Exc. William Allfree, Jacob Caulk and Arthur Moore.

Alexander Eakin. Yeoman. Aug. 14, 1781. Aug. 1, 1783. L. 334. Wife, Elenor; sons, Robert, William and Samuel; grandsons, William Eakin, son of son William; James Eakin, and Alexander, sons of son Samuel; James Cooper, son of dau. Jean Cooper; youngest children of dau. Mary, dec'd; Margaret Adair, youngest dau. of brother Robert; two youngest children of Samuel Allen; two children of John Allen, dec'd. Exc. sons, Robert, William and Samuel.

James Eves. Yeoman. N. C. Hd. Dec. 29, 1777. Aug. 16, 1783. L. 343. Wife, ———; sons, James, Samuel and Abraham; brother, John; dau., Jane, her husband, Moses Girlin; dau., Barbary; son-in-law, Peter Jetton. Exc. son, Samuel Eves.

Peter Vandever. B'wine Hd. Mar. 24, 1783. Aug. 21, 1783. L. 350. Wife, ———; daughters, Elizabeth, Sarah, Mary and Rebeckah; son-in-law, Samuel Milner and Catharine, his wife; son-in-law, David Buxon and Margaret his wife; dau., Rachel, a cripple; children of son Andrew, dec'd. Exc. son, John.

Samuel Eakin. Minister. Aug. 15, 1783. Sept. 10, 1783. L. 366. Wife, Mary; son, Samuel Hunter; his grandfather, Samuel Purviance; son, Alexander Fearis; his grandfather, Alexander Eakin; son, James; daughters, Mary and Susannah. Exc. wife, Mary; brother, Isaac Hazlehurst.

William Elliott. B'wine Hd. Apr. 20, 1778. Sept. 12, 1783. L. 376. Sons, William, Mark, Benjamin; granddau., Mary, dau. of dec'd. son, Joseph; grandson, Edward, son of dec'd. son, John; children of dau., Elinor; children of dau., Jane Huston; granddaughters, Isabella and Elizabeth Clendenin; John Stapler. Exc. sons, William, Mark and Benjamin.

Neill Dougherty. Cordwainer. Bor. of Wil. Sept. 9, 1783. Sept. 15, 1783. L. 368. Housekeeper, Ann McConnell; children by her, Sarah, Mary and John. Exc. Thomas Kean.

Robert Warnock. Aug. 6, 1783. Sept. 24, 1783. L. 370. Children, viz: James, William, Nelly, David and Margaret Moore; grandson, John Low; son-in-law, Nicholas Moore. Exc. Michael Moore and William Warnock.

Cornelius Batchelor. Appo. Hd. Apr. 13, 1779. Oct. 2, 1783. L. 372. Wife, Elizabeth. Exc. wife, Elizabeth Batchelor.

Samuel Clemments. St. Geo. Hd. Sept. 6, 1783. Oct. 17, 1783. L. 381. Wife, Elizabeth; half brother, Reas Nanny; half sisters, Hannah Nanny and Elizabeth Nanny. Exc. wife, Elizabeth; James Miles.

Sarah Belew. Red Lion Hd. June 7, 1783. Oct. 28, 1783. L. 383. Son, Thomas; daughters, Sarah Belew and Elizabeth Gist. Exc. Thomas Couch, Jr.

Allexander Steel. W. Clay Crk. Hd. Aug. 9, 1783. Oct. 31, 1783. L. 404. Two sons, Allen and James; dau., Ruth Buller. Exc. George Gilespie, Jr., son, Allen.

Alexander Elliot. Farmer. Thorow Fare Neck. Sept. 22, 1783. Nov. 11, 1783. L. 385. Wife, Agnes; daughters, Martha Galloway, Sarah Elliot, Agnes Stevenson, Catharine Elkinson and Nancy Elliot; son, James. Exc. Agnes Elliot and John Galloway.

William Williams. Pen. Hd. Mar. 14, 1783. Nov. 15, 1783. L. 387. Wife, Mary; son, Rodger; daughters, Mary Williams, Margret Williams and Isabel Williams; Peter Williams. Exc. son, Rodger Williams.

Evan Rice. Mill Creek Hd. Oct. 15, 1783. Nov. 29, 1783. L. 405. Mother, Elizabeth Rice; father, Thomas Rice, dec'd.; uncle, Jeremia Ball, dec'd.; wife, Elizabeth; her father, Francis Graham, dec'd.; dau., Mary Rice; six sons, Thomas, Evan, William, Washington, Solomon and John. Exc. wife, Elizabeth; brother, Jeremiah Rice.

Catherine Collins. Widow of Thomas Collins. Appo. Hd. Jan. 30, 1782. Dec. 4, 1783. L. 389. Six grandchildren, Thomas, George, Tamer and John Dayken; Mary and Cathren Allfree. "Son George now with the Brittons." Exc. son, John Collins.

Joseph Wheldin. Oct. 27, 1781. Dec. 8, 1783. L. 373. Wife, Sarah; sons, Joseph, Benjamin and Josiah; daughters, Elizabeth and Elida. Exc. wife, Sarah.

Mary Feares. Pen. Hd. Nov. 20, 1781. Dec. 9, 1783. L. 392. Children of dau., Elizabeth Smith, dec'd., viz: John, Robert and William Smith; children of dau., Jean McWhorter, dec'd., viz: Hugh and John McWhorter; children of dau., Mary Henderson,

Mathew, Mary, John, Ebenezer, Elener, Robert and Ann Henderson; children of dau., Ann, dec'd., William, John, James and Elisha James; son-in-law, Rev. Mathew Henderson. Exc. Andrew Muldroh.

Eli Baldwin. B'wine Hd. Dec. 6, 1783. Dec. 27, 1783. L. 395. Wife, Elizabeth; sons, Eli and Samuel; daughters, Margaret, Mary and Elizabeth; William Tallay. Exc. wife, Elizabeth; Samuel Tallay and Henry Little.

William Colesbury. Town of N. C. Nov. 29, 1783. Dec. 29, 1783. L. 397. Brother, Henry Colesbury; brother Swen's two daughters, Sarah and Elizabeth Colesbury; brother Jacob's son, Henry Colesbury; sister Susannah Kirk's son, William; nephew, Andrew Gravenrait Colesbury; sisters, Rachel Smith and Martha Nelson. Exc. brother, Jacob.

John Hook. St. Geo. Hd. Dec. 14, 1783. Jan. 30, 1784. L. 414. Wife, Jean; children, Agnes Hook and Henry Hook. Exc. wife, Jean.

James Boulden, Sr. Pen. Hd. Jan. 4, 1783. Feb. 17, 1784. M. 7. Wife, Elizabeth Boulden; sons, James, Thomas, Nathan and Elisha Boulden; John and Hannah Faries; Robert Lowrey; Sarah Bouldon, widow of son, Elijah; children of son Jesse, dec'd.; children of dau., Augustina; children of son, Elijah, dec'd.; dau., Rachel. Exc. son, James Boulden.

George Smith. N. C. Hd. Jan. 17, 1784. Mar. 1, 1784. M. 12. Sisters, Mary Maxwell, Elizabeth Tobin, Rachel Tobin, Ruth Tobin and Sarah Tobin; Mrs. Elinear Rankin, friend; John Tobin. Exc. Father-in-law, Thomas Tobin.

Michael King. N. C. Hd. Sept. 27, 1783. Mar. 16, 1784. L. 422. Wife, Mary; daughters, Elizabeth Morton and Catharine Vansant; sons, Andrew, David, Michael and George King. Exc. son, George.

Benjamin Boddy. Mar. 23, 1782. Mar. 24, 1784. L. 415. Daughters, Martha ——, Milciah Ann Vandyke and Mary Dorrel; grandsons, Benjamin Mercer, Jeremiah Mercer and Benjamin Dorrel; granddau., Keziah Boddy. Exc. dau., Mary Dorrel.

Alexander Porter, Esq. N. C. Hd. Mar. 22, 1784. Apr. 7, 1784. L. 441. Sons, Alexander and Jonas; dau., Mary Porter; granddau., Eleanor Porter Barclay. Exc. son, Alexander Porter.

Hugh Muldroh. Pen. Hd. Sept. 20, 1783. Apr. 9, 1784. L. 437. Sons, David and Andrew; daughters, Mary Francis and Agnes Robinson; grandchildren, Sarah, David and Mary Henery and Jean and John Muldroh. Exc. sons, David and Andrew.

Elizabeth Ann Herbert. Mar. 8, 1784. Apr. 12, 1784. L. 444. Sons, Barnet, Paul, Isaac and Samuel Vanhorn; daughters, Catherine Herbert and Rachel Herbert; cousin, Mary Vansant. Exc. ——.

John Verner. St. Geo. Hd. Dec. 14, 1783. Apr. 16, 1784. M. 2. Son,

Jacob; daughter, Sarah; wife, Rachel. Exc. wife, Rachel; brother-in-law, John Miller.

William McKinney. Weaver. W. Clay Crk. Hd. Apr. 10, 1784. Apr. 20, 1784. L. 412. Wife, ———; dau., Jane. Exc. James Caldwell.

David Ferris. Yeoman. Bor. of Wil. 5m. 20, 1779. May 7, 1784. L. 424. Wife, ———; two daughters, ———; niece, Rachel Fleaharty; son, Benjamin; daughters, Deborah ———, Sarah Andrews, widow of John Andrews, and Mary, wife of William Lightfoot; grandsons, Isaac and Samuel Andrews; Vincent Bonsall, Nicholas Robinson, Joseph West, John Yarnall and Nathan Wood. Exc. nephews, John and Ziba Ferris.

Hughey Mawhorter. Mill Crk. Hd. Sept. 12, 1783. May 14, 1784. L. 420. Sons, John, Robert, Alexander Mawhorter; daughters, Jannet Crage, Margaret Noble and Sarah Young; grandsons, Alexander and Hughey Young, John Mawhorter, Isaac and Hughey Woods; granddau., Agnes Rankin; sons-in-law, John Woods and Joseph Rankin. Exc. son-in-law, John Woods; grandson, John Mawhorter.

Ann Gozlin. St. Geo. Hd. Mar. 6, 1784. May 22, 1784. L. 418. Son, Jacob Skeer; three youngest children, Mary, James and Ann Gozlin. Exc. son, Jacob Skeer.

Breata Vandever. Widow of Peter Vandever, Sr. B'wine Hd. June 21, 1783. May 26, 1784. L. 434. Four daus., Rachel, Sarah, Mary and Rebecca; Thomas Beeson, Joseph Tatnall, Joseph Stedham. Exc. son-in-law, Samuel Milner.

John Reynolds. Farmer. May 5, 1784. June 1, 1784. L. 432. Wife, Mary; children, George, Benjamin, Mary, Margaret, James and Temperance Reynolds. Exc. wife, Mary.

Isaac Gibbs. May 27, 1784. July 26, 1784. M. 14. Wife, Ingeborg; grandnephews, Isaac and Benjamin Gibbs, sons of nephew, Benjamin Gibbs of Phila.; two nephews, James Nowland and Gibbs Cook; two nieces, Hester Cook and Mary Rogers; sister-in-law, Ann Gibbs; three daughters of nephew, Benjamin Gibbs. Exc. wife, Ingeborg.

James Simpson. Farmer. Newark. Apr. 20, 1784. Aug. 5, 1784. M. 18. Children, John, William, James, Ann, Jean, Hannah, Benjamin and Margaret. Exc. son, William, William Armstrong and Robert Wallace.

John Steel. Mar. 3, 1784. Sept. 14, 1784. M. 23. Wife, ———; children, Allen, John, Mary, Sarah, James and Matthew; " dau.-in-law, relique of my son Joseph." Exc. wife, ———; son, Allen.

Stephen McWilliam. Town of N. C. July 15, 1784. Sept. 18, 1784. M. 25. Elizabeth Spencer, dau. of cousin, William Spencer. Exc. brother, Richard McWilliam.

Thomas McKim. B'wine Hd. Oct. 7, 1782. Sept. 22, 1784. M. 20.

Wife, Agnes; five children, viz: Jean, John, Robert, Alexander and Elizabeth. Exc. sons, Robert and Alexander.

Mary Anderson. Millford Hd. Prov. of Maryland. Sept. 18, 1784. Oct. 8, 1784. M. 27. Dau., Fanny Thomas Anderson; mother, Mary Alexander. Exc. uncle, Starret Gray.

Joseph Jemison. Tayler. Pen. Hd. Sept. 15, 1784. Oct. 16, 1784. M. 29. "Father, Joseph Jemison and my mother, now in Ireland"; brother Allexander's son, Lewes Jemison; brother John Jemison's sons, John and Allexander, and dau., Sarah; Hugh Jeeson, Nancy Lachlin, Richard Johnston. Exc. brothers, John and Allexander.

Adam Buckley. B'wine Hd. Sept. 24, 1760. ———, 1784. M. 33. Wife, Ann; son, John; dau., Elizabeth Williamson; grandson, Adam Williamson; granddau., Ann Price; Adam Clayton; William Grubb, son of John Grubb, dec'd. Exc. son, John Buckley; son-in-law, John Williamson.

Thomas Hockley. Merchant. Phila. Mar. 18, 1776. Nov. 8, 1784. M. 37. Wife, Eleanor; four children, Elizabeth, Thomas, Eleanor and John. Exc. Rev. Jacob Duche; James Reynolds of Phila., gilder and painter; Samuel Smith, mariner; and William Garrigues, carpenter.

Elizabeth Peterson. N. C. Hd. Oct. 16, 1784. Nov. 8, 1784. M. 40. Granddau., Nancy Yanty; great-granddau., Elizabeth Yanty. Exc. nephew, James Eves.

Alexander Moore. Pen. Hd. Oct. 18, 1784. Nov. 11, 1784. M. 41. Wife, Jemima; sons, Jesse, Alexander, Robert and Thomas Moore; daughters, Elizabeth and Margaret Moore. Exc. Jemima Moore.

Joshua Donoho. Cecil Co., Md. Feb. 1, 1773. Nov. 17, 1784. M. 43. Wife, Cornelia. Exc. Cornelia Donoho.

George Robinson. Farmer. B'wine Hd. Dec. 12, 1784. Dec. 23, 1784. M. 47. Wife, ———; four sons, George, John, Joseph and Salkield; daughters, Mary, Margaret and Elizabeth. Exc. wife, Elizabeth; kinsman, Andrew Gibson.

Nathaniel Hanson. Red Lion Hd. Nov. 26, 1782. Jan. 8, 1785. M. 71. Wife, Catharine; brother, John Hanson. Exc. sister, Mary Woods; Robert Porter.

Elizabeth Harvey. N. C. Hd. ———, 1784. Jan. 10, 1785. M. 73. Sons, Alexander and Isaac; daughters, Ann Moulton and Elizabeth Harvey. Exc. brother, Henry Colesberry.

Fanny Hecket. Town of N. C. ———. Feb. 2, 1785. M. 77. "Mary Davis of Phila., formely my servant"; James Millegan and Elizabeth, his wife; James Kinier. Exc. Mary McGrandy.

Thomas Cooch, Jr. N. C. Hd. Dec. 28, 1784. Feb. 3, 1785. M. 78. Wife, Sarah; sons, Thomas, Francis and William; dau., Elizabeth Maxwell. Exc. John Simon and William McMeehen.

John Underwood. Farmer. Pen. Hd. Jan. 9, 1785. Feb. 4, 1785. M. 79. Wife, ————; daughters, Jean, Sarah, Mary and Margaret; sons, John and Joseph; brother, Solomon. Exc. son, John Underwood; Andrew Muldroh.

William Thompson. Yeoman. Pen. Hd. Dec. 18, 1784. Feb. 8, 1785. M. 86. Wife, Jane; son, James; daughters, Ann and Elizabeth Thompson. Exc. wife, Jane; son, James; Isaac Lewes.

Valentine Dushane. Red Lion Hd. Jan. 31, 1785. Feb. 16, 1785. M. 80. Sister, Susanna, married to Alexander McGaughey; half sister, Ann, married to John Wiles; half sister, Esther, married to Daniel Blaney. Exc. brother, Cornelius Dushane.

Jean Gillespie. Village of Newark. Jan. 13, 1783. Feb. 22, 1785. M. 83. Niece, Margary Evans; niece, Margery Platt's three children, viz: Jean, Polly and James. Exc. Dr. Samuel Platt, niece, Margery Platt; Alexander McBeath, Robert Wallace.

Ann Montgomery. Mill Creek Hd. Mar. 15, 1783. Feb. 23, 1785. M. 87. Two daughters, Elizabeth and Mary. Exc. son-in-law, Henry Kitchen.

Francis Way. Maulter. Bor. of Wil. 3m. 10, 1784. Mar. 2, 1785. M. 82. Wife, Mary; sons, Joshua and Francis; daughters, Mary Niles and Sarah Rumford. Exc. wife, Mary; son, Francis.

Jacob Caulk. Feb. 1, 1785. Mar. 24, 1785. M. 88. Wife, Rachel; eight children, Elizabeth, Temperance, Polly, Sarah, Jacob, James, Rachel and William; Dr. Campbell St. Clair; Mr. Edward Tilghman. Exc. wife, Rachel; son-in-law, Jacob Gibson.

Thomas Fossitt. (Nunc.) N. C. Hd. Mar. 10, 1785. Mar. 29, 1785. M. 180. Hannah Mullan, attested by Elizabeth Jacquet and Catharine Bayley. Letters of adm. to John Jacquet.

Elizabeth Bolden. Pen. Hd. Jan. 8, 1785. Apr. 4, 1785. M. 91. Dau., Rachel; sons, Nathan, Elisha, Thomas and James; son-in-law, Richard Bolden; grandson, Nathan; grandchildren, Benjamin and Abigail, children of son, Thomas; children of son, Jesse; children of son, Elijah, dec'd.; children of dau., Augustine, dec'd. Exc. son, James Bolden.

John Adair. Blacksmith. Pen. Hd. Jan. 15, 1785. Apr. 5, 1785. M. 94. Wife, Margaret; sons, John and Joseph; daughters, Agnes Callwell, Mary Adair and Lydia Adair. Exc. wife, Margaret; Isaac Lewis.

Sarah Underwood. Pen. Hd. Mar. 6, 1785. Apr. 5, 1785. M. 96. Sons, Soloman, Nathan, Joseph and Samuel. Exc. dau., Elizabeth and Isaac Alexander.

Ann Armstrong, relict of Archibald Armstrong. Mar. 12, 1779. Apr. 9, 1785. M. 98. Sons, William and John; dau.-in-law, Ann Armstrong. Exc. William Armstrong.

Henry Howell. Pen. Hd. Mar. 21, 1785. Apr. 16, 1785. M. 89.

Grandfather, Joseph Howell, dec'd.; step-grandmother, ———.
Exc. friends, Enoch Jones and John James.

William Clark. Miller. Pen. Hd. Apr. 1, 1783. Apr. 18, 1785. M.
99. Wife, Ann; daughters, Ann and Margaret; grandson, William Clark Frazier; sisters, Ann and Sarah Clark of Ireland;
brother, Joseph Clark; brother-in-law, William Stewart. Exc.
William Clark of Duck Creek, William King of Phila., John King
of Middletown.

Robert McMurphy. Yeoman. St. Geo. Hd. Mar. 13, 1777. Apr. 21,
1785. M. 102. Wife, Jennet; sons, Alexander and Robert; three
grandchildren, Andrew, John and Susannah McMurphy; brother
and two sisters now residing in Ireland; sister, Mary Brading,
her son, Robert Brading; dau.-in-law, Mary McMurphy, widow;
brother John; sisters, Jean and Margaret; Charles and Nathaniel
Bryan. Exc. wife, Jennet; son, Alexander, and George Read.

Adam Nuttall. St. Geo. Village. Feb. 9, 1785. Apr. 23, 1785. M.
107. Wife, Margaret; dau., Margaret; brothers and sisters in
England. Exc. wife, Margaret; John Thompson.

Elizabeth Kirkpatrick. Widow. Red Lion Hd. Apr. 11, 1785. May
2, 1785. M. 109. Daughters, Mary Garrison, Elizabeth McGinnis and Sarah Kirkpatrick; son, Benjamin Elder; granddaughters, Catharine and Elizabeth Laforge; Margaret Harmon. Exc.
John Clarke.

Sarah Scull. Single woman, late of Phila., now of Bor. of Wil. July
1, 1783. May 5. 1785. M. 111. Abigail Scull, dau. of brother,
John Scull; Rebecca Scull, dau. of brother, William Scull; Rebecca Scull, dau. of brother, Joseph Scull; sister, Abigail Angier,
wife of Thomas Angier; children of Joel Lane and sister Esther,
viz: Mary, Jesse, Rebecca, Nathan and William. Exc. Edward
FitzRandolph and Thomas Angier.

Ann Clark. Pen. Hd. Apr. 21, 1785. May 18, 1785. M. 121. Stepmother, ———; sister, Margaret; uncle, Joseph Clark; children
of uncle, William Stewart; Margaret Clark, dau. of cousin, William Clark of Duck Creek; Kezia Lamson, Mary Stewart, Elizabeth Stewart, Rebecca Clark, dau. of Alexander Clark, dec'd.;
nephew, William Clark Frazier. Exc. William Clark of Duck
Creek.

Thomas Ogle. Mar. 10, 1785. May 30, 1785. M. 119. Daughters,
Mary, Judith and Elizabeth; father, Thomas Ogle, dec'd. Exc.
Isaac Lewis, Jehu Davis.

Samuel Patterson, Esq. W. Clay Crk. Hd. May 12, 1785. May 29,
1785. M. 114. Father, William Patterson; brothers, John (now
of Damarora, merchant), William (physician), Benjamin and
Joseph; sisters, Rebecca and Deborth Patterson, Jane Rees and
Mary Gardner; daughters of sister, Jane Rees, to wit: Mary, wife
of James Black, Esq., Catharine Rees, Martha Rees and Elizabeth Rees; children of sister, Mary Gardner, to wit: Mary Gard-

ner, Hester Gardner, Elenor Gardner (who is intermarried with a certain Gustavus Brown), Jane Gardner, William Gardner and Elizabeth Gardner; cousin, Catharine Morgan; housekeeper, Jane Moran; cousin, Abiah McElray. Exc. James Black, Esq., Solomon Maxwell and William McClay.

John See. St. Geo. Hd. Jan. 17, 1781. June 6, 1785. M. 123. Sons, Peter and John; daughters, Sarah, Hannah, Christian and Hester. Exc. dau., Christian and Hester.

Mathias Morton. Farmer. May 18, 1785. June 6, 1785. M. 125. Wife, Abigail, her mother, Mary Treahorn; sons, Ebenezer, Andrew, David, John, Morton, Henery, Adam, Matthias and George; daughters, Elizabeth, Rebeckah, Ann, Christiana and Sarah. Exc. Henery Colesbury, Andrew Morton.

Sarah Brooks. Widow. B'wine Hd. ·Feb. 8, 1785. July 7, 1785. M. 130. Richard Kellam; nephew, Thomas Cartmell, son of brother, William Cartmell; George Cartmell, son of nephew, Thomas Cartmell; Dean Simmons; Thomas and Henery Webster; Thomas Cartmell, Jr., son of Thomas Cartmell, Sr.; John Bird; Charles Robinson; William Cartmell, son of Thomas Cartmell, Jr.; Job Harvey; niece, Ann Shearer, widow; Emmanuel Grubb; Sarah and Hannah Cartmell, daughters of Thomas Cartmell, Sr.; sister, Hannah Kellam; Sarah, Elizabeth and Isaac, children of Rachel and Jacob (son of James Stevenson). Exc. Thomas Babb (neighbor).

Samuel McAntier. W. Clay Crk. Hd. Jan. 3, 1776. Aug. 1, 1785. M. 133. Brother, Alexander McAntier; children of sister, Eleanor Robinson and husband, John Robinson, viz; Jean McColy, Mary Spers, Margaret Robinson and Samuel Robinson; sister Elizabeth Allen's children; brother Robert McAntier's dau., Mary and son, John; cousin, Mary McAntier. Exc. three brothers, Andrew, William and Robert.

Mary Slayter. Widow. Town of N. C. Sept. 6, 1784. Aug. 2, 1785. M. 134. Dau., Martha Copner; children of brother, John Robinson, viz: William and Mary Robinson. Exc. dau., Martha; John Yeates.

Francis Baldwin. Chris. Hd. 3m. 9, 1784. Aug. 5, 1785. M. 148. Wife, ———; sons, John, Eli, William and Levi Baldwin, daughters, Sarah Robinson, Mary Way, and Hannah Chandler; son-in-law, Abner Bradford; grandson, Francis Baldwin, son of son John; grandsons, Eli and Samuel, sons of son Eli. Exc. sons, William and Eli.

Elizabeth Chembers. W. Clay Crk. Hd. 2m. 23, 1775. Aug. 15, 1785. L. 339. Granddau., Elizabeth Johnson, dau. of Robert and Mary Johnson; four children, Mary Johnson, John Chembers, Elizabeth Thompson and Joseph Chembers. Exc. sons, John and Joseph.

Veronica Peterson. St. Geo. Hd. July 15, 1784. Aug. 17, 1785. M. 176. Thomas and Letitia McKain, children of dau. Mary (dec'd.), and her husband, William McKain (dec'd.); Jacob, Richard, John, Henry and Veronica McLean, children of granddau., Nancy McLean; granddau., Mary O'Harra; Henry Peterson, doctor, son of Jacob Peterson, doctor, dec'd. Exc. William Allfree and grandson-in-law, Henry O'Harra.

James Anderson. Sept. 1, 1777. Aug. 19, 1785. M. 143. Brother, Samuel Anderson; sister, Catherine Jameson; Mary, Matthew, Hester and Joseph Anderson. Exc. brother-in-law, Thomas Jameson.

Allexander Faries. Pen. Hd. Sept. 12, 1783. Aug. 19, 1785. M. 145. Sons, John, James, Samuel, William, Robert and Alexander; dau., Jennet McMurphey; grandson, Allexander, son of William. Exc. 3rd son, Samuel.

Margaret Gareson. Sept. 4, ·1783. Aug. 24, 1785. M. 144. Dau., Mary ——; son, Garret Gareson; grandsons, Samuel Wandeware, William Land and Thomas Norris; granddau., Elizabeth Norris. Exc. daughters, Charity Norris and Margaret Ruly.

Francis Smith. Tayler. Wil. May 22, 1785. Aug. 26, 1785. M. 151. Wife, Jane; six children, William, Alexander, Ann, Elizabeth, Sophia and Martha. Exc. wife, Jane, and Andrew Catherwood.

John McMorris. Labourer. Bor. of Wil. July 28, 1783. Aug. 31, 1785. M. 146. Stepmother, Mary McMorris; father, John McMorris; sister, Mary ——; brother and sisters, ——. Exc. James McCorkle.

Andrew Muldroh. Pen. Hd. July 29, 1785. Sept. 5, 1785. M. 152. Children of brother, John Muldroh, John and Jane Muldroh; sister, Mary Frances; sister, Agnass Robinson's children; brother, David Muldroh; Jeremiah Morgan, John McCreary, David Henry, William Robinson, Jr. Exc. Robert McAntier, William Robinson and James Kinkead.

Robert Meers. N. C. Hd. Sept. 5, 1785. Sept. 14, 1785. M. 154. Daughters, Hannah and Catharine Meers; brothers' and sisters' children, ——; sister, Jane Henderson. Exc. James Gallaher and Robert Shields.

John Prole. Captain. Mariner. June 29, 1781. Sept. 20, 1785. M. 147. Wife, Martha; children of sister, Elizabeth Tovey, wife of James Tovey of Bristol, in Great Britain. Exc. wife, Martha.

Isaac Staats. Farmer. Appo. Hd. Mar. 28, 1785. Oct. 1, 1785. M. 158. Sons, George, Levi, Carvel and Elisha; dau., Margaret Staats. Letters of adm. to George Staats.

John Kelso. Laborer. N. C. Hd. Aug. 13, 1785. Oct. 1, 1785. M. 171. Father, Joseph Kelso, in Ireland. Exc. Joseph Rhodes.

Mary Evans (Mrs.) Aug. 9, 1785. Nov. 22, 1785. M. 156. My mother and her brother—both dec'd.; brothers, John, Oswell and Reese, all dec'd.; Mrs. Margaret Knarsborough; Hannah Strawbridge, wife of John Strawbridge, of Phila.; Elizabeth Shakespeare, wife of David Shakespeare, of Phila. Exc. uncles, George Evans, Evan Evans and Peter Evans; uncle George's dau., Polly; Thomas Fleeson; John Boggs; Aunt Margaret Morgan.

Joseph Mortonson. B'wine Hd. Mar. 8, 1770. Nov. 23, 1785. M. 140. Wife, Regina; sons, Joseph and Joshna; daughters, Mary Day, Sarah, Lydia, Ann and Rebecca Mortonson; mother, ——. Exc. son, Joshna.

Isaac Alexander. Husbandman. Pen. Hd. Sept. 6, 1784. Dec. 17, 1785. M. 162. Wife, Jane; son, Isaac; dau., Jane Whan; wife of William Whan; dau., Ann Thomas, wife of David Thomas; sister, Bathiah Miller. Exc. David Thomas, Isaac Alexander

William Allmond. B'wine Hd. Feb. 7, 1781. Dec. 17, 1785. M. 166. Wife, ——; son, Thomas; grandson, William Allmond; Edward Beeson, William and Isaac Tussey, John Staples. Exc. son, Thomas.

Benjamin Caulk. Farmer. Nov. 30, 1785. Dec. 20, 1785. M. 168. Son, Benjamin; two daughters, Temperance and Mary. Exc. James Harris, Jacob Harris and son, Benjamin Slator Caulk.

Mary Morgan. Town of N. C. Mar. 10, 1785. Dec. 30, 1785. M. 169. John Janvier, son of cousin, John Janvier; Mary Ricketts, dau. of sister Sarah. Exc. Francis Janvier, Mary Ricketts.

James Johnston. Red Lion Hd. Jan. 18, 1786. Jan. 23, 1786. M. 178. Brother, John. Exc. John McWhorter.

Haley Pell. Tayler. Dec. 5, 178--. Jan. 27, 1786. M. 181. Wife, Sarah; children, ——. Exc. David Kennedy, Lewis Allfree.

Robert Bryan. Oct. 6, 1784. Jan. 28, 1786. M. 174. Wife, Rebecca; daughters, Martha and Rebecca; sons, John and James; John Eves, James McCullough. Exc. James Booth; wife, Rebecca; son, John.

Jacobus Hinds. Farmer. N. C. Hd. ——. Feb. 10, 1786. M. 183. Wife, Mary; children, Jacob, Isaac, Alice, Mary and Henry; two grandchildren, Elizabeth and John, children of dau. Alice ——. Exc. Jacob and Henry Hinds.

James Harris. Shipwright. Bor. of Wil. Feb. 16, 1785. Feb. 16, 1786. M. 184. James Harris and other children of brother, Barney E. Harris. Exc. Barney E. Harris.

Joseph Hair. Weaver. Chester Co., Pa. Sept. 12, 1778. Mar. 6, 1786. M. 186. Wife, Elinor; six children, to wit: John, James, Elizabeth, Matthew, Joseph and Agnes. Exc. sons, John and James.

William Morrow. Mill Creek Hd. Dec. 28, 1785. Mar. 11, 1786. M. 188. Wife, ——; daughters, Catron Wiley & Sarah. Exc. Allexander Monigle.

Henry O'Harra. Feb. 14, 1786. Mar. 18, 1786. M. 189. Wife, Mary; son, Henry; brother, Hugh O'Harra; nephew, Thady O'Hara, brother John's son; nephew, Edmond; nephew, Thady O'Hara's, sister's son. Exc. Dr. Thomas McDonough Col. Thomas Creig, wife, Mary.

Joseph Lukens. Cooper. Mill Creek Hd. 3m. 9, 1786. Mar. 24, 1786. M. 191. Father, John Lukens; sister, Martha Lukens; brothers, Isaac, Levi and Cadwallader. Exc. father, John; brother, Levi.

Thomas Fitzgerald. Appo. Hd. Mar. 4, 1786. Apr. 4, 1786. M. 193. Son, Philip; brother, James; Thomas Conner, son of John Conner. Exc. brother, James Fitzgerald.

Richard Wild. St. Geo. Hd. Apr. 8, 1786. Apr. 19, 1786. M. 194. Wife, Margaret; children, Elizabeth Wild and Richard Wild. Exc. wife, Margaret Wild.

Samuel Stewart. St. Geo. Hd. Mar. 17, 1786. May 9, 1786. M. 195. Wife, Elizabeth; daughters, Elizabeth and Rebecca; sons, David and James; grandsons, Samuel and Abraham Anderson; granddaughters, Catherine and Elizabeth Runnolds and Elizabeth Anderson. Exc, son, David Stewart.

Richard McWilliam. Town of N. C. Dec. 20, 1785. May 19, 1786. M. 197. Wife, Rebecca; daughters, Ann. Sarah Lewes, Rebecca, Louisa and Hester McWilliams; Richard and Elizabeth Spencer, children of William Spencer; brother, Stephen McWilliam. Exc. wife, Rebecca, Isaac Grantham, and James Booth.

Catherine Mitchell. N. C. Hd. May 29, 1786. June 5, 1786. M. 202. Sister, Mary Cowgill; Samuel Means, Catherine Bruff, Margaret Martin, Charlotta Carney (minor). Exc. William Eakin.

James Jones. Pen. Hd. Jan. 9, 1783. June 7, 1786. M. 203. Wife, Susannah; sons, Enock, Daniel, Abel and James; daughters, Mary Griffith, Jane Buckenham, Hannah Shields, Esther Jones, Susannah James and Margaret ——. Exc. wife, Susannah; sons, Enoch and Daniel.

Andrew Paulson. Mill Crk. Hd. Jan. 17, 1781. June 20, 1786. M. 205. Wife, ——; son, Jacob. Exc. wife ——, Jacob Robertson.

Samuel Gibbons. Dorchester Co., Md. May 15, 1786. June 27, 1786. M. 206. James Moreign. Exc. John Ball.

William B. Clark. Bor. of Wil. 5m. 9, 1786. June 6, 1786. M. 207. Ann Marshall, widow; Elizabeth Haughton, John Townsend, Daniel Britt, Huston Longstreth, William Wareing, Joseph Henzey, Benjamin Jacobs; uncles, Nehemiad Bewsey, George Priest of Great Britain; brother, George; mother, Hannah Clark; Mary Kimble, dau. of Eliner Kimble. Exc. Joseph West and Ziba Ferris.

Andrew Shoel. Yeoman. Town of Port Penn. July 8, 1786. July 19, 1786. M. 214. Wife, Catherine. Exc. Nicholas Van Dyke.

John Merriss. St. Geo. Hd. Sept. 28, 1785. Aug. 8, 1786. M. 215. Sons, Richard and Benjamin Merriss; dau., Sarah Meriss; guardians, William Corbitt and Aaron Oakford. Exc., sons-in-law, John Crow and William Eves.

Mary Garretson. Newport. Aug. 3, 1786. Aug. 29, 1786. M. 217. Aunt, Elizabeth Garretson; dau., Elizabeth; other two minor children. Exc. Hans Stamcast.

Abraham Few. Bor. of wil. Dec. 14, 1784. Sept. 14, 1786. M. 218. Sister, Mary Ray. Exc. Mary Ray.

William Culbertson. Pen. Hd., Mar. 16, 1786. Sept. 16, 1786. M. 219. Wife, Ann; eight children, namely: Ann, David, Jean, William, Robert, Francis, Thomas and John. Exc. wife, Ann.

Abraham Staats. Appo. Hd. Oct. 2, 1786. Oct. 12, 1786. M. 221. Wife, Amy; sons, John, Isaac and Peter Staats; daughters, Elizabeth Bratton and Amy Staats; granddau., Rachel Staats. Exc. wife, Amy; sons, John and Isaac, and George Ward.

William Clark. Appo. Hd. July 15 1786. Oct. 28, 1786. M. 223. Wife, Hannah; children of Thomas and Rachel Goldsborough, viz. Eleanor Clark Goldsborough and William Clark Goldsborough; four daughters, Margaret, Rachel, Jane and Martha; sons, John and William. Exc. son, John.

Benjamin Evans. Yeoman. Cumberland Co., Pa. Dec. 2, 1785. Nov. 4, 1786. Cousin, Benjamin King, son of William King of Penna.; cousin, Caleb Evans. Exc. William King.

John McVay. Appo. Hd. July 12, 1785. Dec. 8, 1786. M. 226. Wife. Mary; cousin, Elizabeth Kees; cousin, John Kees. Exc. wife, Mary, and Peter Hirons.

William Faries. Farmer. Pen. Hd. Oct. 25, 1786. Jan. 5, 1787. M. 228. Wife, ———; sons, William, John and James; daughters, Mary Ann Murphey, Mary Scott, Jane Adair, Hannah Brown and Agness. Exc. sons, William and James.

Richard Sauce. Dec. 17, 1786. Jan. 16, 1787. M. 230. Exc. brother, Thomas Sauce.

Hannah Lewden. Widow. N. C. Hd. 9m. 22, 1786. Feb. 12, 1787. M. 231. Daughters, Margaret Sawyer, Hannah ———; cousin, Mary, wife of Benjamin Worrel; five grandchildren, Susanna Eves, George Sankey, Ruth Vandegrift, Hannah Boggs and Jane McCullough; cousin, John Lewden. Exc. grandson, Robert Middleton.

Joshua Storie. St. Geo. Hd. Dec. 5, 1782. Feb. 13, 1787. M. 233. Wife, Rebecca; brother's dau., Mary Story; Susannah Enos, dau. of Richard Enos. Exc. wife, Rebecca.

Benjamin Rothwell. Feb. 8, 1787. Feb. 16, 1787. M. 234. Wife, ———; son, Jacob; Elizabeth Kelly, dau. of Samuel Kelly. Exc. wife, Elizabeth, Samuel Kelly.

Robert Maxwell. Kent Co., Md. Jan. 12, 1785. Feb. 20, 1787. M. 235. Wife, Ann; sons, Robert, John and William; brother, John Maxwell; dau. Isabel Browning, wife of John Writson Browning;

grandson, Robert Browning, son of John and Isabel. Exc. wife, Ann, and son, John.

Ann Staats. Widow. Appo. Hd. Sept. 6, 1785. Feb 22, 1787. M. 242. Sons, Abraham, Isaac and Ephraim; dau. Rebecca Redman; grandchildren, Elizabeth Staats, Margrate Murphey, Rebecca Cockes, John Best and Abraham Best; other grandchildren. Letters of Adm. to Abraham Staats.

David Williams. Apr. 25, 1786. Feb. 22, 1787. M. 244. Brother's son, Lewis Williams; half sister, Elizabeth ——; three half brothers, Jesse, John and James Nash. Exc. Jesse and John Nash.

Sarah Allison. Bor. of Wil. Feb. 15, 1787. Feb. 26, 1787. M. 245. Daughters, Margaret, Catharine Starret and Sarah Moore; children of dau., Elizabeth Hemphill. Exc., son-in-law, William Hemphill; dau., Margaret Allison.

Nicholas Faus. Bor. of Wil. Oct. 4, 1784. Feb. 26, 1787. M. 247. Wife ——; daughters, Hannah, Eve, Lena and Rebecca Faus; son, Joseph Faus. Exc. Joshua Wollaston.

Esther Jolley. Widow. Wil. Jan. 25, 1787. Mar. 8, 1787. M. 248. Sarah Bennett, Susannah Bennett, Mary Davis. Exc. John Lea.

Robert Robinson. Chris. Hd. Feb. 27, 1787. Mar. 10, 1787. M. 249. Wife, Ann; sons, Aquilla, William, John, Thomas and Ebenezer; daughters, Betty, wife of John Porter; Rebecca, wife of William Moore; and Sarah; Justa Walraven, John Linam, John Nebecker. Exc. son, William.

Henry Stedham. Farmer. B'wine Hd. Mar. 7, 1787. Mar. 22, 1787. M. 253. Wife, Mary; grandchildren, William Low and Hannah Low; Henry Beeson, John Beeson, Edward Beeson and Alice Beeson, children of dau., Mary. Exc. wife, Mary, and Peter Vandevere.

Ann Stewart. Mar. 19, 1787. Mar. 29, 1787. M. 255. Grandsons, Benjamin Stewart, Benjamin Hays and William Stewart. Exc. grandson, Benjamin Hays and Robert Smith.

Abraham Robinson. Feb. 25, 1787. Mar. 30, 1787. M. 257. Wife, Sarah; children, Thomas, Mary, Margaret, Joseph, Sarah, Jane, Anthony, Penrose, and Juliana. Exc. brother, Thomas Robinson; wife, Sarah.

Cornelius Derrickson. Yeoman. B'wine Hd. Feb. 20, 1787. Apr. 7, 1787. M. 259. Wife, Mary; son, Cornelius; three daughters, Jane Senex, Catharine Allmond and Mary Derrickson. Exc. wife, Mary Derrickson. Exc. wife, Mary; son-in-law, Thomas Allmond.

Martin Wert. Waterman. Pen. Hd. Nov. 25, 1783. Apr. 9, 1787. M. 261. Wife, Mary. Exc. Jacob Grantham; wife, Mary.

Richard Nash. Appo. Hd. Mar. 16, 1787. May 4, 1787. M. 263, Wife, Rebecca; sons, Richard, Jesse, James and John; daughters,

Tamar Maccay, Rebecca Maccay, and Elizabeth Fitzgerald; grandson, John Jones. Exc. wife, Rebecca; sons, Jesse and John.

Sarah Haughey. Pen. Hd. May 4, 1787. May 10, 1787. M. 265. Daughters, Pricillah Corwin, Ann Haughey, Ellinor Colvert; son, William Haughey; dau.-in-law, Rosanah Haughey; grandchildren, Levi Haughey, Pricillah Haughey, Nathaniel David, Joshua David and Hugh David; son-in-law, Evin David. Exc. son, William; dau. Ann.

John Vangezell. Shop keeper. Town of N. C. Mar. 2, 1783. June 4, 1787. M. 268. Dau. Gertrude Vangezell; grandson, John Vangezell, son of son, Benjamin. Exc. George Read and Mr. Curtis Clay of Phila.

John Shurmizer. N. C. Hd. July 1, 1787. Aug. 21, 1787. M. 274. Wife, Mary; four children, Catherine, Jacob, Elizabeth and Mary. Exc. Solomon Maxwell and William McClay.

Robert Miller. Red Lion Hd. Aug. 12, 1787. Aug. 22, 1787. M. 275. Brothers, Samuel and Hugh Miller, in Ireland. Exc. Samuel Irelan of Maryland.

Ann Jacquett. Spinster. N. C. Hd. Oct. 9, 1787. Oct. 24, 1787. M. 283. Brother, John Jaquett; sisters, Elizabeth ——, and Ingebur Le Fevre. Exc. Ingebur Le Fevre.

John McDowell. Innkeeper. Chris. Bridge. Mar. 20, 1787. Nov. 5, 1787. M. 284. Wife, Mary. Letters of adm. to wife, Mary.

John Moore. Taylor Chris. Hd. Oct. 5, 1787. Nov. 12, 1787. M. 285. James McLammon, son of Rev. William McLammon; brother, ——; sister, Elizabeth; cousins, Elizabeth Byars, Isack Byars, Benjamin Byars; youngest dau. of William Byars. Exc. Robert Pierce, Sr., and James Crossan.

Hannah Wallace. Chris. Hd. Aug. 15, 1787. Nov. 14, 1787. M. 286. Daughters, Rachel Conden and Elizabeth Wallace; grandson, Joseph Condon. Exc. Elizabeth Wallace.

Neven Caldwell. Mill Creek Hd. May 1, 1787. Nov. 20, 1787. M. 287. Wife, Agnes; son, Thomas; daughters, Mary, Jane, Margaret and Susanna. Exc. wife, Agnes, and James Agen.

Sarah Weldin. Widow. Port Penn. Nov. 3, 1787. Nov. 22, 1787. M. 292. Dau., Lydia, wife of Joseph Harris; dau. Elizabeth, wife of Richard Simmons; sons, Benjamin and Josia Weldin.

James McClintock. Labourer. B'wine Hd. Oct. 29, 1787. Nov. 24, 1787. M. 293. Cousin, James McClintock, Sr.; brother, John; father, James McClintock; sister, Elizabeth, wife of H. Galbraith. Exc. uncle, Samuel McClintock.

Agnes McLonen. Single woman. Bor. of Wil. Sept. 6, 1787. Jan. 7, 1788. N. 10. Margaret Bail and her two daughters, Jane and Ann Bail. Exc. Thomas McKean, Esq.

John Serrill. Wil. May 2, 1781. Jan. 28, 1788. M. 298. Wife, Elizabeth, mother, ——; sister, Hannah Serrill; brothers, Jacob and Isaac; Joseph Shallcross, John Councel, Thomas Williams. Exc. wife, Elizabeth.

Josiah Ash. Appo. Hd. Feb. 2, 1788. Feb. 12, 1788. M. 300. Abraham Taylor, Jr., Mary Whartenby, eldest dau. of William Whartenby; Margaret Hunt, wife of Charles Hunt; Philip Reading; Patrick Lyons and wife; three cousins being mother's brother's daughters, namely, Mary Dohorty, otherways, Mary Delavoli; Elizabeth Dohorty, otherways, Elizabeth Johns; Catherine Dohorty, otherways, Catherine Helons. Exc. William Whartenby.

William Burgess. St. Geo. Hd. Jan. 29, 1786. Mar. 8, 1788. M. 303. Sons, William and Peter; dau., Catherine. Exc. Rev. Thomas Read and brother, Jno. Burgess.

Jonathan Robinson. Wil. Feb. 18, 1788. Mar. 10, 1788. M. 305. Wife, Margaret; niece, Mary, wife of John Chambers; nephews, John, George, and Jonathan Gildersleeve; dau., Mary, by former wife; unborn child; John Betson; niece, Elizabeth Anderson. Exc. John McKinley and William Hemphill.

James Garrison. Feb. 19, 1788. Mar. 12, 1788. M. 307. Wife, Sary. Exc. Sarah Garrison.

Richard Taylor. Appo. Hd. Feb. 7, 1788. Mar. 13, 1788. M. 308. Wife, Martha; two children, Richard and Susanna Taylor. Exc. wife, Martha.

Edward Beeson. Farmer. B'wine Hd. Mar. 8, 1788. Mar. 13, 1788. M. 309. Wife, Mary; sons, Edward, John and Henry; brother, John; dau., Alce. Exc. wife, Mary; brother, Thomas Beeson.

Elizabeth Hanson. Bor. of Wil. 12m. 4, 1787. Mar. 15, 1788. M. 313. Daughters, Elizabeth, wife of James Ballatth; Susannah; Lydia, wife of Nehemiah Tilton; Ann, wife of Daniel Jessup Adams; grandson, Timothy Hanson Adams. Exc. Ziba Ferris and John White.

William Gallaher. Cordwainer. Pen. Hd. Dec. 15, 1785. Mar. 26, 1788. M. 317. Wife, Sarah; sons, Thomas, William and James; dau., Margaret Gray. Exc. sons, William and James.

Henry Grubb. B'wine Hd. Jan. 23, 1788. Mar. 29, 1788. M. 319. Jacob Hutton; Exc. Thomas Bird, Jr., son of John.

Fanny Aiken. Pen. Hd. Mar. 18, 1788. Apr. 1, 1788. M. 320. Dau., Fanny Aiken; sons, James, John, Matthew and Robert. Exc. son, James.

Alexander Adama. Mill Crk. Hd. Mar. 15, 1788. Apr. 2, 1788. M. 321. Wife ———; sons, Jonathan, Thomas and John; daughters, Elizabeth, and Margaret. Exc. James Stroud, Samuel Richards.

James Gamble. Newport. Apr. 15, 1787. Apr. 22, 1788. M. 323. Exc. wife, Catharine Gamble, Swen Justis, Thomas Caldwell.

Thomas Scurry. (Nunc.) St. Geo. Hd. Mar. 29, 1788. May 2, 1788.

M. 323. Attested by James Hanson and Margaret Campbell. Letters of adm. granted to Robert McGuffen.

Thomas B. McKean. Bordentown, N. J. Apr. 2, 1788. May 3, 1788. N. 161. Sister, Letitia McKean; cousins, viz. Joseph B. McKean; Robert McKean, Elizabeth, Letitia and Ann, sons and daughters of Thomas McKean, Esq., of Phila. Exc. Joseph B. McKean of Bordentown.

Alexander Stewart. Oct. 31, 1785. May 9, 1788, M. 325. Wife, Rebecca; unmarried children, Sarah, Mary, Elizabeth and Andrew; son, Alexander and other married children. Exc. wife, Rebecca.

Philip Jones. Bor. of Wil. 5m. 14, 1788. May 26, 1788. M. 327. wife, Edith; sons, Amos and William; daughters, Edith and Phebe; brother, William Jones; Joseph West, John Yarnall, Ziba Ferris, Edward Hewes. Exc. wife, Edith Jones.

William Poole. Feb. 6, 1779. May 26, 1788. M. 329. Mother ————; wife ————; sons, William and Joseph; Joseph West, John Stapler. Exc. Samuel Canby and Joseph Shipley.

Daniel Sharpley. Yeoman. B'wine Hd. May 28, 1788. June 9, 1788. M. 333. Wife, Isabel; sons, William, Daniel and George; brother, William; daughters, Mary, wife of Nathan Millmer; Rachel, wife of Jacob Bratton; Leah, wife of Joseph Ashton and Sarah. Exc. wife, Isabel; son, William.

John Litman. Appo. Hd. 5m. 10, 1788. June 12, 1788. M. 335. wife, Rebecca; sons, Henry and John; dau. Sarah. Exc. wife, Rebecca; son, Henry.

Robert Patterson, steward on Brigantine Don Francine, Hugh Wilson, commander. Oct. 25, 1781. June 30, 1788. M. 338. Niece, Elizabeth Pratt, dau. of George. Exc. George Pratt and Andrew Patterson of Chris. Bridge.

James Stewart, Sr. Farmer. B'wine Hd. Oct. 19, 1787. July 5, 1788. M. 339. Sons, Samuel, James, Robert and William Stewart; wife, Isabella; dau., Isabella Little. Exc. sons, Samuel and James.

John Thompson. Oct. 1, 1786. July 29, 1788. M. 342. Wife, Latiche; children, Elizabeth, Robert, Matthew, Eleanor and Rebecca Thompson. Exc. wife, Latiche Thompson.

Mark Elliott, Jr. B'wine Hd. 3m. 19, 1788. Aug. 1, 1788. M. 342. Sons, John, William and Thomas; dau., Margaret; brother, William Elliot, heir of Joseph Elliott; brother, Benjamin Elliott. Exc. son, John; James Gibbons.

Jean Crossan. Mill Crk. Hd. Apr. 9, 1786. Aug. 20, 1788. M. 345. Exc. 3 brethren, William, Samuel and James Crossan.

James Guttery. Yeoman. Jan. 19, 1782. Aug. 26, 1788. M. 346. Wife, Molly; daughters, Martha McDowel, Margaret Anderson, widow; Isabel Bruce and Jean Guthrie. Exc. son, William Guttery; Alexander Guthrie.

Isaac Weldin. Husbandman. B'wine Hd. Sept. 5, 1788. Sept. 15, 1788. M. 348. Wife ———; children, Jacob Weldin, George Weldin, Isabel Sharpley, Margaret Kinsman, Sarah Smith, Mary Weldin and Eli Weldin. Exc. son, Jacob.

Thomas Scott. May 2, 1788. Oct. 1, 1788. M. 350. Mother, Elizabeth Scott; sisters, Jane, Martha, Elizabeth and Jennet. Christiana Dick. Exc. John Brown.

Harmanus Schee. Yeoman. Appo. Hd. Sept. 26, 1788. Oct. 18, 1788. M. 351. Wife ———; son, James; dau., Mary Schee; brothers, James and Cornelius Schee; brother-in-law, Thomas McMurphey. Exc. brother, Cornelius.

Con Hollahan. Oct. 26, 1788. Nov. 12, 1788. M. 355. Children, John, Margaret and Mary. Exc. son, John; dau., Margaret.

Thomas Cooch. Dec. 17, 1780. Nov. 24, 1788. M. 353. Wife, Sarah; son, Thomas; grandchildren, Thomas, Francis, and William Cooch, Elizabeth Cooch; Sarah, Dorcas and Mary Armitage and William Simonton; dau., Frances Elizabeth Simonton. Exc. son-in-law, John Simonton, Alexander McBeth.

Thomas Babb. B'wine Hd. Sept. 1, 1778. Dec. 1, 1788. M. 358. Wife, Sarah; mother, Mary Babb; daughters, Sarah, Thezia and Margaret Babb. Exc. son, Thomas Babb and Peter Vandever.

John Hyatt, Jr. Village of Port Penn. ——— Dec. 6, 1788. M. 360. Exc. wife, Mary Hyatt.

James Smith. Yeoman. Chris. Hd. Sept. 30, 1788. Dec. 8, 1788. N. 1. Wife, ———; sons, Thomas, William, James and John; six daughters, Rachel Smith, Rebecka Wilson, Elizabeth Lynam; Margaret Smith, Mary Smith, Hanna Smith. Exc., wife, Mary; son, William.

George Vansandt. Oct. 22, 1788. Dec. 10, 1788. N. 4. Wife, Catharine; two children, Chambers and Sally. Exc. uncle Chambers Hall.

Nicholas Moore. B'wine Hd. Aug. 5, 1788. Dec. 12, 1788. N. 5. Two sons, Francis and William; daughters, Ann Griffy, Martha ———, Mary Hart, Sarah ———; granddau., Anna ———, dau. of dau. Elleanor. Exc. sons, Francis and William.

Jonathan Kirk. Chris. Hd. July 12, 1782. Dec. 13, 1788. N. 7. Wife, Jane; children ———. Exc. wife, Jane

Matthew Patten. W. Clay Crk. Hd. Oct. 20, 1784. Jan. 7, 1789. M. 8. Wife, Nancy; brother and sister's children ———. Exc. John Reece, Jr., in place of James Glasgow, dec'd.

Joseph Peirce. Carpenter. B'wine Hd. Jan. 8, 1789. Jan. 20, 1789. N. 11. Sons, Joseph, Amos, George, William and John; daughters, Ann, Elizabeth, and Susannah; brother, Richard Exc. son, Joseph and John Clayton.

David Hughes. Farmer. Mill Crk. Hd. Oct. 23, 1784. Mar. 10, 1789. N. 13. Wife, Phebe; father, William Hughes, dec'd; Guin

Hughes, dau. of brother Isaac Hughes; sister Mary Morgan's children; sisters, Rachel Morrison, and Sarah Whitten. Exc. wife, Phebe; Hugh and Abel Glasford.

Zachariah Vanleuvenigh. Tanner. May 31, 1785. Mar. 13, 1789. N. 15. Wife, Ann; sons, George, John, William, George; daughters, Elizabeth, Rebeccah McWilliam and Mary; Stephen Lewis, grandfather of dau., Rebeccah McWilliam; granddaughters Ann McWilliam, Sarah ———, Rebecca ——— and Louisa ———; niece, Catharine Vanleuvenigh. Exc. wife, Ann.

Robert Wild. Appo. Hd. June 2, 1779. March 18, 1789. N 17. Wife, Elizabeth; children, Thomas, John, Richard and Joseph Wild, and Ann Blackston, wife of Ebenezer Blackston. Exc. wife, Elizabeth, and John Cook.

William Liston. Appo. Hd. 3m. 21, 1789. Apr. 6, 1789. N. 20, Wife, Mary; son, William; sister, Townsend; daughters, Ann and Sarah; nephew, William Townsend, son of James and Ann Townsend; Jane Farson. Exc. Mary Liston and Israel Corbit.

William Peery. Farmer. W. Clay Crk. Hd. Mar. 24, 1788. Apr. 14, 1789. N. 22. Sons, David and Thomas; daughters, Mary Peery and Sarah Hawthorne; grandchildren, Ephraim, William, Thomas and Mary Hawthorne. Exc. sons, David and Thomas.

Sarah Boyd. Widow. Aug. 16, 1785. Apr. 14. 1789. N. 23. Mother, Mary Janvier; niece, Mary Janvier, dau. of brother, Richard Janvier and wife, Mary; children of brother, Thomas Janvier and wife, Jane Janvier; sister's daughters, Mary Bryson and Sally Bryson. Exc. Thomas Janvier and his wife, Jane.

Leonard McKee. Appo. Hd. Nov. 26, 1788. Apr. 15, 1789. N. 25, Wife, Rebecca; sons, Robert, John and Leonard, Richard and Jacob; dau., Sarah. Letters of adm. to Lewis Allfree.

David Pyle, late of Pa. now of Va. Mar. 9, 1789. Apr. 21, 1789. N. 33. Only child, Nathan Pyle, now in Pa.; brother, Amos Pyle. Exc. William Sheppard.

Ann Corbit. Widow. Appo. Hd. ——— May 4, 1789. N. 27. Sons, Joseph, Daniel and John Lea Corbit; four daughters, Abigail, Lydia, Mary Ann, Jamima Corbit; mother, Mary Preston; sister, Hannah Pusey. Exc. brother-in-law, Israel Corbit; brother, Jonas Preston.

Nathaniel Williams. Appo. Hd. Oct. 29, 1788. May 6, 1789. N. 29. Wife, Ann; daughters, Catharine and Mary; sons, John, Isaac, and Nathaniel; William Robertson, Jonas Stedem, John Eveker, Thomas Siniks. Exc. James Shaw.

Israel Corbit. Appo. Hd. 4m. 20, 1789. May 20, 1789. N. 31. Wife, Mary; children, viz: Israel, Hannah, Abraham, Isaac, Deborah, Richard, Elizabeth, Jonathan and Ann. Exc. wife, Mary, and brother, William Corbit.

Rachel Bird, relict of Thomas. B'wine Hd. Feb. 9, 1784. June 2,

1789. N. 34. Son, John; daughters, Elizabeth McClintock, Rachel Reynolds and Sarah Hooten; granddaughters, Rachel Poulson, Rachel Dain; children of dau. Rebecca Bratten, viz. John, Mary, Jane, William, Rebecca, Harman; granddau., Rachel Bird, dau. of Thomas. Exc. son, John.

Henry Curry. May 23, 1789. June 13, 1789. N. 36. Brothers, William and Calven Curry, Rev. Thomas Reed. Letters of adm. to William Curry.

Robert McAntier. W. Clay Crk. Hd. Aug. 16, 1785. June 28, 1789. N. 37. Wife, Ann; sons, John, Samuel, Robert and Alexander Steel McAntier; daughters, Rachel, Hanna and Mary McAntier; brother, Samuel McAntier. Exc. wife, Ann, and son, John.

Ann Clay. Widow. Town of N. C. Mar. 30, 1789. June 29, 1789. N. 42. Sons, Robert, Slator, William, Curtis, George and Thomas Clay; daughters; Mary Clay, Ann Booth, Elizabeth Clay and Sarah Booth, wife of Robert Booth; dau. Mary's grandmother, Mary Van Bibbor; late husband, Slator Clay; granddau. Ann Clay, dau. of son, Slator Clay. Exc. son, William Clay; son-in-law, James Booth.

Michael Pratt, late of Island of St. Eustatius, now of Warm Springs, Va. Apr. 16, 1789. July 31, 1789. N. 47. Wife, Prudence. Exc. ———

Rachel Davidge, Widow. June 2, 1789. Aug. 10, 1789. N. 48. Son, William Ricketts; three daughters, Rebecca Price, Tamor Bowen, Rachel Ward; grandchildren, Rebecca Price, Elizabeth Bowen, Joseph Bowen and John Ward Price. Exc. John Ward, Evert Evertson.

Nathaniel Silsbee, practitioner in physic. Red Lion Hd. Jan. 19, 1789. Aug. 19, 1789. N. 51. Sisters, Ann Mellar, wife of Andrew, and Mary Hunn, wife of John Hunn. Exc. wife, Margaret.

Robert Morton. Merchant. Phila. 5m. 5, 1786. Aug. 20, 1789. N. 39. Father, Samuel Morton, dec'd; mother ———; wife, Hannah; sisters, Sarah and Mary Pemberton; brothers, James and Samuel, both dec'd; cousin, Thomas Greaves; Dr. Thomas Parke; Mary Linton, wife of Jacob Linton; Robert Murdock, son of Samuel Murdock; John Sheridan. Exc. father-in-law, James Pemberton; uncle, John Morton, Caleb Carmalt.

Catharine Bradford. (Nunc.) Feb. 17, 1789. Aug. 22, 1789. N. 232, Nancy Bedford. Attested by Ann Johns and Fidelia Rogerson.

Isaac Cartwright. Feb. 2, 1789. Aug. 24, 1789. N. 52. John Booth, son of Ann Booth; two sons, Abraham and Jacob Cartwright. Exc. stepson, Benedict Jones.

Martin Credy. Yeoman. Appo. Hd. May 12, 1788. Sept. 12, 1789. N. 62. Grandchildren, Elizabeth, Polly, James and Susannah Ferguson, children of James and Hannah Ferguson, his wife; George and Martin Ginniss, children of John and Susannah

Ginniss, his wife; nephew, Jacob Credy, son of brother, John Credy and Elizabeth, his wife. Exc. John Credy and his son, Jacob Credy.

Samuel Preston Moore, practitioner in physic. Phila. 6, 10, 1784. Oct. 8, 1789. N. 59. Wife, Hannah; brothers, Mordecai Moore, Henry Hill, Thomas Moore, Charles Moore, Richard Wells and George Dillwyn; sister, Elizabeth Moore; nephews, Richard and Henry Moore, Stephen and Samuel Moore; nieces, Margaret Jones, Mary Heston, Rachel Morris, Deborah Jackson and Hannah Moore; aunt, Rachel Moore. Exc. wife, Hannah, Charles Moore, Henry Hill and Richard Wells.

William Buckinham. Farmer. Mill Crk. Hd. Mar. 25, 1783. Oct. 13, 1789. N. 65. Wife, Jean; sons, John and William; daughters, Hannah Thomas, and Ruth, wife of William Cloud. Exc. son-in-law, William Cloud.

George Crow. St. Geo. Hd. Nov. 28, 1783. Oct. 22, 1789. N. 66. Wife, Mary; dau. Mary McGinnes; five sons, John, George, Robert, Samuel and Thomas. Exc. wife, Mary, and sons, George and Robert.

Thomas Shipley. Chris. Hd. 1m. 8, 1788. Nov. 6, 1789. N. 68. Wife, Rebecca; sons, Joseph and William; daughters, Mary Buckley, Sarah and Ann Shipley; grandson, Thomas Shipley Byrnes; son-in-law, William Byrnes; wife's dau. Mary Andrews; step-son, John Andrews; nephew, William Canby, John Buckley, Joseph Tatnall, Cyrus Newlin. Exc. son, Joseph Shipley, Samuel Canby.

Benjamin Alricks. Carpenter. Bor. of Wil. Oct. 26, 1789. Nov. 10, 1789. N. 75. Wife, Margaret; brothers, Jonas and Joseph Alricks. Exc. wife, Margaret, and brother, Jonas.

Hugh Huston. Mill Crk. Hd. Apr. 19, 1773. Nov. 16, 1789. N. 77. Wife, Jean; son, Alexander's children; son, Samuel. Letters of adm. to Samuel Huston.

Lawrence Higgins. Red Lion Hd. Apr. 1, 1789. Nov. 21, 1789. N. 78. Wife, Susannah; sons, Jesse, Anthony, David, and Samuel; dau. Susannah; two grandchildren, Susannah and John Armstrong, children of dau. Elizabeth and James Armstrong; John Read Higgins, son of son, Jesse. Exc. son, Jesse and George Read, Jr.

John Deakyne. Appo. Hd. Nov. 1, 1789. Dec. 2, 1789. N. 81. Exc. brother George Deakyne.

Jacob Cartwrite. Farmer. Appo. Hd. Oct. 25, 1789. Dec. 19, 1789. N. 82. Sons, Joseph, Stephen and Jacob. Exc. wife, Mary and Abraham Cartwrite.

William Bedford. Town of N. C. Mar. 31, 1786. Dec. 26, 1789. N. 84. Dau. Ann; grandson, William Cannan. Exc. son, Gunning Bedford; George Read, Miss .Catharine Bradford.

John Bowen. Yeoman. Aug. 27, 1789. Jan. 11, 1790. N. 91. Grandchildren, Ozweld and Jean Bowen; stepdau. Hester David. Exc. Daniel Jones and Shem James.

Edward Tatnall, B'wine Hd. Sept. 5, 1789. Jan. 25. 1790. N. 94. Daughters, Elizabeth Tripp, Mary Marshall and Sarah Richardson. Exc. son, Joseph Tatnall.

Abraham Taylor. Appo. Hd. Nov. 1, 1789. Feb. 18, 1790. N. 96. Dau. Dianer Taylor; son, William Taylor; two sisters; brothers children; Abram Tayler. Exc. John Runels.

John Crawford. Appo. Hd. Feb. 11, 1790. Mar. 1, 1790. N. 98. Daughters, Mary, Agnes, Margaret; sons, John, Alexander, and Andrew; Thomas Rothwell, Joseph Stidham, Rebecca Moore, Duncan Beard. Exc. son-in-law, Elias Walraven; son, James.

Elizabeth Baldwin. Widow. B'wine Hd. Oct. 28, 1789. Mar. 6, 1790. N. 100. Sons, Samuel and Eli; daughters, Margaret, Mary and Elizabeth Baldwin. Exc. dau. Margaret, William Smith and Samuel Talley.

Elizabeth Rice, widow of Thomas Rice, later of Mill Crk. Hd. Yeoman. Feb. 9, 1788. Mar. 10, 1790. N. 101. Five children now living, viz: Thomas, Joseph, Solomon, Jeremiah and Mary Rice; chillren of dau. Hannah. dec'd, viz: Jane Boggs, William and Rice Boggs; children of son, Evan, dec'd, viz: Thomas, Evan, William, Washington, Solomon and Mary Rice. Exc. sons, Joseph and Jeremiah.

Thomas Moore. Dec. 23, 1789. Mar. 13, 1790. N. 103. Wife, Mary; daughters, Mary Murdock, Ruth Smith and Eleanor; sons, Lewis, Samuel and Thomas. Exc. Sons, Samuel and Thomas.

Isaac Dushane. Red Lion Hd. Feb. 26, 1790. Mar. 17, 1790. N. 105. Wife, Elizabeth. •Exc. wife, Elizabeth, and Christopher Vandegrift.

Mary Springer. Chris. Hd. May 22, 1786. Mar. 23, 1790. N. 107. Children, Charles, Dorcas Bell, Mary Armstrong, Nicholas, Ann Jamison, Elizabeth Paulson, Jacob, John and Thomas Springer. Exc. Nicholas Springer and John Armstrong.

William Phillips. Sr. Mill Crk. Hd. Nov. 15, 1789. Mar. 23, 1790. N. 108. Wife, Mary; sons, William, James, Robert and John; dau. Hannah, wife of George Taylor; niece, Hannah Thatcher; children of dau. Sarah (dec'd) wife of Moses Palmer; children of dau. Hannah Taylor, viz. Mary, Lydia, Maris and Evan. Exc. son, William.

William Veazey. Dec. 9, 1789. Mar. 23, 1790. N. 113. Daughters, Sarah Loutitt, Mary Veazey and May Veazey; nephew, John Cornan, son of Samuel Cornan. Exc. Edward H. Veazey and William Ward of Sassafras Neck.

Thomas Beeson. Farmer. B'wine Hd. 2m. 13, 1787. Apr. 12, 1790. N. 117. Wife, ———; sons, David, Jonathan, and Thomas;

daughters, Parthena, Alice and Rebeccah. Exc. sons, Jonathan, and Thomas Beeson. Joseph Tatnall, Samuel Canby, William Canby and Vincent Bonsall.

William Patterson. (Nunc.) Mar. 28, 1790. Apr. 12, 1790. N. 120. Jesse Bunker, son of Benjamin Bunker; Stephen Biddle, Veazey Edwards, Hannah Fearis, wife of John Fearis. Exc. Thomas Bartholomew. Attested by David Hayes and Samuel McKinley.

Abel Davis. Mason. Newark. Apr. 13, 1780. Apr. 29, 1790. N. 122. Wife, Sarah; daughters, Rachel, Mary, and Hannah; sons, Benjamin and John. Exc. wife, Sarah, and son, Benjamin.

John Cloud. Chris. Hd. Apr. 17, 1790. May 5, 1790. N. 123. Wife, Phebe; nephew, John Cloud, eldest son of brother, Joseph Cloud; second son of brother, Joseph. Exc. wife, Phebe.

Mary Wirt. May 4, 1789. May 17, 1790. N. 125. Samuel Wirt, son of Thomas; sister's sons, George and Conrad Bird; husband, Martin Wirt, dec'd. Exc. Benjamin Bravard, Margaret Dollinson.

John Basset. Appo. Hd. Jan. 4, 1790. May 25, 1790. N. 126. Sons, Thomas, James, Elias and John; wife, Susannah and unborn child. Exc. son, Elias.

James Robinson. Tanner. Bor. of Wil. 11m. 16, 1787. May 28, 1790. N. 128. Wife ———; daughters, Mary and Rachel; sons, Francis, James and Thomas; two granddaus. Mary and Eleanor Hamilton, daughters of dau. Rachel; grandsons, James and Caleb Robinson, sons of son, Francis; sister, Elizabeth Robinson of Ireland; present wife of son Francis; Archibald Little; Robert Taylor, Edw. Tatnall, William Shipley, Joshua North. Exc. brother, Nicholas Robinson, Joseph West and dau. Mary.

Joseph Jackson Sr. Yeoman. B'wine Hd. Apr. 27, 1790. June 4, 1790. N. 134. Son, George; Mary and Joseph Jackson, children of son Philip; Joseph, son of son Joseph; daughters, Elizabeth Askew and Mary Murphey; John Askew; James Murphey; Isabel Jackson, relict of son Philip. Exc. son Joseph and William Sharpley.

Isaac Miller. Yeoman. W. Clay Crk. Jan. 8, 1772. June 8, 1790. N. 136. Wife, Jennet; sister, Agnes Caldwell and her son Neven; sister, Mary Hutchison and her sons; sisters, Martha Hays, Margaret Miller, Elizabeth Fulton and Jennet Ogle. Letters adm. granted to Joseph Barton, (wife Jannet being dec'd) during minortity of next of kin.

Thomas Read. Mariner. Phila., Pa. May 13, 1783. June 11, 1790. N. 264. Exc. wife, Mary Read.

Joseph West Tanner. Wil. Jan. 12, 1781. June 19, 1790. N. 139. Nephew, Joseph West; sisters, Rachel and Elenor; brothers' and sisters' children; William Starr; Rebecca Jones; Hannah Cathrel; David Ferris; Samuel Starr; Thomas Swain; Garrett Blackford and Mary his wife. Exc. wife, Hannah; bro.-in-law, John Stapler.

Isaac Turner. Cecil Co. Md. Dec. 28, 1787. July 21, 1790. N. 90.
Son, George Chick Turner; father, Peter Turner, dec'd; sister,
Margaret Chick; brothers and sisters ————. Exc. brother,
Daniel Turner.

Elijah Hooten. B'wine Hd. May 25, 1790. July 20, 1790. N. 145.
Wife, Sarah; son, Jacob. Exc. wife, Sarah and William Sharpley.

Griffith Griffith. Farmer. Pen. Hd. July 3, 1790. Aug. 5, 1750. N.
147. Wife, Elizabeth; daughters, Hannah and Mary. Exc. wife,
Elizabeth; brother-in-law, John Armstrong.

Thomas Bellew. Pen. Hd. Aug. 10, 1790. ————. Filed. Wife,
Elizabeth; cousins, Elizabeth and Sarah Pryor, Patty and Sarah
Gest, John Dougherty. Exc. wife Elizabeth and William Hend-
erson, Jr.

Christianah Morton. N. C. Hd. ———— 1790. Aug. 11, 1790. N. 149.
Sister, Ann Morton; Sarah Morton, George, Adam and Ellot
Morton. Exc. Andrew Morton.

Esther Mack. Widow. Town of N. C. July — 1790. Aug. 17, 1790.
N. 150. Mary Dowdle; Esther Mangin, late Esther Blackburn;
Esther Torrent, minor dau. of Thomas and Mary Torrent; Joseph
Tatlow, Esq. Exc. relation, Thomas Torrent.

Bridget Filpot. Widow. Chris. Hd. July 26, 1790. Sept. 1, 1790. N.
152. Exc. dau. Ledenna Springer.

Deborah Williams. Single lady. St. Geo. Hd. Sept. 22, 1790. Sept.
28, 1790. N. 154. Mother ————; kinswoman, Thomas Shortt, his
sister Mary Elliott; Rev. John Boggs. Exc. Thomas Shortt.

Lydia Springer. Mill Creek Hd. July 31, 1790. Oct. 1, 1790. N. 155.
Sisters, Rebecca Horner, Catharine Springer, Rachel Springer,
Sarah Springer and Mary Springer; aunt, Lydia Springer. Exc.
brother, Peter.

William Hutchison. Yeoman. Chris Hd. Sept. 25, 1790. Oct. 19,
1790. N. 156. Wife, Ann; sons ————; daughters ————. Exc.
brother, John Hutchison, John Garret.

John Hadley. Mill Creek Hd. Nov. 2, 1789. Oct. 23, 1790. N. 158.
Wife, Margaret; grandfather, Simon Hadley dec'd; sons, Simon
and Samuel; daughters, Elizabeth Dixson, Emmy Dixson and
Mary Pennock. Exc. sons, Simon and Samuel.

Ann Tate. Wil. Nov. 24, 1790. Jan. 22, 1791. N. 168. Sons, Levi
and William; daughters, Dinah Jackson and Martha Painter.
Exc. son, Levi.

George Grubb. Mason. Mill Creek Hd. Nov. 16, 1788. Feb. 22,
1791. N. 169. Wife, Susanna; sons, George, Richard and James;
daughters, Mary, Ann, Susanna and Margaret. Exc. wife Susanna and brother, Richard Grubb.

John Wood. Farmer. Chris. Hd. Feb. 11, 1791. Feb. 23, 1791.
N. 170. Wife, Sarah; dau. Hannah; sons, Samuel, John and
Joseph. Exc. Jacob Broom and Joseph Summerl.

Ann Gilpin. Widow. Bor. of Wil. 7m. called July 3, 1777. Mar. 3, 1791. N. 174. Vincent Gilpin, son of brother-in-law Joseph Gilpin; Betty Gilpin, dau. of brother-in-law George Gilpin, dec'd; daughters of sister Betty Bailey, dec'd, namely, Betty, wife of Francis Swain; Ann, wife of David Hays; Mary, wife of Samuel Mendinhall and Phebe, wife of Benjamin Mendinhall; sisters, Hannah Walker, Mary Gilpin and Betty Gilpin; Joshua, Sarah and Thomas Gilpin, children of exc. Thomas Gilpin; Thomas Gilpin son of Samuel; Margaret Heath; Lydia Gilpin, widow of Thomas, exc; cousin Betty Dickison, wife of John Dickinson; cousin Ann Dewee. Exc. Thomas Gilpin, Lydia Gilpin and Joseph Shallcross; sister-in-law, Esther Paintor.

John Taylor. Trader. Appo. Hd. Mar. 5, 1789. Mar. 11, 1791. N. 178. Son, John; daughters, Mary Coombs, Hester Hanson, Lumigha Bilderback; Elizabeth Coombs, dau. of dau. Mary; grandson, John Coombs. Exc. son John; son-in-law John Hanson. Abraham Staats app't exc. in place of son John dec'd.

Joseph Bilderback. Appo. Hd. Mar. 31, 1789. Mar. 11, 1791. N. 183. Wife, Lumigha; sons, Hance and Abraham; John Taylor. Exc. wife, Lumigha and son Hance.

Benjamin Canby. Yeoman. Bor. of Wil. 5m. 22, 1789. Mar. 12, 1791. N. 185. Children ———; Nathan and John Melner; William Jones; brother, Thomas Canby. Adm. by Harlin Cloud, Thomas Canby, Caleb Harlan, Frederick Craig.

John Hall. St. Geo. Hd. Mar. 5, 1791. Mar. 15, 1791. N. 187. Dau., Mary Hall; son, Chatwood Hall; brother William's son. Exc. brother, Clement Hall.

Levi Pierce. B'wine Hd. Feb. 12, 1790. Mar. 28, 1791. N. 188. Wife, Mary; sons, George and Lazarus; daughters, Mary, Honour, Susanna, Rebecca and Hannah. Exc. wife, Mary and Joseph Pierce.

Sarah Robinson. Widow. B'wine Hd. Feb. 27, 1791. Apr. 20, 1791. N. 190. Children, Thomas, Mary, Margaret, Sarah, Joseph, Jane, Anthony, Penrose and Juliana Robinson. Exc. Sharp Delleney, Francis Johnson.

Joseph England, Sr. Miller. Mill Creek Hd. June 12, 1789. May 6, 1791. N. 192. Wife, Abigail; brother-in-law, Joseph Rotheram; son, Joseph; daughters, Elizabeth Wollason, Sarah Kirkwood, Johannah England and Abigail England. Exc. wife, Abigail, son Joseph and son-in-law Williiam Wollason.

William Johnston. Mill Creek Hd. Dec. 20, 1787. May 17, 1791. N. 194. Wife, Margaret; grandson, William Johnston; children of dau. Margaret Porter viz; Margaret, Eleanor, Mary, Elizabeth, Susannah, David and William Porter. Exc. dau. Margaret Porter.

Ralph Walker. Wil. Apr. 16, 1791. May 26, 1791. N. 196. Wife,

Hannah; kinsman, Stephen Falp, Jr., now in England. Exc. wife, Hannah; John Lea.

John Clark. Red Lion, Hd. Mar. 1, 1791. June 7, 1791. N. 197. Wife, Mary; sons, George, John, Thomas and Levi; daughters, Elizabeth Boots, Mary and Sarah. Exc. son, George.

William Rothwell. May 8, 1791. June 9, 1791. N. 200. Wife, Ann; sons, Thomas and William; four daughters ———. Exc. wife, Ann.

George Wright. Appo. Hd. May 17, 1791. June 11, 1791. N. 201. Son, John; son-in-law, Charles Haverin; dau. Elinor Haverin; grandsons, William and James Simpson. Exc. Charles Haverin.

John Simonton. Mill Creek Hd. June 27, 1791. July 20, 1791. N. 202. Sons, William and John; dau. Frances; brother, William Simonton; Mrs. Dorcas Lewis; Rev. John McCrery. Exc. Alexander McBeath, William Simonton, Sr., William Thompson.

Rachel Vandyke. Widow. St. Geo. Hd. May 6, 1790. Aug. 31, 1791. N. 204. Daughters, Mary Stewart and Rachel Foster; granddaughters, Eliza, Mary and Margaret Stewart; grandchildren, Nancy Johns, Nicholas and Mary Vandyke; son, Abraham Vandyke. Exc. son-in-law, Dr. David Stewart and his wife, Mary.

Morgan Jones. Yeoman. Pen. Hd. Dec. 10, 1759. Sept. 5, 1791. N. 164. Dau. Ann, wife of Peter Delap; sons, David, Abel, Joshua, Zachariah, Morgan and John; daughters, Lettice and Esther; grandson, Morgan, son of son, Zachariah. Exc. sons, Zachariah and David.

Letitia Richardson. Widow. Appo. Hd. Sept. 2, 1791. Sept. 30, 1791. N. 206. Son, William; dau., Rebecca Bennet; grandchildren, Benjamin Herman, Elijah and Richardson Staats and Lydia Ann Moore. Exc. Robert Johnson.

Josiah Barlow. Appo. Hd. Sept. 8, 1791. Oct. 1, 1791. N. 208. Daughters, Susannah and Mary Barlow. Exc. wife, Elizabeth Barlow.

Jacob Pugh. Gentleman. St. Geo. Hd. Sept. 15, 1791. Oct. 1, 1791. N. 209. Cousin, Philip Reading, only son of Rev. Philip Reading. Exc. Philip Reading.

John Pryor. Red Lion Hd. Nov. 1, 1791. Nov. 15, 1791. N. 223. Four children, Sarah, Elizabeth, Thomas Ellot and Margaret Pryor. Exc. James Delap.

Justa Walraven. Yeoman. Chris. Hd. Sept. 29, 1791. Nov. 18, 1791. N. 224. Wife, Mary; Rachel Pluright, wife of William Pluright. Exc. son, John.

Robert Allen. W. Clay Crk. Hd. Oct. 28, 1791. Nov. 24, 1791. N. 227. Half brother, James Magee. Exc. brother, John Allen.

Evart Evertson. Dec. 2, 1791. Dec. 19, 1791. N. 229. Wife, Susanna; her brothers, George and John Ward; her father, John

Ward; five children, George, Sarah, Henrietta Maria, Jeremiah and Rebecca. Exc. wife, Susanna and John Ward.

Samuel Stewart. St. Geo. Hd. Jan. 3, 1792. Jan. 9, 1792. N. 233, Sister, Nancy; children of Jamimah Hanson, dec'd., viz: Joseph, Samuel and Sophia. Exc. brother, William.

Miss Mary Kneasborough. St. Geo. Hd. Dec. 29, 1791. Jan. 12, 1792. N. 237. God-dau., Mary Ann Moore, widow of James Moore and dau. of Mary Cheek; cousins, Francis, Thomas and John Reynolds, sons of Francis Reynolds, dec'd. Exc. cousin, John Reynolds.

John Hood. Gentleman. N. C. Hd. Dec. 26, 1791. Jan. 12, 1792. N. 239. Dau., Mary, now wife of Thomas Skillington; three grandchildren, Abraham, William and Marian Hood Rothwell, children of dau. Mary and Abraham Rothwell, dec'd.; widow of John Nowland of Hartford Co.; grandchildren, Dennis, James, Larabet, John and Marriot Nowland, children of dau. Nancy by James Nowland. Exc. Robert Maxwell.

Elizabeth Dushane. Widow. Town of St. Geo. Red Lion Hd. Dec. 6, 1790. Jan. 23, 1792. N. 234. Isaac and Elizabeth Dushane, children of Andrew Peterson Dushane; granddaughters of Samuel Alricks, viz: Elizabeth, dau. of Dr. David Thompson and Elizabeth Dushane; cousins, Elizabeth Reese, Rachel Reese and John Reese, children of uncle, Reese Reese, my mother's brother; George, Lewis and Mary Reese, children of Lewis Reese, dec'd., son of my mother's oldest brother. Exc. John Reese, millwright; Samuel Eccles.

Timothy Piece, Sr. B'wine Hd. Dec. 10, 1791. Jan. 30, 1792. N. 240. Exc. wife, Mercy; two sons, Timothy and William.

James Matthews. Jan. 16, 1792. Feb. 2, 1792. N. 242. Two nephews, James Scanlon and James Knight. Exc. brother, Arthur Matthews.

Leven Justis. Mill Crk. Hd. Apr. 27, 1791. Feb. 3, 1792. N. 243. Daughters, Debora Robeson, Ann Justis and Mary Justis. Exc. sons, Aaron and Abenor.

Jona William Faries. Feb. 4, 1792. Feb. 10, 1792. N. 246. Mother, ————. Exc. brother, Isaiah; sister, Mary Higgins.

Robert McCreery. Pen. Hd. Jan. 14, 1792. Feb. 11, 1792. N. 247. Sister, Rachel; mother, Elenor. Exc. Joseph Thomas.

John Rouse. Newport. Feb. 7, 1792. Feb. 16, 1792. N. 248. Wife, Hannah; mother, Patience McGlasskie; sister, Rebecca Grunden's children; sister, Rachel Hazlewood. Exc. wife, Hannah.

Alexander McMurphey. Widower. St. Geo. Hd. Feb. 3, 1792. Feb. 21, 1792. N. 249. Three children, Agnes, Robert and Elizabeth. Exc. brother, Robert McMurphey and Robert Haughey.

Robert Shields. N. C. Hd. Feb. 11, 1792. Feb. 21, 1792. N. 251.

Wife, Hannah; four daughters; brothers, James and Caleb; sister, Mary Ligget. Exc. wife, Hannah and Daniel Jones.

Rachel Handson. St. Geo. Hd. Dec. 2, 1791. Feb. 24, 1792. N. 258. Daughters, Mary King, Suffiah Vandyke, and Rachel Miles; granddaughters, Alice Hanson, Rachel Vandyke and Rachel Hanson, dau. of Lawrence Hanson. Exc. William Frazer.

Thomas May. Wil. Nov. 8, 1791. Feb. 29, 1792. N. 253. Wife, Sarah; nephew, James May; niece, Rachel Jones, formerly Rachel May; sister, Mary and husband, Christopher Garrett; sister, Sarah McClintock; cousin, Mary Brook; aunt, Hannah Brook, Rebecca Patrick, Deborah Palmer, Samuel Potts. Exc. John Brook and brother, Robert May.

Richard Shepherd. Mar. 8, 1792. Mar. 27, 1792. N. 261. Stepdau., Joan Allen; sons, William and Samuel; daughters, Sarah and Mary. Exc. John Gillmore.

David Caldwell. Red Lion Hd. Mar. 18, 1792. Mar. 29, 1792. N. 262. Wife, ———; children, William, Elizabeth, James, John and others. Exc. Capt. William McKennan, Anthony Dushane.

Thomas Hanaway. Yeoman. Mill Crk. Hd. Jan. 25, 1791. Mar. 31, 1791. N. 263. Wife, Elizabeth; dau., Elizabeth; sons, Samuel, Thomas, Jesse, David and John. Exc. son, John.

William Moore. Yeoman. B'wine Hd. Mar. 24, 1792. Apr. 23, 1792. N. 268. Niece, Anna, dau. of sister, Eleanor, dec'd.; four sisters, Ann Griffey, Martha Moore, Mary Hart and Sarah Moore. Exc. brother, Francis Moore.

John Springer. Wil. Apr. 5, 1792. Apr. 25, 1792. N. 269. Wife, Sarah; sons, John and Benjamin; daughters, Mary and Sarah; Elizabeth McKinny. Exc. wife, Sarah and Peter Brynberg.

Margery Stedham. B'wine Hd. Sept. 27, 1790. Apr. 30, 1792. N. 271. Children of dau., Ann Wiley; two daughters, Sarah Webster and Mary Whitsel; son-in-law, George Whitsel. Exc. son-in-law, Henry Webster.

Robert Hood. Appo. Hd. May 4, 1792. May 14, 1792. N. 273. Sister, Susannah, wife of James Peterson; half brothers, John and James Hood; Nicholas Barlow. Exc. brother, Thomas Hood.

Charlotte Pearce. Red Lion Hd. Dec. 16, 1791. May 21, 1792. N. 274. Exc. sister, Susanah Hance.

David Muldroh. Farmer. Pen. Hd. Apr. 30, 1792. May 22, 1792. N. 275. Sister, Ann Robinson; nephews, John Muldroh, David Henery, William Robinson and Joseph Sharpe; nieces, Jane Brian and Sarah Henery. Exc. Morgan Jones, John Muldroh and John Moore.

David Howell. Pen. Hd. May 22, 1792. June 5, 1792. N. 277. Wife, Sarah; sons, David, Thomas, Oliver and Samuel; daughters, Dinah and Nancy. Exc. wife, Sarah and William James.

Samuel Ruth, Sr. N. C. Hd. Feb. 17, 1792. June 16, 1792. N. 280.

Wife, Ann; sons, William, Samuel, Moses, Benjamin, Robert and George; daughters, Mary, Elizabeth, Eleanor and Frances; William Scot and Robert Bryan. Exc. sons, William and Samuel.

Sarah McCallmont, Jr. Newport. July 26, 1791. June 18, 1792. N. 283. Mother, Sarah McCallmont; late father, John McCallmont; brother, Arthur McCallmont. Exc. brother, James McCallmont.

Elizabeth Yarnall. Shopkeeper. Wil. 8m. 29, 1791. July 10, 1792. N. 284. Exc. sister, Esther Yarnall.

Isaac Pierce. Bor. of Wil. 7m. 3, 1792. July 20, 1792. N. 286. Exc. wife, Phebe.

Henry Reynolds. Wil. July 17, 1792. July 30, 1792. N. 287. Wife, Mary; sons, Joseph and Benjamin; daughters, Sarah and Betty; Joseph Shallcross, Jacob Fussel, Samuel Canby. Exc. Isaac Hendrickson.

Jane Kirkpatrick. St. Geo. Hd. May 30, 1792. July 31, 1792. N. 289. William and Samuel, sons of John Moody. Exc. John Moody.

John Wott. Yeoman. Mill Crk. Hd. Mar. 4, 1790. Aug. 2, 1792. N. 290. William Montgomery, Mary Montgomery, John McBath, Robert Barr, William Gettis; brother, James Wott; Rev. William McKanon. Exc. brother, Robert McFerson.

Isabella Hyatt. Aug. 26, 1791. Aug. 23, 1792. N. 294. Sister, Mary Smith, wife of William Smith; David Lebo, Archibald Fowler. Exc. Thomas McDonough.

Joseph Dickinson. Tanner. Sept. 29, 1792. Oct. 2, 1792. N. 296. Dau., Mary Webster; grandchildren, Joseph, Duncan, Dickinson, John, Evan, Betsy, Judah and Polly Webster. Exc. son-in-law, Evan Webster, grandson; Joseph Webster.

Catharine Vanleuveneigh. Spinster. N. C. Hd. Sept. 25, 1792. Oct. 22, 1792. N. 298. Children of sister, Elizabeth Carter, viz: Catharine, Betsey, Susanna and Hannah; relation, Eliza Vanleuvenigh, dau. of Ann Vanleuvenigh. Exc. Joseph Tatlow of New Castle.

John Deakyne. Appo. Hd. Nov. 1, 1792. Nov. 6, 1792. N. 301. Wife, Elizabeth; six children, Thomas, Elizabeth Curry, William, Catherine, George and John; cousin, Jacob Deakyne. Exc. son, Thomas and Archibald Murphy.

Mary Summerville. Bor. of Wil. Dec. 7, 1791. Nov. 14, 1792. N. 377. Dau., Isabella Jane Richardson, her husband, Nicholas Richardson; grandchildren, David and Isabella Jane Campbell. Letters of adm. granted to Samuel Erwin in absence of Nicholas Richardson.

William Armstrong. W. Clay Crk. Hd. June 7, 1788. Nov. 20, 1792. N. 303. Wife, Ann; sons, Edward, David, George, John and James; daughters, Rebeckah, Ann, Jean and Margaret. Exc. sons, Edward and David; dau., Rebeckah and brother-in-law, John Beaty.

William Wooderson. Farmer. Appo. Hd. Nov. 23, 1792. Dec. 6, 1792. N. 305. Wife, Martha; children, Richard, Sarah and unborn. Exc. wife, Martha and Jacob Reynolds.

David Clark. Storekeeper. Bor. of Wil. Oct. 8, 1792. Dec. 8, 1792. N. 306. Exc. brother, William Clark.

James Adams, Sr. Wil. Nov. 14, 1792. Jan. 7, 1793. N. 308. Late wife, Martha; graves of son Hans and daughters, Martha and Sarah; sons, James, Samuel and John; dau., Mary Keith; granddaughter, Martha Adams, dau. of Hans; brother, Robert Adams, dec'd. Exc. Capt. Patrick O'Flinn and sons, Samuel and John.

William McClure. B'wine Hd. Aug. 15, 1792. Jan. 16, 1793. N. 310. Wife, Jane; children of John and Elinor Newbary, Joseph, John, Caleb, Mary Flower and Ann Butterfield; Francis Day, Joseph Day, Elinor Day and Joseph Day, children of Francis Day; Samuel and Jane Russell, children of Ephraim Russell; Jane, Isabel and Mary Simonson, daughters of William Simonson. Exc. Joseph Day and Edward Simonson.

Richard See. Dec. 20, 1792. Jan. 19, 1793. N. 312. Exc. sons, Abraham and William.

Robert Mercer. Red Lion Hd. July 25, 1786. Jan. 22, 1793. N. 313. Wife, Sarah; sons, Simon and Jeremiah. Adm. Simon Mercer.

Joseph Gilpin. Yeoman. Chris. Hd. Dec. 2, 1788. Feb. 4, 1793. N. 314. Wife, ———; sons, Joseph, Israel, Gideon, Thomas and Vincent; daughters, Orpah Shallcross, Betty, Hannah and Mary; sons-in-law, Joseph Shallcross and Daniel Stubbs; grandchildren, Edward Gilpin (son of Vincent), Orpah Gregg, Mary Reese Gilpin and Mercy Gilpin. Exc. son, Vincent or Edward Gilpin and John Ferris.

Chambers Hall. Pen. Hd. Feb. 4, 1793. Mar. 2, 1793. N. 320. Brother's dau., Elizabeth Hall; brother's son, Alexander Hall; sister's son, Asa Vansant; Sarah Vansant, dau. of Rhody Vansant. Exc. Alexander Hall, Asa Vansant.

Jane Farsons. Widow. 10m. 7, 1785. Mar. 2, 1793. N. 321. Next of kin of late husband, Robert Beeby; children of nephew, Jacob James. Exc. James Pemberton and Nicholas Waln of Phila., Joseph West and James Lee of Wil.

James Buckingham. Joyner. Wil. 8m. 19, 1786. Mar. 6, 1793. N. 323. Wife, Mary; sons, Richard, John, Joshua and Gloveyer; dau., Eleanor; grandchildren, Marib, Hasial and Mary Chandler; dau., Hannah, dec'd. wife of David Chandler. Exc. sons, Richard and John.

David Bush, Sr. Feb. 28, 1792. Mar. 21, 1793. N. 325. Sons, George, John and David Bush, Jr. Exc. son, George.

George Robinson. Miller. B'wine Hd. Feb. 25, 1793. Apr. 2, 1793. N. 327. Three sisters, Mary, Margaret and Elizabeth; two brothers, Joseph and Salkeld. Exc. John Grubb.

Margaret Robinson. B'wine Hd. Mar. 4, 1793. Apr. 2, 1793. N. 328. Mother, Elizabeth Robinson; Rebeckah Orr, minor dau. of James Orr; brothers and sisters, Mary, Joseph, Elizabeth and Salkeld Robinson. Exc. John Grubb.

Amy Staats. Appo. Hd. Mar. 9, 1793. Apr. 16, 1793. N. 331. Sons, John, Isaac and Peter; dec'd husband, Capt. Abraham Staats; dec'd father, John Barker. Exc. three sons, John, Isaac and Peter.

William Jones. Tayler. Wil. May 13, 1793. May 25, 1793. N. 334. Wife, Esther; sons, George, Ellis and Asbury; daughters, Jane, Mary and Esther. Exc. wife, Esther.

Mary Price. Widow. Village of Newark. May 30, 1793. June 28, 1793. N. 335. Nephews, Lewis, Joseph, Josiah, Elisha and Thomas Lunn; nieces, Elis Lunn, Mary Parnel Eaton and Martha Eaton. Exc. Margaret Knaresborough; niece, Mary Parnel Eaton.

John Gythen. Farmer. Appo. Hd. Sept. 14, 1791. July 16, 1793. N. 337. Wife, Elizabeth; dau., Hester; sister's children, Elizabeth and Jean Egleson. Exc. wife, Elizabeth and Garret Staats.

Edward Davis. Mariner. Late of Great Britain. July 18, 1793. July 24, 1793. N. 339. Adm. Mrs. Sarah Singleton.

Sarah Whitelock. Wil. Apr. 12, 1793. July 27, 1793. N. 340. Son, George Rasin; grandchildren, Sarah Wallis, Joseph Rasin, Isaac Whitelock (son of Charles), Mary McLean, Sarah McLean, George McLean and Joseph McLean. Exc. John Hayes and Joseph Rasin.

Joseph Cannon. Yeoman. Mill Crk. Hd. Mar. 6, 1792. Aug. 16, 1793. N. 343. Wife, Mary; children, William and Martha; sister, Martha ——. Exc. wife, Mary and son, William.

John Counsil. Grazier. B'wine Hd. Aug. 18, 1793. Aug. 31, 1793. N. 345. Ann and Jane Crampton, daughters of dec'd. dau., Esther Crampton; sons, William, Joseph and James; dau., Sarah Gilpin; son-in-law, Thomas Gilpin. Exc. Peter Vandever.

Robert Meldrum. St. Geo. Hd. Aug. 19, 1793. Aug. 31, 1793. N. 347. Wife, Sarah; four children, Joseph, Elizabeth, Kezia and Rebeckah. N. B. "Elizabeth and Kezia Meldrum mentioned in this will are wives of Benjamin and Richard Flinton." Exc. wife, Sarah; son, Joseph.

Thomas Short. Husbandman. (Nunc.) St. Geo. Hd. Sept. 4, 1793. Sept. 7, 1793. N. 349. Attested by Rebecca Read and James Haggerty; Hugh Colhoun and his wife, Mary Colhoun, mother of testator; Israel Elliott and Mary, his wife, late Mary Short, sister of testator; half-brothers and sisters. Exc. mother, Mary Colhoun; brother, John Colhoun.

John Stapler. Wil. June 29, 1792. Sept. 9, 1793. N. 351. Wife, Jemima; grandchildren, Sarah Gilpin, John Stapler Littler, and

Sidney Littler; Charles Robinson, Jonas Canby, Robert Pierce, John Lea. Exc. kinsman, George Sterne, Samuel Canby and Edward Gilpin.

Jacobus Anderson, Sr. Weaver. Chris. Hd. June 8, 1793. Sept. 17, 1793. N. 354. Wife, Mary; children, John, Elizabeth Jackson, Jacob, Mary Chandler, Joseph, Ann, Catharine, Rachel, William, Isaac and Peter. Exc. wife, Mary, and son, Joseph.

Jean Graham. Mill Crk. Hd. Sept. 17, 1793. ———. Filed. Son, William; daughters, Elizabeth Springer and Ann Ogle; son John's daughter, Mary Graham. Exc. son, John.

Richard Kellam. Farmer. B'wine Hd. Dec. 28, 1786. Oct. 4, 1793. N. 356. Son, David; grandson, Isaac Weldon, son of dau. Mary; dau., Margaret Rambo. Exc. son, David, and John White.

Andrew McKee. B'wine Hd. Feb. 7, 1789. Oct. 5, 1793. N. 358. Wife, Mary; children of sons, William, James and Andrew; dau., Isabel Bail, her son, Andrew; David, son of dec'd. son, David. Exc. son-in-law, Samuel Bush; son, Andrew; son, John.

David Stewart. Port Penn. Jan. 15, 1792. Oct. 16, 1793. N. 362. Dau., Rachel, dec'd.; sons, James and David; four daughters, Elizabeth, Mary, Ann and Margaret. Exc. wife, Mary.

Mary Gordon. Wil. July 12, 1793. Oct. 17, 1793. N. 365. Ann Hazel, her son, William; brother, John Gordon; children of John Fairs of Kent Co., by his first wife. Exc. Eleazer McComb and Thomas Bellach.

Sarah Garretson. Newport. Chris. Hd. Dec. 28, 1776. Oct. 22, 1793. N. 368. Brother, Jediah Garretson; nephew, Eliakim Garretson. Exc. sister, Elizabeth Garretson.

William Pearson. June 16, 1792. Oct. 22, 1793. N. 431. Son, Richard; dau., Margaret. Exc. wife, Avia.

Nathan Wood. Wil. 10m. 11, 1793. Oct. 25, 1793. N. 369. Dau., Rachel; son, Joseph. Exc. wife, Rebecca.

James Partridge. Farmer. Jan. 8, 1793. Nov. 4, 1793. N. 371. Sons, Francis, John, Eaton Rudolph, James and Christopher; daughters, Susanna and Margaret. Exc. sons, Francis and John.

Catharine Marra. May 1, 1793. Nov. 5, 1793. N. 373. Nieces, Mary Reed and Sarah Ryland; nephews, John and William Reed; Margaret, Catharine and Marra Ryland, children of Benjamin and Sarah Ryland. Exc. Benjamin Ryland.

Francis Kinsey. Weaver. Appo. Hd. Jan. 2, 1793. Nov. 5, 1793. N. 375. Sons, Benjamin, Francis and Abraham. Exc. wife, Rebecca.

Frederick Wirt. Taylor. Wil. July 6, 1786. Nov. 22, 1793. N. 379. Half sister, Dorothy Hidren. Exc. wife, Anna Dorothy.

John Pierce. Weaver. B'wine Hd. Nov. 17, 1793. Nov. 22, 1793. N. 380. Sons, Jehu, Jonathan and Aaron; dau., Deborah. Exc. wife, Margaret and son, Jonathan.

John Toppin. Farmer. Red Lion Hd. June 11, 1793. Nov. 28, 1793. N. 382. "Young lad named James Toppin, who I have hitherto brought up"; wife, Rebecca; grandchild, John McCormick, son of dau., Anna. Exc. sons, Samuel, John and George.

John Bratten. Yeoman. Chris. Hd. May 12, 1784. Dec. 2, 1793. N. 384. Dau., Ann, intermarried with George Craghead; grandchildren, Isabella, Esther, Elizabeth, Milly, Thomas and William Craghead. Exc. wife, Isabella.

Sarah Andrews. Widow. Bor. of Wil. 5m. 19, 1790. Dec. 27, 1793. N. 387. Sons Samuel, Isaac and Benjamin; daughters, Deborah and Mary; former husband, John Andrews. Exc. Edward Hewes and George Spackman.

Thomas David, Sr. Pen. Hd. Nov. 16, 1790. Dec. 30, 1793. N. 390. Dau., Margaret Pierce. Exc. sons, Davidson and Thomas.

Thomas Connarroe. Phila., Pa. Oct. 6, 1791. Jan. 10, 1794. N. 392. Dau., Abigail Curtis, wife of Thomas Curtis; dau., Rebecca Trotter, wife of Daniel Trotter. Exc. sons, Thomas and Antrim.

Robert Haughey. Husbandman. St. Geo. Hd. Dec. 22, 1779. Jan. 27, 1794. N. 394. Wife, Christian; sons, Francis and John; nephew, Robert Haughey, son of brother James. Exc. brothers, Marimus and James Haughey.

Caleb Byrnes. Stanton, Mill Crk. Hd. 1m. 2, 1794. Jan. 28, 1794. N. 398. Wife, Mary; sons, Jonathan and Daniel; daughters, Martha Strond and Rachel Byrnes. Exc. son, Jonathan and son-in-law, Joshua Strond.

Alexander Cummins. W. Clay Crk. Hd. Jan. 7, 1794. Feb. 5, 1794. N. 400. Wife, Agnes; children, Alexander, Jean and Hannah. Exc. James Barr and James Griffin.

Benjamin Hays. May 22, 1791. Feb. 18, 1794. N. 402. Wife, Katharine; dau., Martha. Exc. Samuel Elcles and wife, Katharine.

John Morgan. Mill Creek Hd. Apr. 23, 1790. Mar. 11, 1794. N. 403. Son, William; daughters, Rachel Hamilton, Sarah Scott, Mary Henery, Given Dinsmore; John and Mary Morgan, children of son, William. Exc. son, William and Heath John.

Grace Peterson. N. C. Aug. 13, 1793. Mar. 13, 1794. N. 406. Son, Henry Peterson; grandchildren, Mary, Hester Catholina and Harriet Grace Wynkoop and Andrew Jacob Peterson; son, Philip Reading. Exc. Henry Peterson.

Sarah Seccondiron. St. Geo. Hd. Sept. 10, 1789. Mar. 13, 1794. N. 410. Fanny Toland, dau. of Philip Toland. Exc. John Brown and Margaret, his wife.

Sarah Richardson. Widow. Sept. 2, 1791. Mar. 31, 1794. N. 412. Son, John; daughters, Mary and Ann; Ann's child, Sarah; Mary Bonsall; Samuel Canby; Nicholas Waln. Exc. dau., Mary.

John Ford (alias **Benson**). Merchant. Wil. Mar. 28, 1794. Apr.

2, 1794. N. 414. Son, Jacob Ford. Exc. Joseph Shallcross, Caleb Seal, Joshna Seal.

John French Finney. Town of N. C. Mar. 27, 1793. Apr. 2, 1794. N. 416. Aunt Elizabeth ——; Anna Dorothea, wife of John Finney of Penna.; grandfather, Dr. John Finney of New Castle; brothers, Davis T. and Washington L. Finney; sisters, Elizabeth Miller, Anna J. Miller and Sarah Maria. Exc. father, —— and mother, ——.

Rebecca Bennett. Jan. 16, 1794. Apr. 10, 1794. N. 419. Children, Samuel, Lydia, Vincent and John Moore. Exc. Richard Taylor.

Thomas Nichols. Yeoman. Chris. Hd. Oct. 10, 1788. Apr. 18, 1794. N. 421. Wife, Lydia; three daughters, in Va., Rachel Heald, Mary Janney, Dinah Walter; sons, Isaac, Eli, William, Henry, Amor, David and Daniel; youngest dau., Judith Nichols. Exc. son, Daniel.

Ziba Ferriss. Bor. of Wil. 4m. 22, 1794. May 5, 1794. N. 424. Wife, ——; sons, John, Benjamin and Ziba; daughters, Deborah and Edith. Exc. wife, Edith and cousin, John Ferriss.

David Thomas. May 5, 1794. May 9, 1794. N. 429. William Pearce, James Monro; relatives, David, James, Enoch and Nathan Thomas and Mary Laroux. Exc. John Laroux and James Thomas.

Ann McAntier. W. Clay Crk. Hd. Mar. 31, 1794. May 13, 1794. N. 433. Three daughters, Mary, Rachel, and Hannah McAntier. Exc. Alexander McBeath.

James Bently. Taylor. Appo. Hd. Mar. 6, 1794. May 20, 1794. N. 434. Mrs. Mary Allfree; John Williams Allfree. Exc. William Allfree.

Edith Jones, widow of Philip Jones. Wil. 10m. 24, 1793. May 28, 1794. N. 436. Sons, Amos and William; daughters, Edith and Phebe Jones; grandson, Phillip Jones, son of son Amos; grandson, Phillip Jones, son of son William. Exc. James Brian and George Speakman.

Cornelius Naudain, Jr. May 25, 1794. June 3, 1794. N. 438. Two daughters of brother Henry Naudain, viz. Mary and Jean Naudain. Exc. James Thomas and Thomas Booth.

John Hance. May 12, 1794. June 10, 1794. N. 439. Sons, William, Peter and Nicolis. Exc. son, William.

Ranier Penton. N. C. Hd. Oct. 29, 1793. June 23, 1794. N. 440. Sons, John, Joseph and William; daughters, Eliza and Mary. Exc. wife, Elizabeth; son, John.

Deborah White. June 11, 1794. June 25, 1794. N. 442. Brother's dau., Anna Falconer; sister, Anna White, widow; granddaughters Deborah and Henrietta Ward. Exc. son-in-law, George Ward.

John Brown. Appo. Hd. Sept. 11, 1794. July 17, 1794. N. 444.

Three nephews, viz: Edmond Chance, Edmond Brown and John Robinson; cousin, George Brown; Mary Parsons, Charlotte Hirons and Catherine Conner. Exc. Joseph Parsons.

Alexander Hall. N. C. Hd. June 29, 1794. July 23, 1794. N. 445. Wife, Sarah; two sons, Asa and William Hall. Exc. Ezikeal Britton.

John Bond. Phila. ————. Aug. 11, 1794. N. 447. Wife, Sarah; children of sister, Ann Shelley. Exc. wife, Sarah and ‑William Lees.

Peter Jaquet, Sr. N. C. Hd. Apr. 22, 1793. Aug. 14, 1794. N. 448. Sons, John Paul, Jesse and Nicholas; daughters, Ann Trent Jaquett, Mary Cairns, late Mary Jaquett and Sabrina Murray, late Sabrina Jaquett. Exc. John Paul Jaquett; James Eves.

Mary Allmond. Widow. B'wine Hd. July 31, 1794. Aug. 16, 1794. N. 450. Son, John; daughters, Elizabeth Elliott, Mary McKee, Margaret Brooks, Ann Derrickson, Sarah Allmond, Rebecca Allmond and Isabel Jackson. Exc. Isaac Stevenson.

William McClay. Aug. 7, 1794. Aug. 30, 1794. O. 1. Wife, Frances; daughters, Mary, Sarah and Eliza; sons, William, Samuel, John and Robert; Mary's husband, Thomas Moore. Exc. wife, Frances and William McMechen.

William Patterson. July 7, 1794. Sept. 16, 1794. O. 4. Wife, Susanna; sons, John (of Damarara), Samuel, Benjamin and Joseph; dau., Jane Rice; granddaughter, Elizabeth Rice; son-in-law, Capt. Archibald Gardner and dau. Mary's (dec'd.) children, viz: Mary Eleanor, Nancy, Elizabeth, William, James, Dorcas, Archibald, and Hester Gardner; daughters, Deborah Dixon, and Rebecca Adams; Levi Adams; grandson, William Parkinson, of Damarara; granddau., Mary Black, wife of James Black; granddau., Elizabeth Patterson, dau. of son John; child of late granddau., Catharine Hyatt, dec'd.; sisters-in-law, Elizabeth Boon and Hannah Janvier; dau. of Isaac Cannon, by his late wife, whose maiden name was Alice Danford. Exc. wife, Susanna; James Latimer and James Black.

James Broom. Yeoman. Wil. July 15, 1791. Sept. 17, 1791. O. 14. James and Ann Broom, children of son, Jacob; James Broom, Hetty Willes Broom, Eliza Broom, Harriott Rumsey Broom and other children of son Abraham; Elizabeth, wife of Abraham. Exc. sons, Jacob and Abraham.

David McMechen. May 5, 1794. Oct. 10, 1794. O. 18. Brother's, William and James McMechen; sisters, Mary Kenedy, Margaret Cochran, Jane Smith, Rebeckah Cochran and Tabitha Nivin; James Mitchel Cochran, son of Rebecca and Samuel Cochran; Samuel Nivin. Exc. brother, James McMechen.

Benjamin Robinson. Mill Crk. Hd. Oct. 17, 1792. Oct. 10, 1794. O. 20. Brother-in-law, Robert Boggs; nephews, Moses, James,

Joseph and John Boggs; John Robinson in Virginia. Exc.
nephew, Moses Boggs.

Benjamin Burgin. Oct. 3, 1794. Oct. 22, 1794. O. 23. Exc. wife,
Sarah Burgin.

James Black. Miller. Mill Crk. Hd. Feb. 27, 1792. Nov. 18, 1794.
O. 24. Daughters, Mary, Nancy, Sally, Catharine, Jean Black
and Elizabeth Wallace; Samuel Patterson, Jane Rice, James
Glasko, Dr. William McCrea. Exc. wife, Mary; sons, James R.
and George; son-in-law, Dr. George Wallace and Thomas Montgomery.

Hester Reading. Appo. Hd. Dec. 22, 1785. Nov. 25, 1794. O. 47.
Dau., Catharine Anne Reading. Exc. son, Phillip.

William Shipley. Bor. of Wil. Oct. 10, 1794. Nov. 26, 1794. O. 28.
Wife, Sarah; children, Samuel, William, Robert, John, Joseph,
Thomas, James, Elizabeth (married to Joseph Gist), Susanna
(married to Savin Hamilton, dec'd.), Sarah and Mary. Exc. wife,
Sarah; and sons, John and Thomas.

Francis Ennos. B'wine Hd. Aug. 25, 1794. Dec. 8, 1794. O. 32.
Exc. wife, Mary Ennos.

Francis King. St. Geo. Hd. Jan. 3, 1794. Dec. 9, 1794. O. 34. Wife,
Ann; sons, Francis and Isaac; dau., Ann, wife of John Kreeson;
grandson, Abraham Vandegrift. Exc. son, Isaac.

Thomas Montgomery. St. Geo. Hd. Apr. 30, 1787. Dec. 26, 1794.
O. 37. Brothers and sisters. Exc. wife, Mary.

James Stevenson. Weaver. B'wine Hd. Dec. 15, 1794. Dec. 29,
1794. O. 39. Wife, Elizabeth; sons, Jacob, William, Isaac,
James; daughters, Hannah Dempster, Mary Orr, Rebeckah
Stevenson; grandson, Aaron, son of dau. Margaret, dec'd. Exc.
sons, Jacob and James.

Jacob Vanhorn. St. Geo. Hd. Dec. 3, 1794. Dec. 30, 1794. O. 43.
Children, Elizabeth, Samuel, Jeremiah and John Mansfield Vanhorn. Exc. Mrs. Jemima Mansfield, her dau., Elizabeth. Guardian, Samuel Mansfield, son of Jeremiah.

Ebenezer Morton. (Nunc.) Husbandman. Pen. Hd. Dec. 22, 1794.
Jan. 22, 1795. O. 48. Daughters, Sarah and Anna. Attested by
Andrew Morton and Patience Morton, widow of Ebenezer.

Allen Palmatory. (Nunc.) Husbandman. Appo. Hd. Jan. 3, 1795.
Feb. 12, 1795. Filed. Wife, Ann; sons, Allen and John. Attested by Thomas Hartup and John Hartup. Letters of adm.
granted to John Francis, in right of his wife Ann, widow of
Allen Palmatory.

Mary Thomson. Widow. N. C. Jan. 20, 1795. Feb. 21, 1795. O.
50. Sons, John, Joseph and Samuel; daughters, Catharine and
Mary; dec'd brother, John Silsbee. Exc. Joseph Tatlow.

James Black. Farmer. Jan. 22, 1789. Mar. 6, 1795. O. 54. Sisters,
Rebeckah and Ann Black. Exc. brother, John Black and Robert
McAntaren.

Sarah Meldrum. St. Geo. Hd. Feb. 13, 1794. Mar. 6, 1795. O. 55. Dau., Rebeckah Meldrum. Exc. son, Joseph Meldrum.

Rev. Morgan Edwards, clerk of Pen. Hd. Apr. 17, 1792. Mar. 7, 1795. O. 57. First wife, ——; sons, William and Joshua; Rev. David Davis. Exc. son, Joshua and John Prichard.

Jonas Porter. Red Lion Hd. Sept. 9, 1794. Mar. 21, 1795. O. 59. Daughters, Mary, Nancy and Hannah; sons, Alexander, Jonas and David. Exc. wife, Margaret and brother, Alexander.

Andrew Miller. Nov. 2, 1794. Mar. 23, 1795. O. 61. Wife, Ann; four daughters, Elizabeth, Mary, Ann and Sarah; son, Joseph. Exc. wife, Ann.

Abner Alston. St. Geo. Hd. 3m. 14, 1795. Mar. 30, 1795. O. 63. Wife, Hannah; dau., Hannah; nephew, Abner Alston, son of brother Zoab; brothers, John, Zoab and Israel; sister, Elizabeth. Exc. John Hirons and John Alston.

John Bell. Farmer. B'wine Hd. Jan. 23, 1795. Mar. 31, 1795. O. 65. John and Jacob McKeever, sons of Alexander McKeever; Jacob Stevenson. Exc. Isaac Stevenson.

David Caldwell. Planter. Mar. 10, 1795. Mar. 31, 1795. O. 67. Wife, Mary; daughters, Jane and Frances Caldwell; son-in-law, Enoch Morris; grandsons, James Morris, Isaac Melcor (son of Isaac), David Kelley (son of Benjamin). Exc. son-in-law, Benjamin Kelly; nephew, Joseph Guir.

Margaret Heath. Single Woman. Bor. of Wil. Mar. 3, 1795. Apr. 1, 1795. O. 69. Brother, Samuel Heath's dau. Margaret (a widow), Margaret Lewis; Susanna, dau. of Hance Naff and Mary, his wife. Exc. relation, Hance Naff.

Thomas Ford. Weaver. B'wine Hd. Mar. 8, 1795. Apr. 1, 1795. O. 71. Daughter, Ann; Turvil Ford, son of brother, James Ford. Exc. wife, Mary.

Sarah Cazier. Pen. Hd. Dec. 27, 1794. Apr. 4, 1795. O. 72. Brothers, Matthias and Isaac Cazier; half sister, Susannah; Elizabeth Sebo, dau. of David Sebo; niece, Rachel Bryan; nephews, Andrew Bryan, John Conway, and Henry Conway. Exc. John Conway.

Thomas Cochran. Mill Creek Hd. May 4, 1793. Apr. 8, 1795. O. 74. Exc. sister, Margaret Cochran; nephew, William Rankin; nephew, Joseph Rankin.

Catherine Miles. Red Lion Hd. Dec. 30, 1794. Apr. 24, 1795. O. 77. Mother, ——; half-sisters, Elizabeth Glenn, Mary and Grace Van Dyke; half-brother, John Van Dyke; sisters, Susanna Lowber, Sarah Miles, and Lidea Miles. Exc. uncle, James Miles.

Rev. John Thompson. Presby. Minister. Mar. 15, 1795. May 4, 1795. O. 79. Son, Thomas McK. Thompson. Exc. wife, Latitia, and brother, Thomas McK. Thompson.

Jane Lewellen. Widow. Pen. Hd. Mar. 30, 1795. May 7, 1795. O. 80. Friend, Thomas Bradley. Exc. friend, Andrew Fisher.

Joseph Rotheram. Farmer. W. Clay Crk. Hd. Oct. 10, 1794. May 16, 1795. O. 81. Dau., Catherine Wilson, her son, Joseph Wilson; three grandchildren, Lydia Foreman, Joseph Rotheram Foreman, and John Foreman, children of my late daughter, Elizabeth Foreman; late wife, Lydia; niece, Catherine Rotheram, dau. of late brother, Jacob. Exc. Solomon Maxwell, Joel Lewis, James Stroud, Abel Glassford.

John Kendall. Cordwainer. Bor. of Wil. Sept. 23, 1783. May 27, 1795. O. 85. Dau.-in-law, Mary Kendall, widow of son, Jesse Kendall; three grandchildren, Isaac, John and James; brother-in-law, Isaac Collier; son-in-law, Samuel Hollingsworth; dau., Hannah. Exc. wife, Mary. Cod. May 5, 1792, son, Samuel; dau., Ann.

Andrew Miller. Red Lion Hd. Apr. 26, 1794. June 22, 1795. O. 90. Daughters, Deborah Stewart and Ann Miller; son, John. Exc. wife, Mary.

Jane Reynolds. Widow. B'wine Hd. May 2, 1795. July 17, 1795. O. 93. Mother-in-law, Rachel Reynolds; sister-in-law, Sally Reynolds; father, Thomas Wilson; sons, William and John Reynolds; bro.-in-law, Jacob Reynolds; kinsman, Thomas Bird, son of John Bird. Exc. bro.-in-law, Thomas Reynolds, Jr.

Dr. Henry Peterson. St. Geo. Hd. Dec. 28, 1794. July 18, 1795. O. 99. Wife, Elizabeth; late mother, Grace Peterson; three nieces, Mary Wynkoop, Hester Catholena Wynkoop, and Harriot Grace Wynkoop; son, Andrew Jacob Peterson. Exc. Philip Reading.

John Arthur Clark. (Nunc.) Weaver. Pen. Hd. June 19, 1795. July 20, 1795. O. 100. Attested by William Whan and Robert Faries, mother, Jannet Clark. Est. adm. by Robert Clark.

Rebecca Kearny. Talbot Co., Md. Sept. 24, 1794. July 28, 1795. O. 178. Niece, Rebecca George; daughters of dec'd nephews, Abraham and James Wynkoop; grandnephew, Dyre Sharpe Wynkoop. Exc. grandnephew, Nicholas Hammond.

Benjamin Pearce. St. Geo. Hd. Oct. 10, 1794. Sept. 9, 1795. O. 103. Son, John Pearce; dau., Sarah Meanor, wife of John Meanor. Exc. son, Benjamin Pearce.

William Hall. Yeoman. St. Geo. Hd. Mar. 10, 1792. Sept. 29, 1795. O. 105. Children of dau., Mary Hagerty; her son, William Walker; children of dau., Hannah Acton; dau., Sarah Hall; son, Samuel Hall. Exc. son, John Hall; son-in-law, Clement Acton.

Robert Creighton. Farmer. Mill Crk. Hd. Apr. 22, 1793. Oct. 16, 1795. O. 107. Wife, Mary; sons, William and Robert; daughters, Mary and Elizabeth. Exc. son, Robert.

Samuel Platt, Jr., M. D. Newark. Mar. 1, 1795. Nov. 4, 1795. O. 110. Sisters, Elizabeth Evans, Martha Duraghan; bro.-in-law, John Duraghan; Samuel Anderson, Mary and Ann Anderson, children of sister, Ann Anderson; half brother, George Platt; half sisters, Jane and Mary Platt. Exc. George Russell.

Mary Ferriss. Oct. 24, 1795. Nov. 5, 1795. O. 112. "Children all dead." Rebecca Ward; son, Isaiah, dec'd; Catherine Faries, dau. of Samuel Faries; Mary Williams, dau., Roger Williams; granddau., Mariah Williams Higgins. Exc. son-in-law, David Higgins.

Rhoda Webb. Widow of Joshua Webb. Bor. of Wil. Apr. 21, 1795. Nov. 7, 1795. O. 114. Exc. mother-in-law, Lydia Webb.

John Stidham. Chris. Hd. Sept. 23, 1795. Nov. 10, 1795. O. 115. Sons, David, John, Jonas and William. Exc. son, David Stidham.

John Moore. Pen. Hd. Oct. 31, 1795. Nov. 10, 1795. O. 116. "Three minor children." Exc. son, William Moore, Morgan Jones.

William Price. Blacksmith. Pen. Hd. Oct. 22, 1795. Nov. 17, 1795. O. 118. Five grandchildren ——, children of dec'd son, John; granddau., Deborah; "My children, viz, Sarah, Mary, Morton, and Ann." Exc. William James, and dau., Ann Price.

William See. St. Geo. Hd. Nov. 6, 1794. Nov. 17, 1795. O. 120. Son, William; two grandsons, William See Stilwell and Richard See Stilwell; Peter Jetun, eldest son of bro.-in-law Peter Jetun. Exc. wife, Fanny, and bro.-in-law, Robert Armstrong.

Isaac Hollingsworth. Chris. Hd. Jan. 25, 1792. Nov. 23, 1795. O. 124. Wife, Hannah, sons, Jesse, Joseph, Benjamin, Job, Eli; daughters, Judith and Hannah Hollingsworth. Amor Hollingsworth. Exc. sons, Job and Jesse.

Margaret Gray. Mill Crk. Hd. Aug. 3, 1793. Dec. 3, 1795. O. 128. Niece, Margaret Latimer, wife of George Latimer; grand niece Elizabeth Poe, wife of Capt. James Poe. Exc. nephew, William Cathcart.

James Russell. W. Clay Crk. Hd. Feb. 9, 1792. Dec. 22, 1795. O. 131. Five children, Isabella, Hannah, Ann, Andrew and James Russell; two eldest daughters by first wife, Margaret and Mary Russell. Exc. wife, Margaret.

Isaac Thomas. Yeoman. Appo. Hd. Dec. 12, 1795. Jan. 4, 1796. O. 96. Wife, Elizabeth; bro, William Mansfield, Hannah Howell's child; brother, Edward Mansfield's children; brother, John Thomas's children. Exc. cousin, Thomas Mansfield.

Sarah Davis. Pen. Hd. June 4, 1795. Jan. 9, 1796. O. 133. Daughters, Rachel, Mary and Hannah; granddaughters, Sarah and Mary Perry; Abel, Sarah and Hannah Davis, children of son, Benjamin. Exc. John and Mary Davis.

Joseph Clayton. Sept. 12, 1794. Jan. 25, 1796. O. 135. Dau. Margaret Clayton; grandson, Isaac Clayton. Exc. son, Isaac.

Vincent Bonsall. Wil. Jan. 1, 1796. Jan. 25, 1796. O. 136. Wife, Mary; dau., Hannah Bonsall; son, Philip Bonsall; grandsons, Vincent, Caleb and Isaac Bonsall. Exc. James Brian and Samuel Canby.

Walter Fullam. Jan. 18, 1796. Jan. 28, 1796. O. 140. Present wife, Mary Fullam; cousin, Thomas Fullam. Exc. Richard Ford and James O'Donnel.

Benjamin Bunker. St. Geo. Hd. Feb. 22, 1796. Feb. 29, 1796. O. 142. Children, Benjamin, Josiah, Elizabeth, Emelia and Sarah, children of Sarah Bantim; grandchildren, Benjamin and Abigail Bouldin, children of Thomas Bouldin. Exc. son-in-law, Thomas Bouldin.

Rachel McEntire. W. Clay Crk. Hd., Sept. 3, 1795. Mar. 14, 1796. O. 144. Sisters, Polly and Hannah; Bros., Samuel and Robert. Est. Adm. by James McCallmont and James Caldwell.

Georgre Wood Crow, M. D., St. Geo. Hd. Jan. 28, 1796. Mar. 14, 1796. O. 145. Exc. bro., Robert Crow.

Nicholas Sellars. Brickmaker. Wil. Feb. 14, 1796. Mar. 15, 1796. O. 146. Wife, Susanna; sons, George, Jacob and John; Susanna and Catherine Sellars, daughters of son, George. Exc. sons, Jacob and John.

Samuel Underwood. Cecil Co., Md. Apr. 6, 1795. Mar. 23, 1796. O. 148. Wife, Elizabeth; only son, Ezekiel. Exc. Robert Armstrong and William Lees.

Rebecca Moore. Widow. Pen. Hd. Mar. 24, 1796. Apr. 1, 1796. O. 150. Sons, John, Jeams, Francis and William; daughters, Rebecca Bracan, Jean Bracan, Rebecca Enos, and Margaret Short; John Enos, Henery Bracan. Exc. son, Jeams Moore, and son-in-law, Abraham Short.

David Devou. N. C. Hd. Jan. 9, 1796. Apr. 6, 1796. O. 153. Wife, Rachel; sons, Frederick, Samuel and James. Exc. bro., Jesse Devou.

Jesse McDonough. St. Geo. Hd. Apr. 15, 1791. Apr. 6, 1796. O. 476. Sons, Thomas, Patrick and Micah; grandsons, James and Joseph Anderson. Exc. son, Thomas.

Thomas Connor. Laborer. (Nunc.) Mar. 11, 1796. Apr. 9, 1796. O. 156. Joseph Mills. Attested by James Ratcliff. Letters of adm. to William Kelley.

John Lindsey. Mill Crk. Hd. Oct. 24, 1795. Apr. 27, 1796. O. 157. Children ——. Exc. wife, Jane Lindsey, and Samuel Jorden.

Samuel Kelly. Yeoman. Mill Crk. Hd. June 2, 1794. May 3, 1796. O. 159. Children, Elizabeth, William, Rebecka, Ezemy, Lydia and Margaret; Samuel Kelly, the miller; late wife, Rebecka, mother of said Elizabeth and William. Exc. wife, Margaret, Thomas Montgomery, Esq., and Robert Crawford, Gent.

Charles Springer. Mill Crk. Hd. May 27, 1791. May 19, 1796. O. 163. Wife, Mary; daughters, Elizabeth Springer, Hannah and Rachel McDonald; sons, Christopher, Jeremiah and Benjamin. Exc. sons, Jeremiah and Christopher.

Hugh Smith. Late of Pen. Hd. Apr. 3, 1796. May 21, 1796. O. 165. Son, David; dau., Polly Exc. wife, Elizabeth and William Robertson.

Robert Eakin. June 6, 1795. May 24, 1796. O. 166. Son, John; nephew, Robert, son of bro. William Eakin; nephew, James, son of bro. Samuel Eakin, dec'd. Exc. wife, Mary, and James Thomas.

Mary Gilpin. Chris. Hd. Feb. 13, 1793. May 27, 1796. O. 168. Four daughters, Orpah, Betty, Hannah and Mary; son-in-law, Joseph Shallcross; grandson, Edward Gilpin, son of Vincent Gilpin. Exc. son, Vincent.

Sarah Price. N. C. Sept. 20, 1795. May 28, 1796. O. 169. Daughters, Catherine and Elenor Price. Exc. John Groves.

Abraham Brown. Chris. Hd. Apr. 23, 1791. June 23, 1796. O. 172. Wife, Sarah; sons, Isaac, Andrew, William, Abraham and John Brown; dau., Margaret Brown. Exc. son, Andrew Brown.

Samuel Niles. Mar. 8, 1796. June 28, 1796. O. 174. Exc. mother, Mary Niles, and bro., Hezekiah Niles.

Jemima Stapler. Widow of John Stapler. Wil. July 28, 1796. Aug. 2, 1796. O. 175. Niece, Jemima Dickinson, dau. of David and Rebecca Dickinson; sister, Rachel Jeffris; sister, Sarah Newlin, wife of Thomas Newlin; Samuel Grubb, son of bro. Isaac; uncle, Caleb Hewes (mother's bro.); Sarah Wilson, widow of Nicholas; Samuel Chandler, son of Christopher and Prudence Chandler; Phebe Chandler, wife of Christopher; Rebecca and Hannah Grubb, daughters of bro., Isaac Grubb; sister, Mary Marshall; bro., Samuel Grubb, dec'd. Exc. cousin, Edward Hewes.

John Donnald. Bor. of Wil. July 10, 1796. Aug. 22, 1796. O. 180. Samuel and Sarah Dixson, children of wife's brother, Samuel Dixson. Exc. wife, Elizabeth.

Arnold Naudain. Appo. Hd., ———, Aug. 26, 1796. O. 182. Wife, Catherine; three sons, Elias, Arnold and Andrew; four daughters, Mary, Lydia, Rachel and Rebeccah. Letters of adm. granted to Elias Naudain.

Joseph Trimble. Late of Ireland, now of Wil. Aug. 8, 1796. Sept. 9, 1796. O. 183. Wife, Rebecca (in Ireland); three children, Robert, Matthew and Thomas; kinsman, John Trimble. Exc. Isaac Hendrickson.

John McKinley, M. D. Bor. of Wil. Aug. 27, 1796. Sept. 14, 1796. O. 185. Exc. wife, Jane.

Thomas Wollaston. Farmer. Mill Crk. Hd. 2m. 6, 1781. Sept. 19, 1796. O. 186. Wife ———; sons, Joshua, James and Jeremiah; bro., George Wollaston; daughters, Sarah and Catherine; bro.-in-law, Joseph Rutheram; nephew, Jacob Wollaston. Exc. son, Joshua.

Thomas Evans. Farmer. Sept. 4, 1796. Sept. 29, 1796. O. 191. Wife, Frances Lowan Evans; son, Thomas; dau., Elizabeth; sister, Jane Thompson; three nephews, Joseph, Thomas, Nathaniel Evans David, sons of sister, Ann David; Jane Thompson's son-in-law, John Jones. Exc. Robert Middleton and William Cooch Simonton.

Allen Steel. July 24, 1793. Oct. 7, 1796. O. 193. Bro., John; sister, Polly ———; mother ———. Exc. George Gillespie, Jr.

Bethiah Boldin. St. Geo. Hd. Sept. 30, 1796. Oct. 24, 1796. O. 195. Sisters, Charlotte Glenn, Ann England, Elizabeth and Martha Bouldin; four half-sisters, (daughters of late mother by last husband, Elijah Cole), Sarah, Mary, Abigail and Hannah Cole. Exc. uncle, Elisha Bouldin.

James Dunlap. Pen. Hd. Oct. 27, 1796. Nov. 7, 1796. O. 197. Daughters, Sarah and Mary; sons, Samuel and William. Exc. son, William Dunlap.

Thomas Carter. Oct. 29, 1796. Nov. 10, 1796. O. 198. Wife, Elizabeth; son, John; dau., Elizabeth McDonnal; sons in Ireland, Alexander and Thomas Carter. Exc. Peter Williams.

Joseph Capelle. Bor. of Wil. Oct. 13, 1796. Nov. 15, 1796. O. 199. Wife, Mary; children, Marcus and Maria. Exc. Isaac H. Starr and William Robinson, (tanners) renounced. Court app't John Stockton and William Stidham.

John Grubb. Wil. June 24, 1792. Nov. 23, 1796. O. 202. Sisters, Charity, Sarah and Lydia. Exc. bro.-in-law Edward Gilpin.

Stewart Thompson. N. C. Oct. 10, 1796. Nov. 25, 1796. O. 202. Son, George Morris Thompson. Exc. wife, Mary Ann Thomson.

Paul Vanhorn. Appo. Hd. Dec. 3, 1796. Dec. 13, 1796. O. 205. Two children, Elias and James Vanhorn. Exc. bro., Barnott Vanhorn.

Eleanor Calvert. Pen. Hd. Oct. 2, 1793. Dec. 14, 1796. O. 210. Dau. Sally's son, Jonathon Calvert; bro., William Haughey; bro., Thomas Haughey's children, Levi and Priscilla Haughey; sister Priscilla Cowen's children, Thomas, Nancy, John, William, Sally and Priscilla Cowen; sisters, Hannah Davidson and Nancy Haughey; Hugh David. Exc. Lewis Thomas.

John King. Village of Middletown. Jan. 2, 1797. Feb. 7, 1797. O. 212. Children of bro., William King, late of Balto., viz John King and others. Exc. Elias Naudain.

Rebecca Shipley. Widow. Bor. of Wil. 12m. 12, 1796. Feb. 16, 1797. O. 215. Dau.-in-law, Martha Andrews; niece, Rebeckah Robinson; relation, Ann Robinson, widow of Francis Robinson; Rebeckah Wood; dau., Mary Bonsall and husband, Abraham Bonsall; sons, John and James Andrews; bro., Nicholas Robinson; relations, Samuel Canby and William Poole. Exc. son, James Andrews and nephew, William Robinson.

Mary Penrose. Widow. Naman's Creek, B'wine Hd. July 11, 1791. Mar. 4, 1797. O. 256. Dau., Sarah Robinson; son-in-law, Abraham Robinson. Exc. Thomas Robinson and Francis Johnston.

Thomas Almond. B'wine Hd. Jan. 31, 1797. Mar. 8, 1797. O. 218. Wife, Catherine; son, William; daughters, Elioner, Mary, Margaret, and Elizabeth. Exc. Isaac Stevenson.

Robert Porter. Red Lion Hd. Aug. 21, 1796. Apr. 17, 1797. O. 222. Daughters, Martha Porter, Anne Maria Porter and Mary Porter; son, David; cousin, Ann Glenn; uncle, Richard Pensh, of Phila. Exc. William McMeehen.

Jannat English. Mill Crk. Hd. Mar. 10, 1787. Apr. 21, 1797. O. 223. Dau., Agnes McGregor; dau., Elizabeth; dau. Nancy's children; dau. Rebecca's children; dau., Sarah, and dau., Jennet; David English. Exc. dau., Sarah Nivin.

George Crouding. Appo. Hd. Feb. 28, 1797. Apr. 22, 1797. O. 225. Wife, ——; dau., Ingeby; son, Jacob. Est. adm. by widow, Ede Crouding, and Benjamin Holliday.

Benjamin Mendenhall. Merchant. Chris. Hd. Nov. 28, 1795. Apr. 25, 1797. O. 226. Wife, Hannah; dau., Ruth Nichols, wife of Samuel Nichols; dau., Lydia, wife of John Webster. Exc. son, Eli.

Allen Fields. Appo. Hd. Apr. 21, 1797. May 9, 1797. O. 230. Sons, William, Henry and Benjamin. Exc. wife, Mary and bro., Benjamin Field.

Abraham Fields, Sr. Feb. 17, 1797. May 9, 1797. O. 231. Exc. dau., Sarah Fields, and son-in-law, Abraham Fields, grandchildren, Sarah and Joseph Vance.

Sleighter Boushelle, M. D. Formerly of Cecil Co., Md., but for some yrs., of Burke Co., North Carolina. May 14, 1795. May 16, 1797. O. 233. Nephews, sons of bro., Thomas Bouchelle, John, Sleighter, Jr., and Peter Boushelle; five grandchildren, David, Thomas, John, Mary and Martha Witherspoon, children of dau, Susanna Witherspoon; niece, Mary Boushelle. Exc. James Byard, John Carnan, nephew, Sleighter Boushelle, Jr.

Margaret Thomas. Widow. St. Geo. Hd. Mar. 25, 1797. May 25, 1797. O. 238. Sons, James, Nathan and Enoch; grandchildren, Margaret Thomas, Mary Bird, David Thomas, Rebecca Thomas, Elizabeth Thomas and Nathan Thomas; grandson, James Bird. Exc. Nathan Thomas.

Jesse Moore. Potters's Twp., Mifflin Co., Pa. Mar. 5, 1797. June 6, 1797. O. 208. Wife, Rebeccah; children, ——. Exc. Robert Smith and William Hickey.

Matthew Griffin. Appo. Hd. Apr. 4, 1797. June 6, 1797. O. 240. Sons, Joseph and Matthew; daughters, Elizabeth Benn and Temperance Griffin. Exc., wife, Eleanor, and bro., Ebenezer Griffin.

William Elliott, Jr. Farmer. B'wine Hd. May 16, 1797. June 8, 1797. O. 242. Mother, Jean Elliott, five sisters, Elizabeth McKee, Jane Elliott, Leah Steel, Rachel Hamilton and Hannah Anderson; nephews, Joseph, Andrew and William McKee, sons of sister Elizabeth, and William McKee; niece, Mary Clark, late Mary Elliott. Exc. wife, Elizabeth and Isaac Stevenson.

John Erwin. Bor. of Wil. May 12, 1797. June 20, 1797. O. 245. Children, Samuel, William, John, George, James, Hannah Israel, and heirs of dec'd dau. Margaret Laforge. Exc. wife, Letitia Erwin.

James Miles. Red Lion Hd. Jan. 25, 1796. June 23, 1797. O. 247. Wife, Rachel; son, James; children of sister Margaret, wife of John Hanson. Exc. son, Lawrence Hanson Miles.

Duncan Beard. Appo. Hd. ——. June 29. 1797. O. 257. Wife, Rebekah; Duncan Webster, son of Evan Thomas Webster; Mary Cleaver, dau. of John Cleaver; Duncan Beard, son of John Beard. Exc. Archibald McMurphey, Chirstopher Weaver and Richardson Armstrong.

Nicholas Campbell. Laborer. Chris. Bridge. June 27, 1797. June 30, 1797. O. 250. Bro.'s sons' children, Jean, Nancy and Sally Campbell, (near Phila.); sister Mary Murray, (in Ireland). Testator died at house of Andrew Smith before signing.

John Evans. Pen. Hd. Feb. 15, 1790. July 6, 1797. O. 251. Six children, Robert, Samuel, David, Rachel, Nancy and Margaret. Exc. wife, Jean, and son, Robert.

Hugh Dougherty. N. C. Hd. Aug. 4, 1797. Aug. 16, 1797. O. 260. Exc. Samuel Ruth.

Joseph Vance. St. Geo. Hd. Apr. 15, 1796. Aug. 21, 1797. O. 262. Dau. Sarah Vance, nephews, Benjamin Vance Merrit and John Merrit. Exc. Dr. Benjamin Merrit and wife, Rachel Vance.

Richard Richardson. 8m. 27, 1797. Sept. 16, 1797. O. 266. Wife, Sarah, (dau. of Edward Tatnall); sons, Joseph, Ashton, and John; dau. Ann, dau. Elizabeth Stroud. Exc. wife, Sarah, sons, Joseph and Ashton.

Jacob Colesberry. N. C. Hd. Aug. 15, 1797. Sept. 19, 1797. O. 272. Wife, Catharine; sons, Andrew Gravenrat Colesberry, Dr. Henry Colesberry, William, Jacob and Levi; daughters, Margaret Colesberry and Mary Walraven. Exc. son, Levi.

James Anderson. Farmer. W. Clay Crk. Hd. June 1, 1797. Sept.

21, 1797. O. 275. Children of nephew, James Anderson and Mary, dec'd, Jane, Isabel Kilgore, James, William, Mary Whan, Martha Anderson, and Margaret Anderson; Martha Kinkead, and Joseph her husband, their son, James Anderson Kinkead; bro. William. Exc. step-son, Samuel Evans, George Gillespie, and bro. William's grandson, Alexander Anderson.

Samuel Hogg. Tallow-chandler. Bor. of Wil. 11m. 25, 1794. Oct. 13, 1797. O. 282. Wife, Catharine. Samuel, son of son, Andrew, John Hogg, son of Samuel, grandson, Samuel Poak, granddau. Elianor Lindsay. Exc. son, James Hogg.

Robert Veazey. Cecil Co., Md. Sept. 12, 1797. Oct. 25, 1797. O. 254. Nephew, Samuel M. Veazey, bro., Samuel's daughters, Ann and Elizabeth. Exc. George Lewis.

John Antrim. St. Geo. Hd. Oct. 30, 1797. Nov. 7, 1797. O. 287. Wife, Susannah, unborn child, mother ———. Exc. bro.-in-law, Alexander McFarland.

Arthur Penny. Farmer. B'wine Hd. July 13, 1797. Dec. 11, 1797. O. 292. Sons, David and William. Exc. wife, Hannah, and Isaac Stevenson.

Robert Armstrong. Nov. 27, 1797. Dec. 13, 1797. O. 295. Son, Robert Washington Armstrong, other children ———. Exc. wife, Elizabeth.

Stephen Stapler. Stanton, Mill Crk. Hd. June 12, 1792. Dec. 16, 1797. O. 298. Elizabeth and Stephen Woolston, children of dec'd dau., Mary, wife of Joshua Woolston, of Bucks Co., Pa; children of son Thomas; Ann Dennis; kinswoman, Hannah Erwin, Charles Byrnes, cousin Stephen Stapler, son of William Stapler. Guardians, nephew, John Stapler, Jr., and cousin, Samuel Smith. Exc. son, Thomas and Simon Hadley.

John Laroux. St. Geo. Hd. Dec. 19, 1795. Dec. 29, 1797. O. 302. Cousin, John Laroux; friends, Patrick McDonough, Dr. Nathan Thomas, George Armstrong, Dr. William Carpenter's son, John, Enoch Thomas. Exc. James Thomas and Dr. William Carpenter.

Nathaniel Cannady. B'wine Hd. Apr. 19, 1796. Jan. 15, 1798. O. 307. Children, Benjamin, Mary, Ann, John and James. Exc. wife, Mary.

Charles Paulson. Carpenter. Newport. ——— 1797. Feb. 11, 1798. O. 311. Sons, Joel, Peter, Samuel and Aaron. Exc. wife, Susannah and son, Aaron.

Joseph Thomas, Jr. Pen. Hd. Jan. 24, 1798. Feb. 15, 1798. O. 318. Son, Daniel Howell Thomas; dau., Elizabeth Thomas. Exc. wife, Eleanor Thomas, and Oliver Howell.

Margaret Russell. Widow. W. Clay Crk. Hd. Aug. 9, 1796. Feb. 23, 1798. O. 321. Children, Isobal, Nancy, Hannah, Andrew, and James Russell. Exc. bro., James Kerr.

John Linn. Store-keeper. Aug. 18, 1797. Feb. 24, 1798. O. 322. Father and mother, William and Mary Linn, in Ireland, bros., William, David, Cunningham, and Henry; sisters, Rebecca and Mary. Exc. John Miller, Phila., and Andrew Catherwood, Wil.

Archibald McMurphy. Appo. Hd. Dec. 5, 1797. Mar. 19, 1798. O. 327. Sons, Thomas and Joseph. Exc. wife, Ann and son, Thomas.

Richard Pearson. June 24, 1796. Mar. 27, 1798. O. 331. Sons, John and Richard Pearson; grandchildren, Richard, Margaret, Charles and Elizabeth Pearson, and Nancy ———, dau., Nancy Bostick. Exc. dau., Elizabeth Pearson, widow.

Elizabeth Chandler. Widow of Isaac. Chris. Hd. Dec. 1, 1797. Apr. 7, 1798. O. 333. Grandchildren, Benjamin Chandler, Betty, Jane, Ann, and Isaac Cann, Thomas Strode and Ann Strode. Exc. son-in-law, Joseph Chandler.

Daniel Britt. Wil., late of Phila. Mar. 1, 1798. Apr. 12, 1798. O. 335. Dau., Mary Britt; son, George Britt; mother-in-law, Elizabeth Mecom; sisters of late wife, Sarah Smith, wife of Benjamin Smith, Abia Mecom, and Jane Mecom; first cousins, Mary Britt and Daniel Cox, in England; John Field and Deborah his wife; Daniel Britt, Jr., John Britt; children of Sarah Smith; Edward Mecom Carr, son of Mary Carr, dec'd. Exc. John James and Benjamin Smith.

John Wright. Jan. 15, 1798. May 11, 1798. O. 340. Children, Isaac and three others not named. Exc. wife, Mary and William Cradick.

William Foott. Mill Crk. Hd. May 11, 1797. June 5, 1798. O. 344. Dau., Ann Foott; son-in-law, Robert Giffin; grandchildren, Mary, Jean, and James Giffin, children of said Robert and dau., Rachel Giffin, dec'd. Exc. wife, Esther Foot, William Barker, and Abraham Barker.

William Carpenter, Sr. St. Geo. Hd. May 9, 1798. June 25, 1798. O. 347. Sons, Richard, James and William; dau., Elizabeth Skeer; son-in-law, Harmonus Alrich. Exc. sons, Richard and James.

Daniel Nickols. Mill Crk. Hd. Apr. 7, 1795. June 30, 1798. O. 350. Nephew, Thomas Dixson, son of Isaac, dec'd; grandson Daniel Gregg, son of William, dec'd; great-nephews, Thomas, Jesse and Isaac Dixson, sons of Thomas; late wife's children, Charles and Grace Gause; Samuel Dixson's three daughters, Mary, Jane and Martha; David Pusey's four children, Ann, David, John and Lydia; James and Annie Wilson; Robert and Ann Phillips; nephews, Isaac, Silas, and Jehu Dixson, sons of Isaac, dec'd.; Sister Ann's four other children, Dinah Jackson, Levi and William Tate and Martha Painter; nephews, Jacob and Thomas Nickols, sons of John; Charity Cherry, wife of William Cherry, and Hannah Brown, dec'd, daughters of bro. John; William Brown, son of said Hannah; bro., John's grandson, Robert Clendenon; bro.,

Isaac; bro., Thomas's widow, and son Daniel Nickols; bro., Joseph's
son Samuel, and his sister Hannah, wife of Stephen Logue; bro.,
Samuel's widow, and children, Ellis Nickols, Susannah ――――, and
Edith Sharpless; Isaac Dixson, son of nephew John, dec'd; late wife's
grandson, Daniel Gregg; Stephen Wilson; Ann Greave; Margaret
Lockard; Phebe Cherry, dau., of William and Charity. Exc. sons-in-
law, James Wilson and Robert Phillips.

Hugh Means. Chris. Hd. May 10, 1797. Aug. 1, 1798. O. 356. Rev.
William McCannon, Rev. William Smith, sister, Jane Divett, nieces,
Ann Armstrong, wife of Hugh Means; Jane Armstrong, wife of
Robert Shields; Mary Armstrong; Elizabeth Knox, formerly Means;
Leatitia Woodcock, wife of William Woodcock; and Margaret Cars-
well, wife of Samuel Carswell; sister, Ann Crawford; bro., William;
nephews, William Divett, James and John Crawford, Hugh Means,
William and Samuel Beaty; bro., Samuel Means's four children,
Elizabeth, Leatitia, Hugh, and Margaret. Exc. Henry Latimer and
Samuel Carswell.

Robert McFerson. Yeoman. Mill Crk. Hd. Sept. 4, 1794. Sept. 4,
1798. O. 365. Dau., Mary and Martha; sons-in-law, James Fitzgerald, Benjamin Montgomery, and John McBeth; grandson, Robert,
and others, children of John McBeth. Exc. John McBeth and Robert
Montgomery.

William Derrickson. Chris. Hd. June 3, 1797. Sept. 25, 1798. O.
368. Wife, Elizabeth; son, Zacharias; daughters, Susanna, (her
child), Mary, Elizabeth, and Sarah. John Lynam. Exc. son, Peter
Derrickson, and John Armstrong, Jr.

William Rice. Grocer. Wil. Sept. 10, 1798. Sept. 27, 1798. O. 371.
Wife, Sarah; bro., Edward Rice of Ireland, and sister, Charity
Cluff. Exc. bro., James Rice and John Sellers; sister-in-law, Eliza-
beth Keerns.

Joshua Clayton. June 8, 1785. Oct. 6, 1798. O. 374. Sons, James
Lawson Clayton, Richard and Thomas Clayton; dau., Mary; bro.,
John; friends, Peter Lawson and Richard Bassett. Exc. wife, Rachel.

Mary Hyatt. Red Lion Hd. Sept. 21, 1798. Oct. 16, 1798. O. 377.
Friend, Isabel Lawrence. Exc. bro., John Hyatt.

David Van Dyke. St. Geo. Hd. Sept. 23, 1798. Oct. 19, 1798. O.
379. David Van Dyke, son of David Van Dyke; John Van Dyke,
son of Isaac Van Dyke; children of bro.-in-law John Hanson, James
and Mary Hanson. Exc. wife, Mary and Elias Naudain.

Francis Janvier. N. C. Hd. Oct. 24, 1798. Nov. 14, 1798. O. 386.
Wife, Sarah; sister, Sarah; Maria Golden, dau., of John Golden
of Balto. Exc. bros., John and Philip Janvier.

Peter Derrickson. Chris. Hd. Oct. 3, 1798. Nov. 15, 1798. O. 390.
Bros., and sisters, Zacharias, Mary, Elizabeth, Sarah, and Susannah
Derrickson. Exc. John Armstrong.

James McDonald. Bor. of Wil. Sept. 18, 1798. Nov. 15, 1798. O. 391. Bro., John McDonald in Scotland; John Mackneill. Exc. Robert Hamilton.

Timothy Hanson. Cabinet-maker. Bor. of Wil. Sept. 6, 1798. Nov. 16, 1798. O. 393. Wife, Mary; daughters, Susanna and Elizabeth; sons, Samuel and Thomas; Eli Mendinhall, Thomas Littler, Bridget Woodward, Thomas Davis, William Wilson, John Simpson, Thomas Wilson, Joseph Warner, James Brobson, John White. Exc. son-in-law, William Robinson and Peter Brynberg.

John Robinson. Street-paver. Wil. Sept. 9, 1798. Nov. 17, 1798. O. 396. Son, John, and other children. Exc. wife, Mary and James Hogg.

Martha Williams. St. Geo. Hd. Jan. 17, 1795. Nov. 17, 1798. O. 398. Exc. Gamaliel Turner.

James Lea. Yeoman. Bor. of Wil. 3m. 10, 1786. Nov. 19, 1798. O. 400. Wife, Margaret; four daughters, Elizabeth, Margaret, Sarah, and Frances. Exc. son, James Lea, and son-in-law, Samuel Canby.

Jane Hartley. Widow. Bor. of Wil. Jan. 1, 1798. Nov. 27, 1798. O. 406. Dau.-in-law Sarah Hartley, widow; grandson, Joseph Hartley; sisters, Ann Grimes, and Sarah Abraham, of Ireland; Sarah Alderdice; kinsman, Jacob Ford; son, Benjamin dec'd; Firm of Benson and Hartley; John Benson, alias Ford. Exc. Joseph Warner.

Joshua Pedrick. Wil. Sept. 10, 1798. Nov. 28, 1798. O. 410. Late wife, Elizabeth; three children, Jonathan, Thomas, and Maria Pedrick; bros., Elijah and Jonathan Pedrick; sisters, Margaret Stanton, and Rebecca Pedrick. Exc. Isaac Pedrick, Gideon Scull and Stephen Hays.

Regina Mortonson. Widow. B'wine Hd. Feb. 26, 1795. Dec. 6, 1798. O. 415. Daughters, Sarah Mortonson, Lydia Rawson, Ann Mortonson, and Rebekah, wife of Joshua McLean; granddaughters, Mary McLean and Regina Rawson. Exc. son-in-law, Joshua McLean.

George Spackman. Bor. of Wil. 8m. 7, 1796. Dec. 8, 1798. O. 417. Sisters, Susanna Pouel, Mary Kenny and Elizabeth; bros., Thomas and Isaac; children, Ann, Samuel, and Hester Spackman, and Mary Downing; son-in-law, Thomas Downing. Samuel Canby, William Poole. Joseph Warner, Isaac Dickson. Exc. wife, Thomzin.

Thomas Robinson. Farmer. W. Clay Crk. Hd. Nov. 10, 1790. Dec. 12, 1798. O. 421. Children, Richard, Margaret, and Elizabeth, unborn child. Exc. William Wollaston, and Thomas Montgomery. Est. adm. by David Morrison.

Eleazer McComb. Wil. Sept. 6, 1798. Dec. 12, 1798. Father-in-law, Thomas Irons, Esq.; daughters, Jannett, and Elizabeth; son, James Bellach Macomb; sister, Mary Macomb. Exc. son, Thomas Irons Macomb and friend, John Bellach.

Joseph White. Bor. of Wil. Oct. 26, 1798. Dec. 12, 1798. O. 427. Sisters, Esther Currin, Jane Way, Elizabeth Phillips, and Ann White. Mother, Ann White; niece, Ann Phillips, dau. of William and Elizabeth Phillips; nephew, Joseph Currin, son of James and Esther Currin. Exc. bro., John White, and bro.-in-law, John Way.

Samuel Platt, M. D. W. Clay Crk. Hd. Mar. 26, 1798. Jan. 4, 1799. O. 434. Daughters, Dinah Worth, Margaret McCrea, Elizabeth Evans, Ann Anderson, Martha Durgan, Jane, and Mary; son, George; grand-dau., Ann Ross. Exc. wife, Margery and William McMechen.

Henry Garretson. Newport. Jan. 16, 1799. Jan. 31, 1799. O. 440. Wife, Sarah; grandson, Henry Garretson. Letters of adm. to Peter Garretson.

Joseph Springer, Sr. Chris. Hd. June 1, 1791. Mar. 11, 1799. O. 446. Son, Joseph. Grandson, Joseph Lynam. Daughters, Sarah Springer, Ann Lynam, Beyatoy Hendrixson, Mary Hendrixson, Cathrian Backhous, Rebecca Stidham, Rachel Armstrong, Elenar Boman, and Hannah Justis. Exc. son, Charles.

Ann Armstrong. Widow. Bor. of Wil. Feb. 20, 1799. Mar. 13, 1799. O. 499. Exc. Joseph and John Richardson.

Aaron Daniel. St. Geo. Hd. Mar. 5, 1799. Apr. 15, 1799. O. 451. Daughters, Elizabeth, Sarah, and Mary; sons, John and Aaron. Exc. wife, Martha Daniel and Barzilla Jefferis.

Jane Elliott. Widow. Sept. 19, 1797. Apr. 16, 1799. O. 453. Daughters, Elizabeth McKee, Jane Elliott, Leah Steel, Rachel Hamilton, Hannah Anderson and Martha Anderson, dec'd.; grandchildren, Mary Clark (late Elliott), John Anderson, Elizabeth, Mark, Jane, James, Alexander, Martha, Leah and Rachel Anderson. Exc. daughters, Jane and Leah.

Thomas Hollingsworth. Chris. Hd. 3m. 27, 1790. Apr. 7, 1799. O. 455. Wife, Jane; children, Thomas, John Err, Levi, Joshua, Nathaniel, Susanna, Mary and Jane. Exc. sons, Thomas and Levi.

James Montgomery. N. C. Hd. May 6, 1790. Apr. 18, 1799. O. 458. Exc. mother, Elizabeth Montgomery.

Charles Williams. Chris. Hd. May 25, 1797. Apr. 18, 1799. O. 460. Seven grandchildren, Charles Ogle, Thomas Ogle, William Ogle, Mary Ogle, Sarah Brindly, James Brindly, and Susanna Brindly, all being the children of dau. Elizabeth. Exc. son-in-law, James Brindly and Thomas Ogle.

Catherine Hyatt. St. Geo. Hd. Jan. 23, 1798. May 22, 1799. O. 465. Sons, John, Francis and Thomas Hyatt; daughters, Mary and Catherin Hyatt. (No exc. or adm. given).

William Elliott, Jr. B'wine Hd. June 1, 1799. June 8, 1799. O. 467. Sister, Margaret, wife of John Welsh; brother, Thomas Elliott;

nephew, William Elliott, son of brother John. Exc. brother-in-law, John Welsh.

Ann Chandler. Widow of Thomas Chandler. Chris. Hd. May 22, 1799. June 15, 1799. O. 470. Grandson, Jesse Chandler; dau., Dinah Gregg; Elizabeth Webb. Exc. son, Thomas Chandler.

Tamer James. Pen. Hd. May 31, 1798. June 18, 1799. O. 471. Jane Cahoon, dau. of Thomas Cahoon and Elizabeth, his wife. Exc. Tamer Edwards, dau. of John Edwards and Jane, his wife.

Charles Evans. Chris. Hd. June 30, 1799. July 17, 1799. O. 474. Children, Sarah Foot, Jonathan Evans, Oliver Evans, Margaret Ringold, Theophilus Evans, Joseph Evans, Evan Evans, and Elizabeth Bracken; grandchildren, Ann Bracken, Ann Ball, Joseph and John Ball. Exc. son, John Evans, and John Armstrong.

Emanuel Grubb. Yeoman. B'wine Hd. Jan. 1, 1799. Aug. 17, 1799. O. 482. Wife, Anne; sons, Benjamin, Peter, James, Nicholas. Exc. son, William Ford Grubb, and nephew, Amer Grubb.

Samuel Byars. Bor. of Wil. July 7, 1799. Aug. 13, 1799. O. 484. Children, James, Rebekah, Samuel, Martha, Robert, Joseph and Elizabeth. Exc. wife, Elizabeth.

Samuel Delaplain. Chris. Hd. Nov. 8, 1797. Aug. 31, 1799. O. 486. Children, Nehemiah, Sarah, Elizabeth, Joseph and Lydia; mother-in-law, Elizabeth Tomlinson. Exc. wife, Rachel.

Sarah Janvier. Town of N. C. (Now of Darby, Pa.) 6m. 8, 1799. Sept. 2, 1799. O. 480. Brother, Richard Maris; Elizabeth Bird, wife of John Bird; Margaret Colesberry, Ann Oakford, wife of Aaron Oakford, of Darby; Ann Stockton, wife of John Stockton. Exc. John Stockton.

John Clark Vansant. Mill Crk. Hd. Aug. 14. 1799. Oct. 1, 1799. O. 490. Sons, Isaac and James; daughters, Hannah, Mary and Sarah. Exc. wife, Mary, and son, John.

John Yarnall. Wil. 9m. 21, 1799. Oct. 5, 1799. O. 501. Daughters, Phebe, Rachel, and Edith; son, John. Exc. wife, Elizabeth, and Zachariah Jess.

Isaac Starr, Jr. B'wine Hd. 9m. 6, 1799. Oct. 22, 1799. O. 503. Wife, Margaret; children, Elizabeth Tatnall Starr, and Isaac Starr. Exc. father, Isaac Starr, Sr.

William Williams. Yeoman. Oct. 13, 1729. ———. Copy recorded, Nov. 27, 1799. O. 493. Son, William. Exc. wife, Catherine.

Thomas Montgomery. Yeoman. Mill Crk. Hd. May 17, 1794. Dec. 10, 1799. O. 508. Wife, Mary; sons, Benjamin, William, Alexander, Thomas, James, Robert, Daniel, Samuel, David and Moses; son John's three children, Minta, Mele and James; dau., Margaret, married to William Faron; dau., Mary. Exc. son, Moses.

Alexander Foster. W. Clay Crk. Hd. Oct. 19, 1798. Dec. 20, 1799.
O. 494. Sisters, Catherine Moore (wife of Jason Moore), Sarah
Gill, and Ann Rogers, widows, all in Ireland; niece, Sarah Killingher,
dau. of Elizabeth Killingher; nephew, Christopher F. Killingher;
cousin, Maurice Rogers, son of Mary Rogers (widow); nephew, John
Moore. Exc. Samuel M. Fox, George Read.

Rachel Flharty. Bor. of Wil. 5m. 6, 1794. Dec. 28, 1799. O. 512.
Daughters, Deborah and Elizabeth Flharty. Exc. Edward Hewes.

William McGarvey. Farmer. N. C. Hd. Dec. 22, 1799. Dec. 28,
1799. O. 514. Son, David; Joseph Scott, son of late wife; Mary
Pike (housekeeper); sister, Margaret McGarvey. Exc. brother, John
McGarvey.

INDEX

INDEX

www.ingramcontent.com/pod-product-compliance
Lightning Source LLC
Chambersburg PA
CBHW062025270326
41929CB00014B/2315